ASTONIS

X-MEN
XENOGENESIS

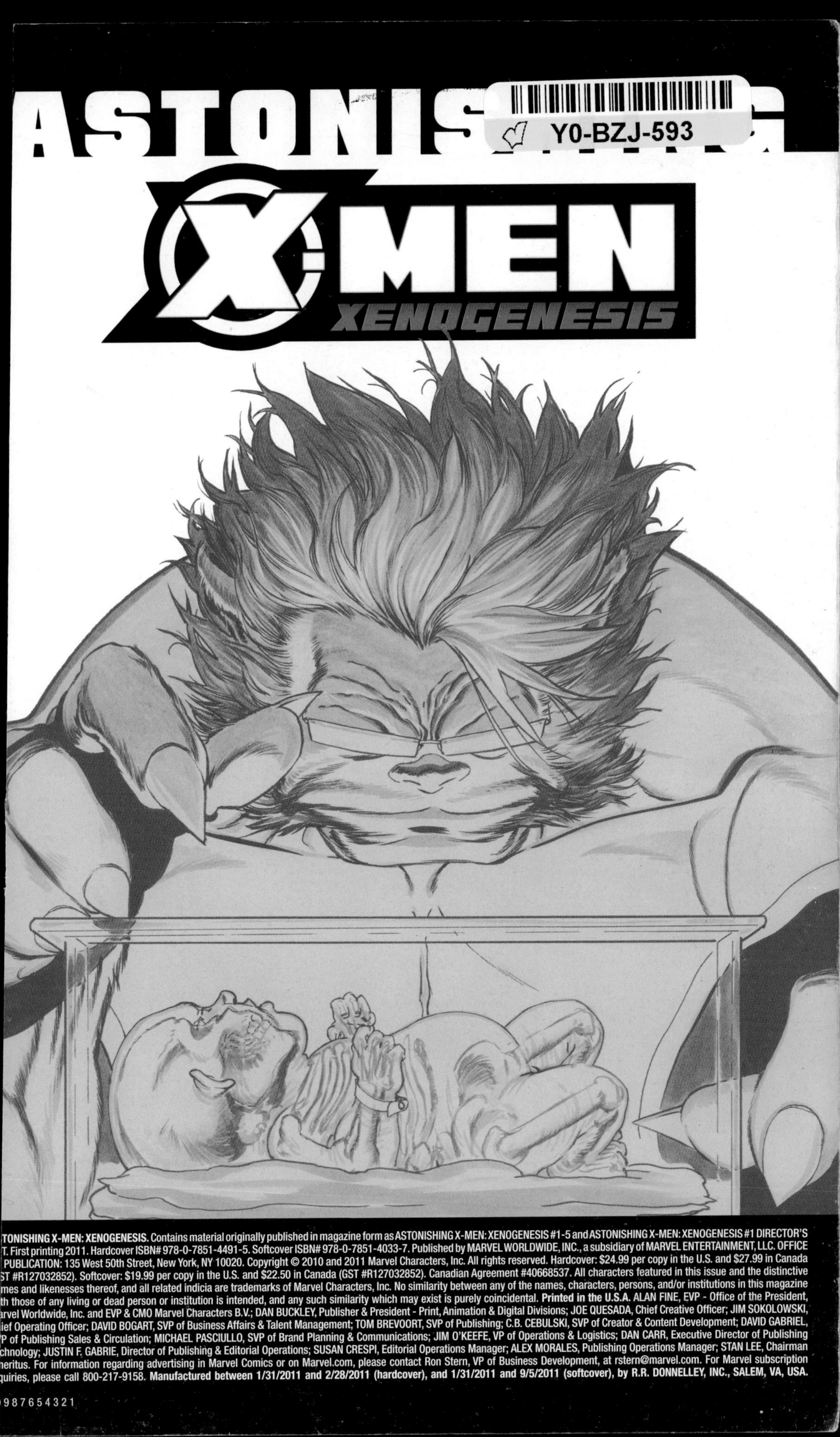

TONISHING X-MEN: XENOGENESIS. Contains material originally published in magazine form as ASTONISHING X-MEN: XENOGENESIS #1-5 and ASTONISHING X-MEN: XENOGENESIS #1 DIRECTOR'S
T. First printing 2011. Hardcover ISBN# 978-0-7851-4491-5. Softcover ISBN# 978-0-7851-4033-7. Published by MARVEL WORLDWIDE, INC., a subsidiary of MARVEL ENTERTAINMENT, LLC. OFFICE
PUBLICATION: 135 West 50th Street, New York, NY 10020. Hardcover: $24.99 per copy in the U.S. and $27.99 in Canada
ST #R127032852). Softcover: $19.99 per copy in the U.S. and $22.50 in Canada (GST #R127032852). Canadian Agreement #40668537. **Printed in the U.S.A.** ALAN FINE, EVP - Office of the President,
arvel Worldwide, Inc. and EVP & CMO Marvel Characters B.V.; DAN BUCKLEY, Publisher & President - Print, Animation & Digital Divisions; JOE QUESADA, Chief Creative Officer; JIM SOKOLOWSKI,
ief Operating Officer; DAVID BOGART, SVP of Business Affairs & Talent Management; TOM BREVOORT, SVP of Publishing; C.B. CEBULSKI, SVP of Creator & Content Development; DAVID GABRIEL,
P of Publishing Sales & Circulation; MICHAEL PASCIULLO, SVP of Brand Planning & Communications; JIM O'KEEFE, VP of Operations & Logistics; DAN CARR, Executive Director of Publishing
chnology; JUSTIN F. GABRIE, Director of Publishing & Editorial Operations; SUSAN CRESPI, Editorial Operations Manager; ALEX MORALES, Publishing Operations Manager; STAN LEE, Chairman
neritus. For information regarding advertising in Marvel Comics or on Marvel.com, please contact Ron Stern, VP of Business Development, at rstern@marvel.com. For Marvel subscription
quiries, please call 800-217-9158. **Manufactured between 1/31/2011 and 2/28/2011 (hardcover), and 1/31/2011 and 9/5/2011 (softcover), by R.R. DONNELLEY, INC., SALEM, VA, USA.**

987654321

WRITER **WARREN ELLIS** ARTIST **KAARE ANDREWS**

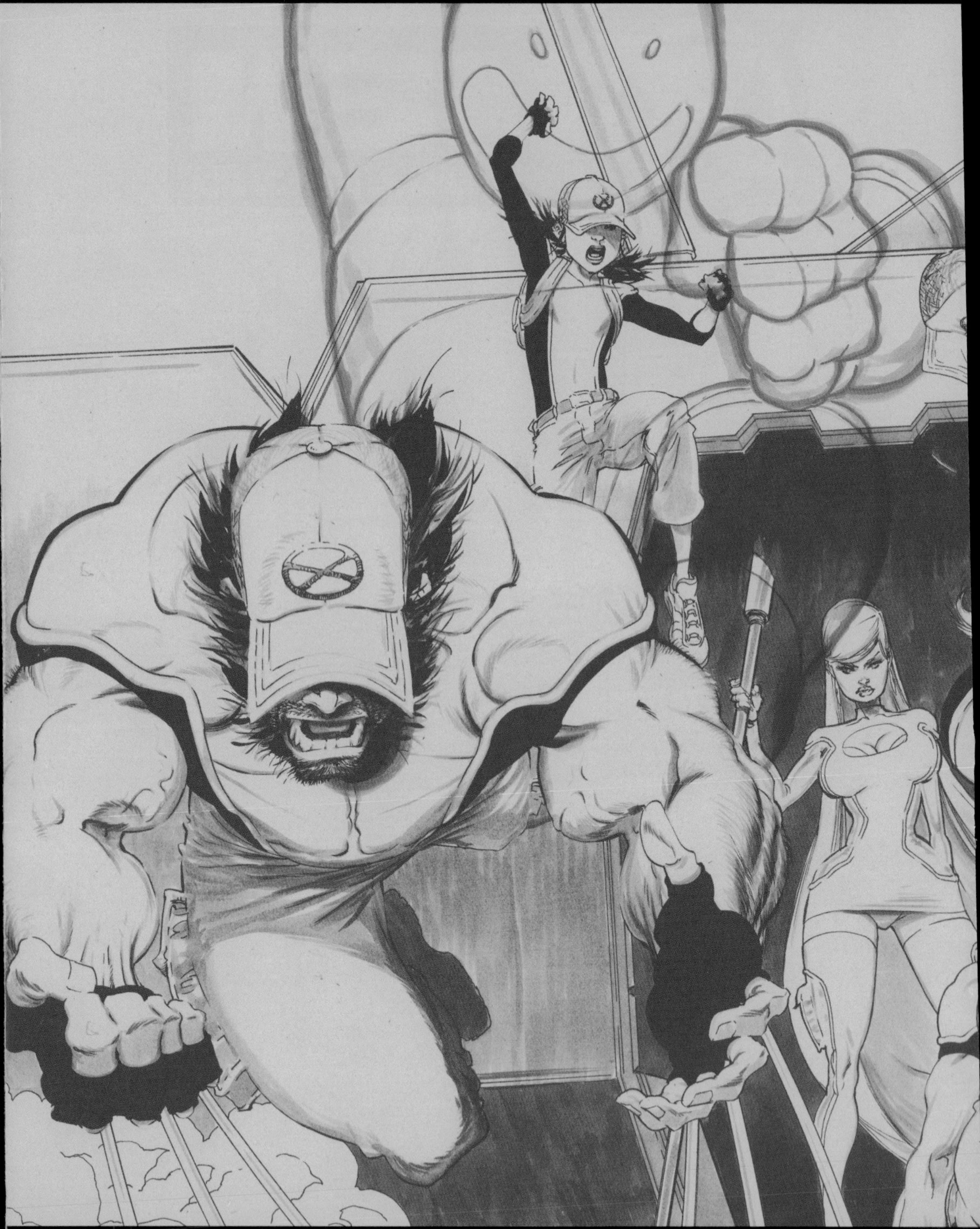

COLORIST **FRANK D'ARMATA**

LETTERERS **VIRTUAL CALIGRAPHY'S JOE CARAMAGNA & CLAYTON COWLES**

ASSOCIATE EDITOR **DANIEL KETCHUM** EXECUTIVE EDITOR **AXEL ALONSO**

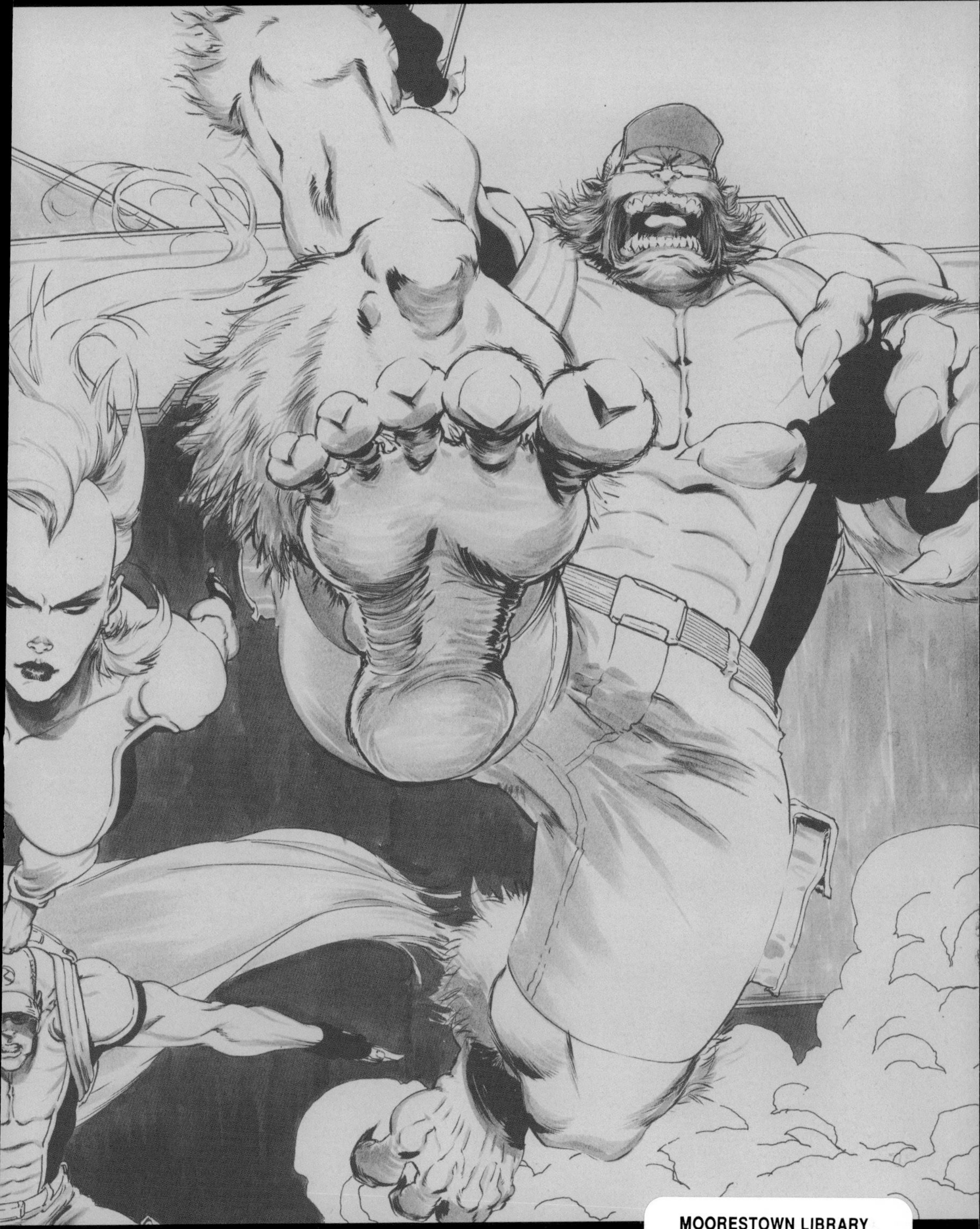

COLLECTION EDITOR **JENNIFER GRÜNWALD** EDITORIAL ASSISTANTS **JAMES EMMETT & JOE HOCHSTEIN** ASSISTANT EDITORS **ALEX STARBUCK & NELSON RIBEIRO**
EDITOR, SPECIAL PROJECTS **MARK D. BEAZLEY** SENIOR EDITOR, SPECIAL PROJECTS **JEFF YOUNGQUIST** SENIOR VICE PRESIDENT OF SALES **DAVID GABRIEL**
BOOK DESIGN **JEFF POWELL** EDITOR IN CHIEF **AXEL ALONSO** CHIEF CREATIVE OFFICER **JOE QUESADA** PUBLISHER **DAN BUCKLEY** EXECUTIVE PRODUCER **ALAN FINE**

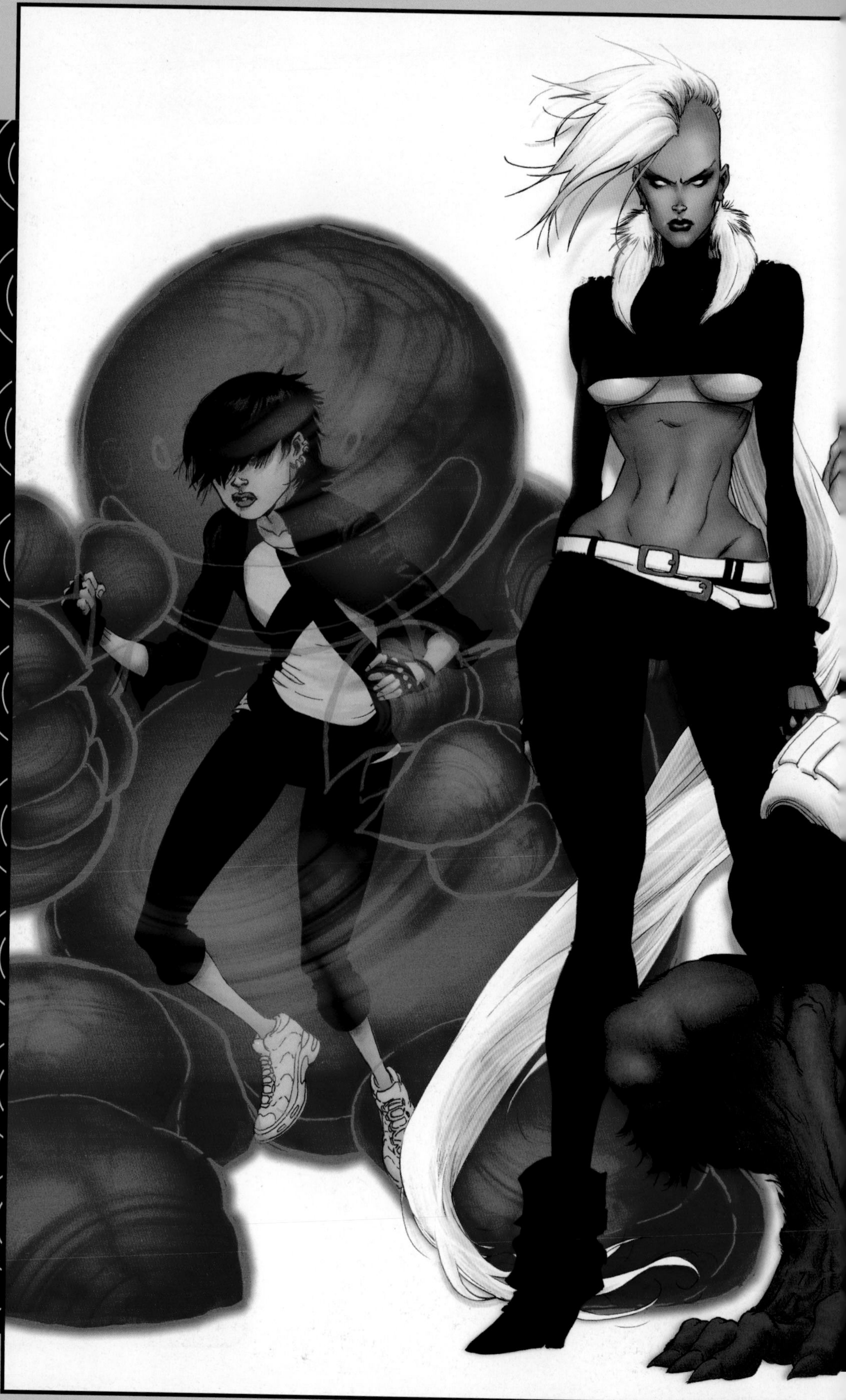

ONE

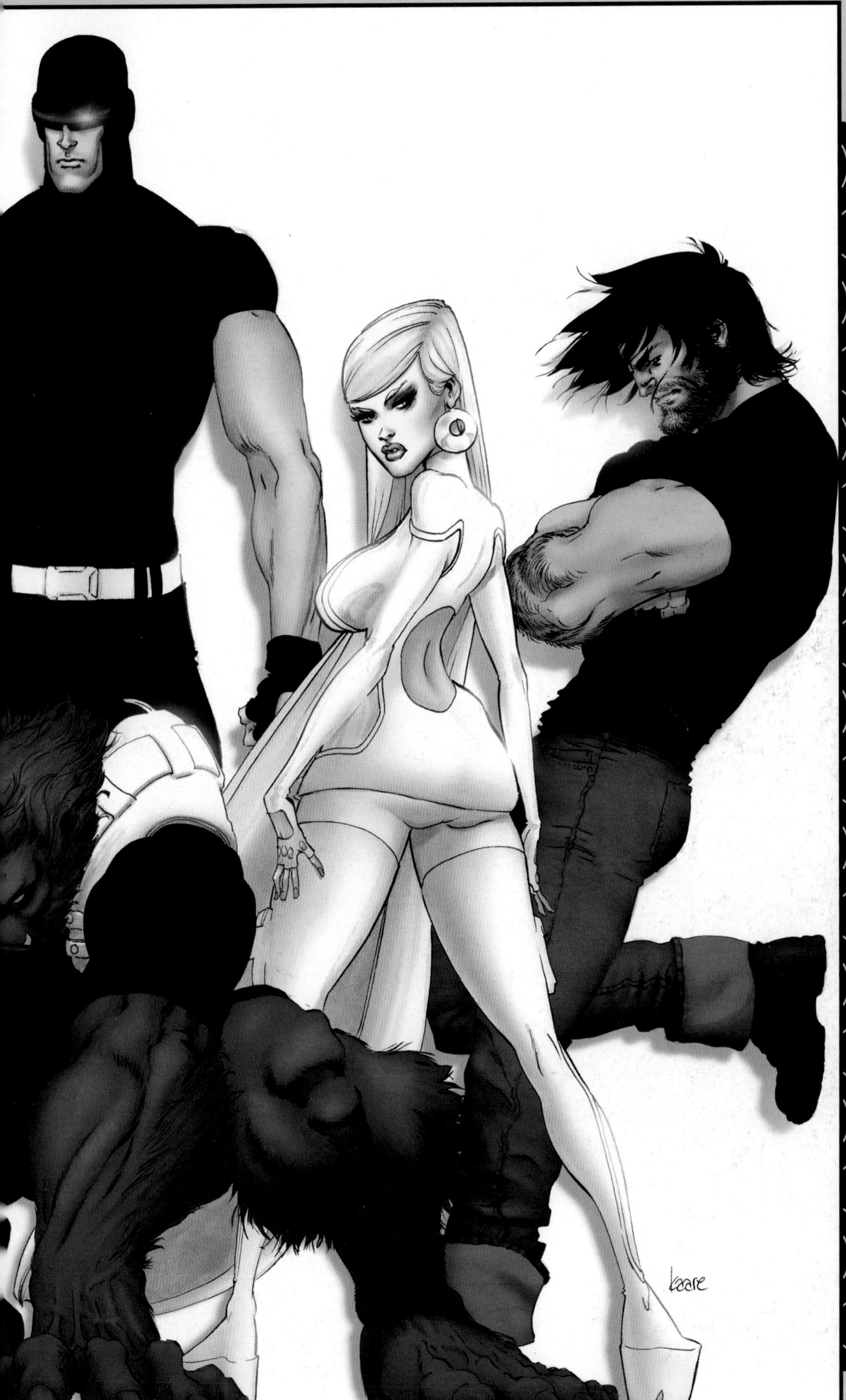
kaare

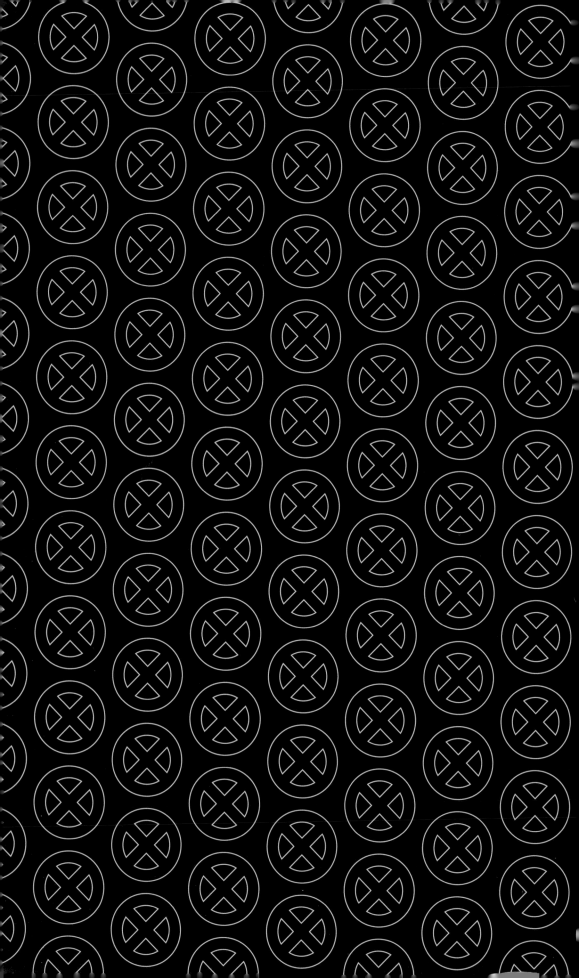

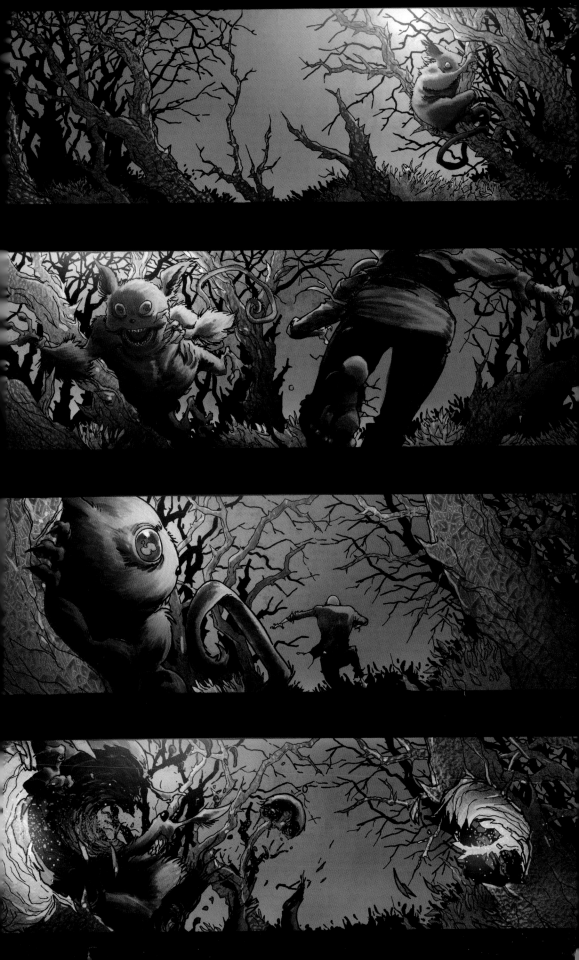

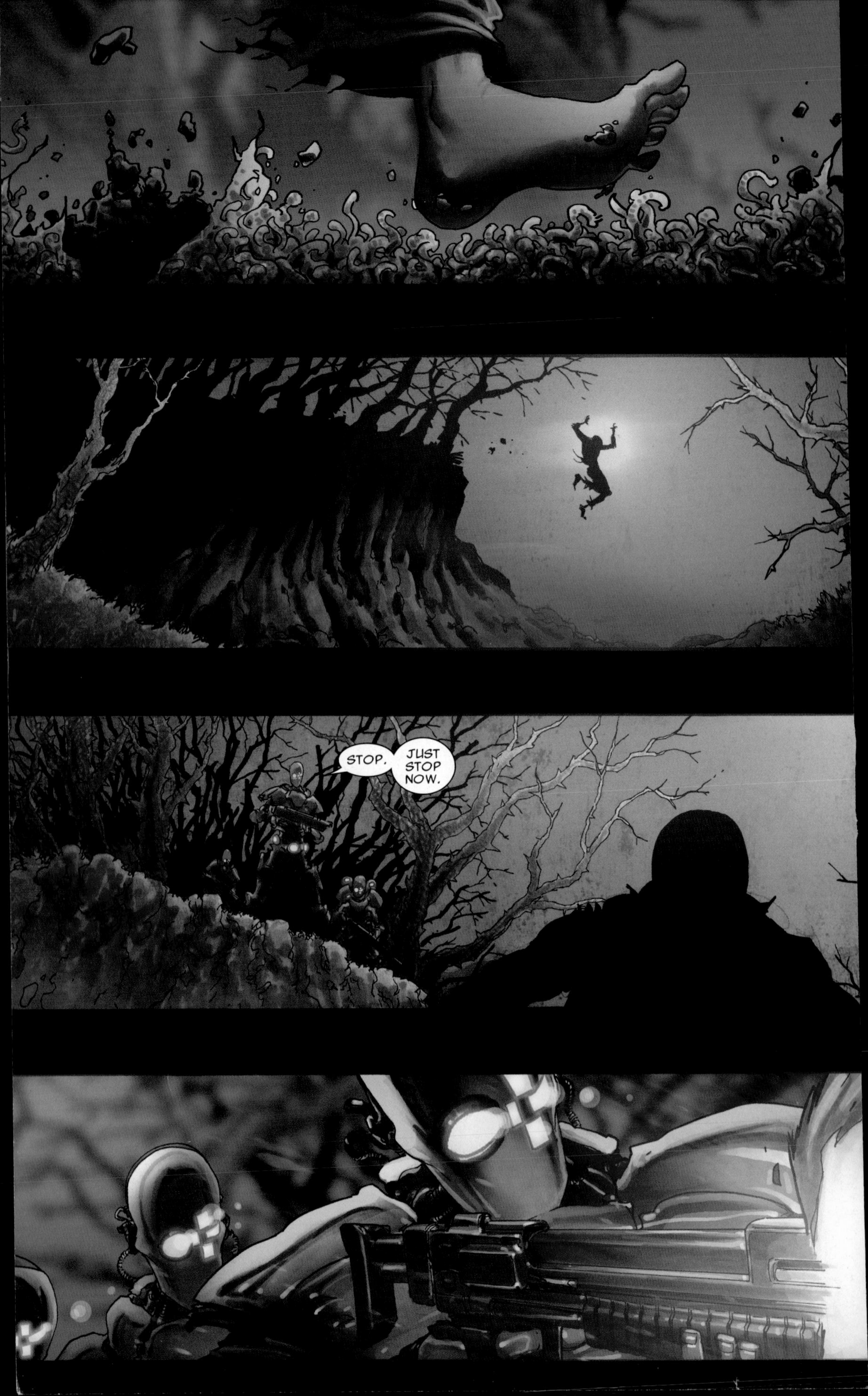
STOP.
JUST STOP NOW.

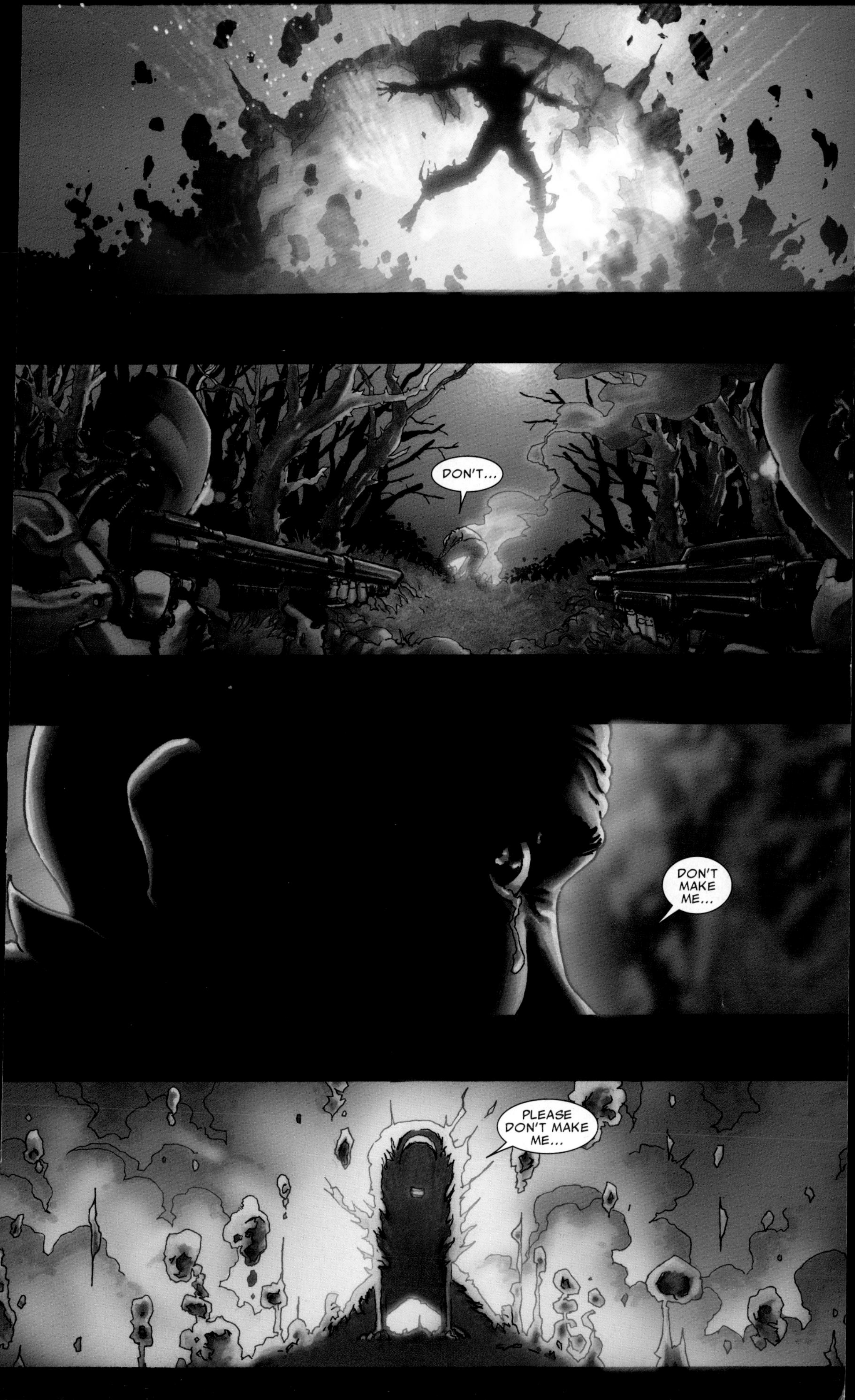
DON'T...
DON'T MAKE ME...
PLEASE DON'T MAKE ME...

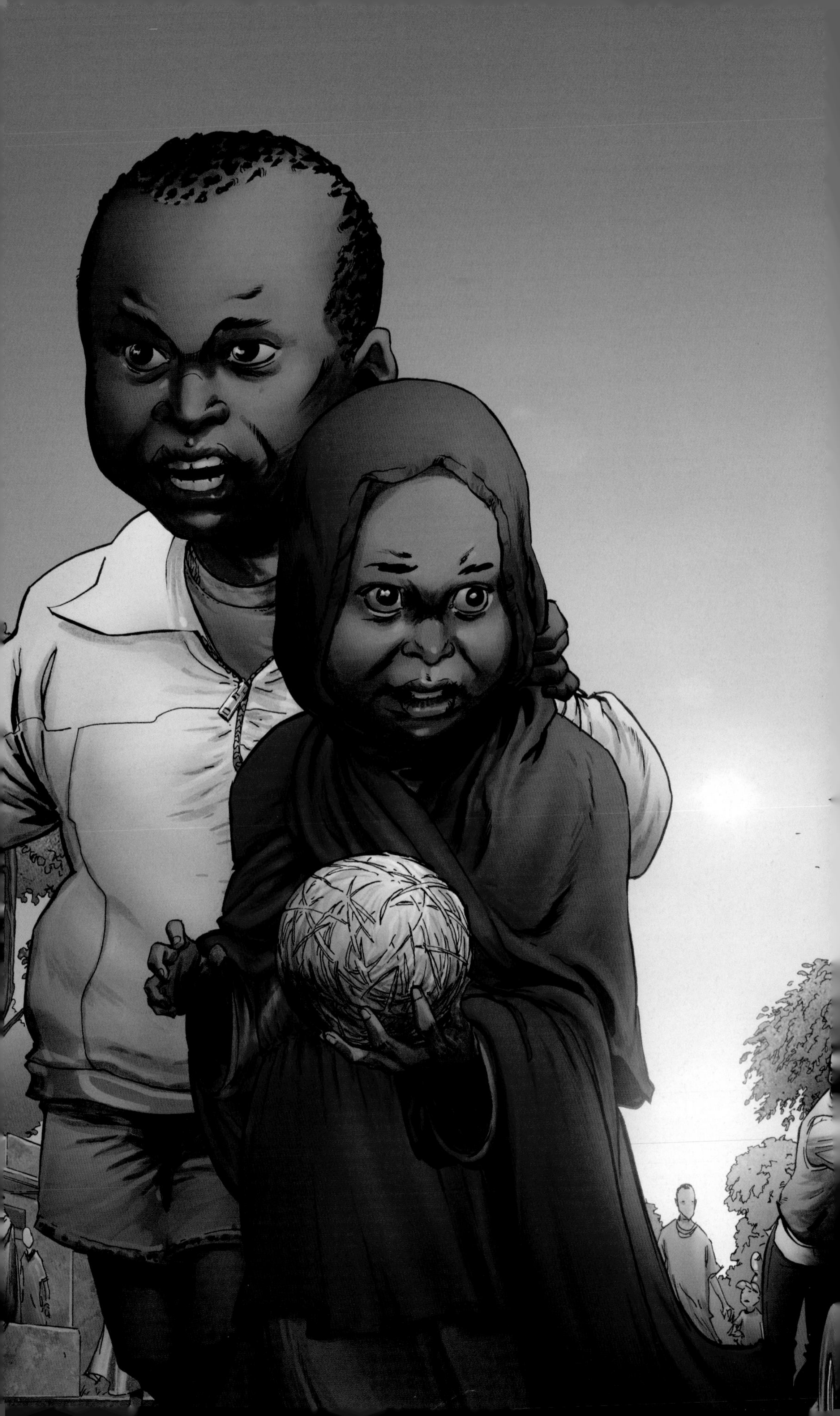

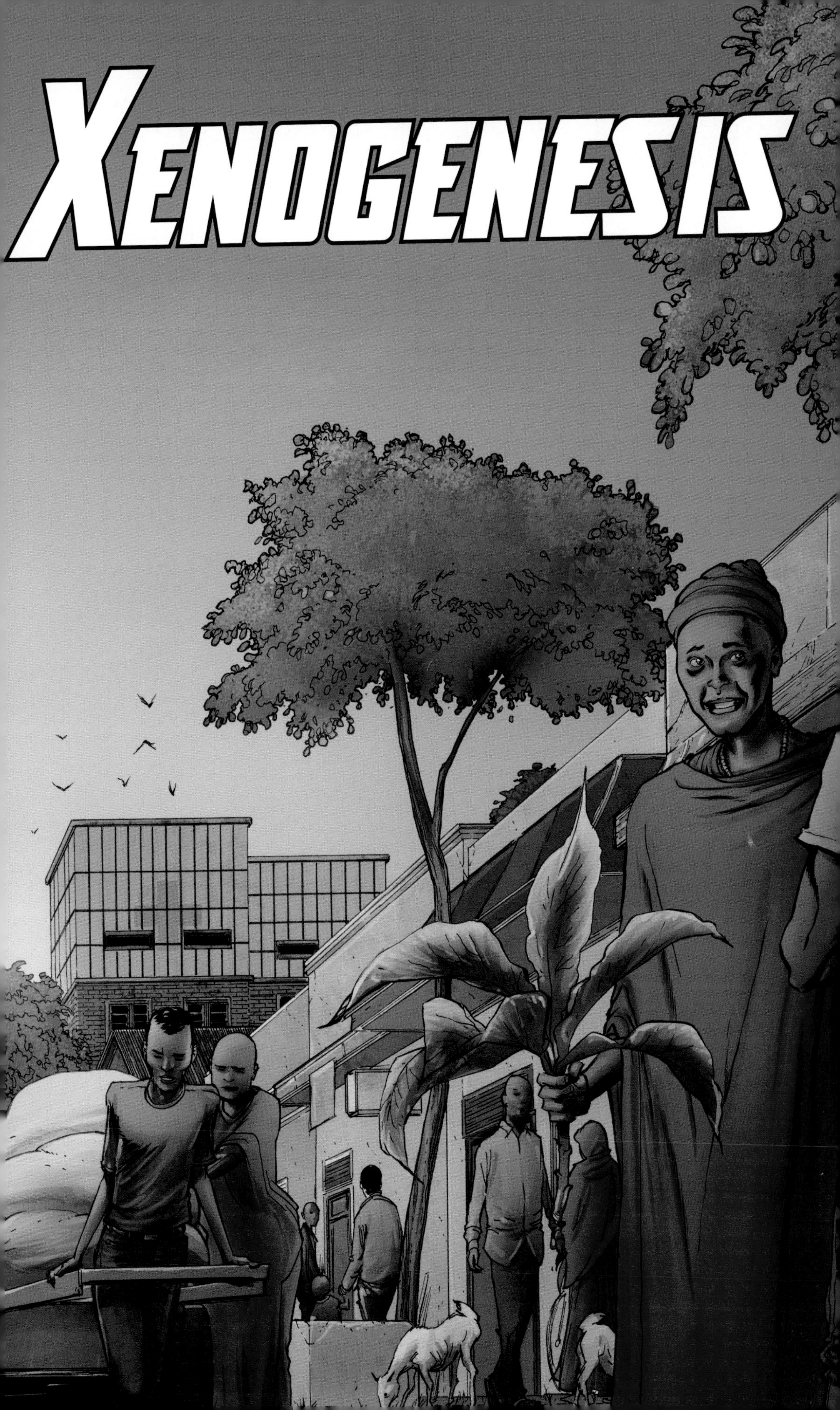
XENOGENESIS

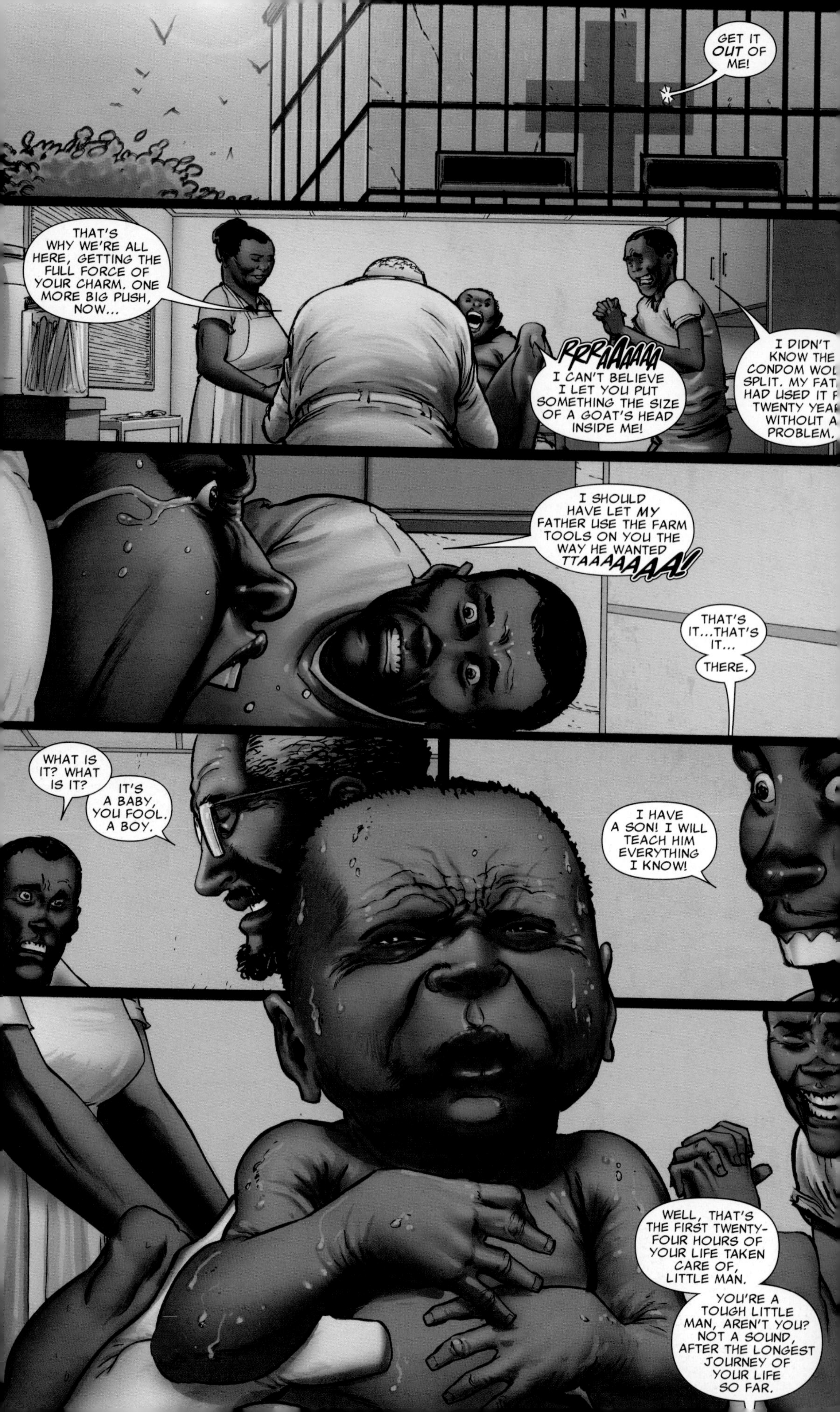
GET IT OUT OF ME!
THAT'S WHY WE'RE ALL HERE, GETTING THE FULL FORCE OF YOUR CHARM. ONE MORE BIG PUSH, NOW...
RRRAAAAAA
I CAN'T BELIEVE I LET YOU PUT SOMETHING THE SIZE OF A GOAT'S HEAD INSIDE ME!
I DIDN'T KNOW THE CONDOM WOU SPLIT. MY FAT HAD USED IT F TWENTY YEAR WITHOUT A PROBLEM.
I SHOULD HAVE LET MY FATHER USE THE FARM TOOLS ON YOU THE WAY HE WANTED TTAAAAAAA!
THAT'S IT...THAT'S IT...
THERE.
WHAT IS IT? WHAT IS IT?
IT'S A BABY, YOU FOOL. A BOY.
I HAVE A SON! I WILL TEACH HIM EVERYTHING I KNOW!
WELL, THAT'S THE FIRST TWENTY-FOUR HOURS OF YOUR LIFE TAKEN CARE OF, LITTLE MAN.
YOU'RE A TOUGH LITTLE MAN, AREN'T YOU? NOT A SOUND, AFTER THE LONGEST JOURNEY OF YOUR LIFE SO FAR.

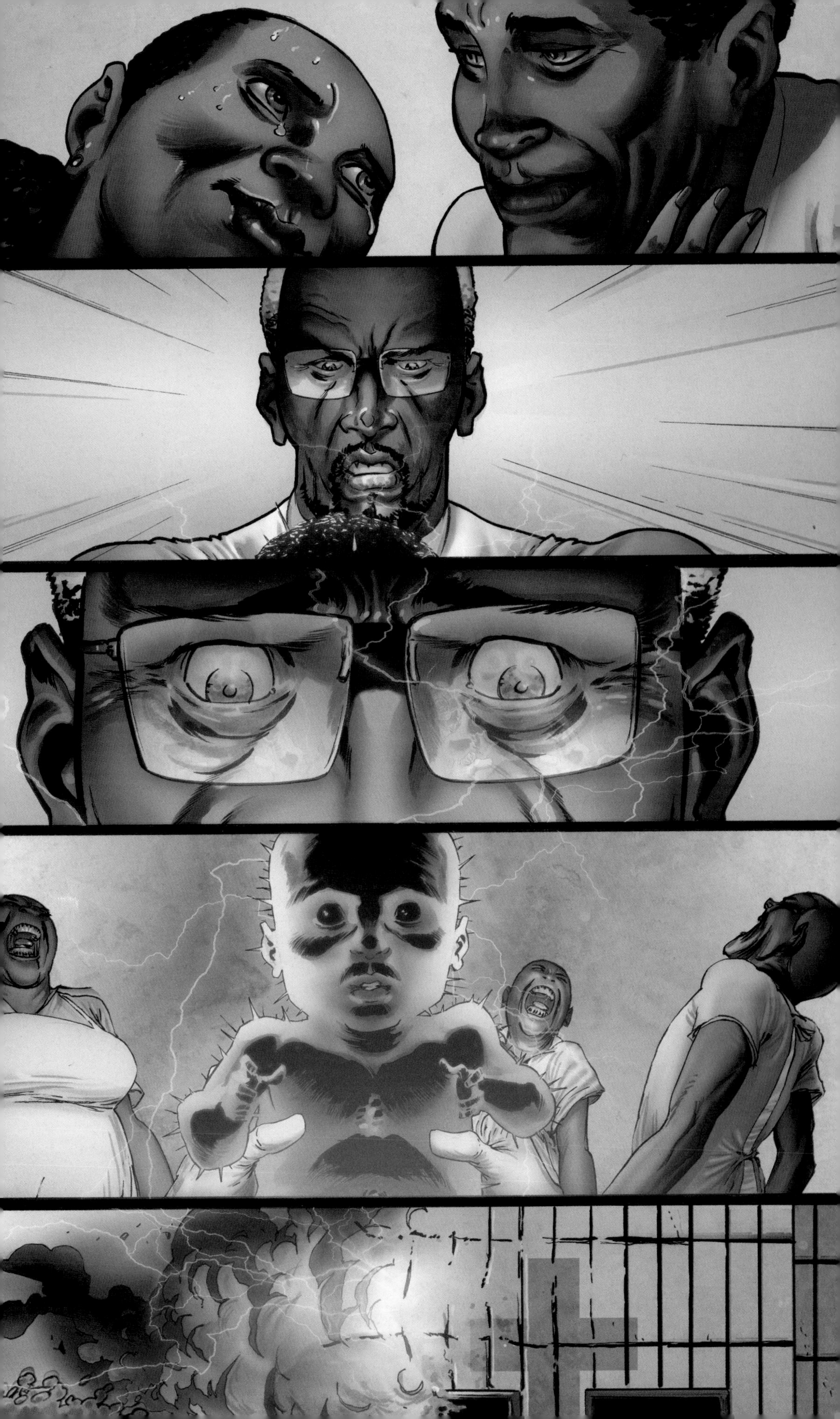

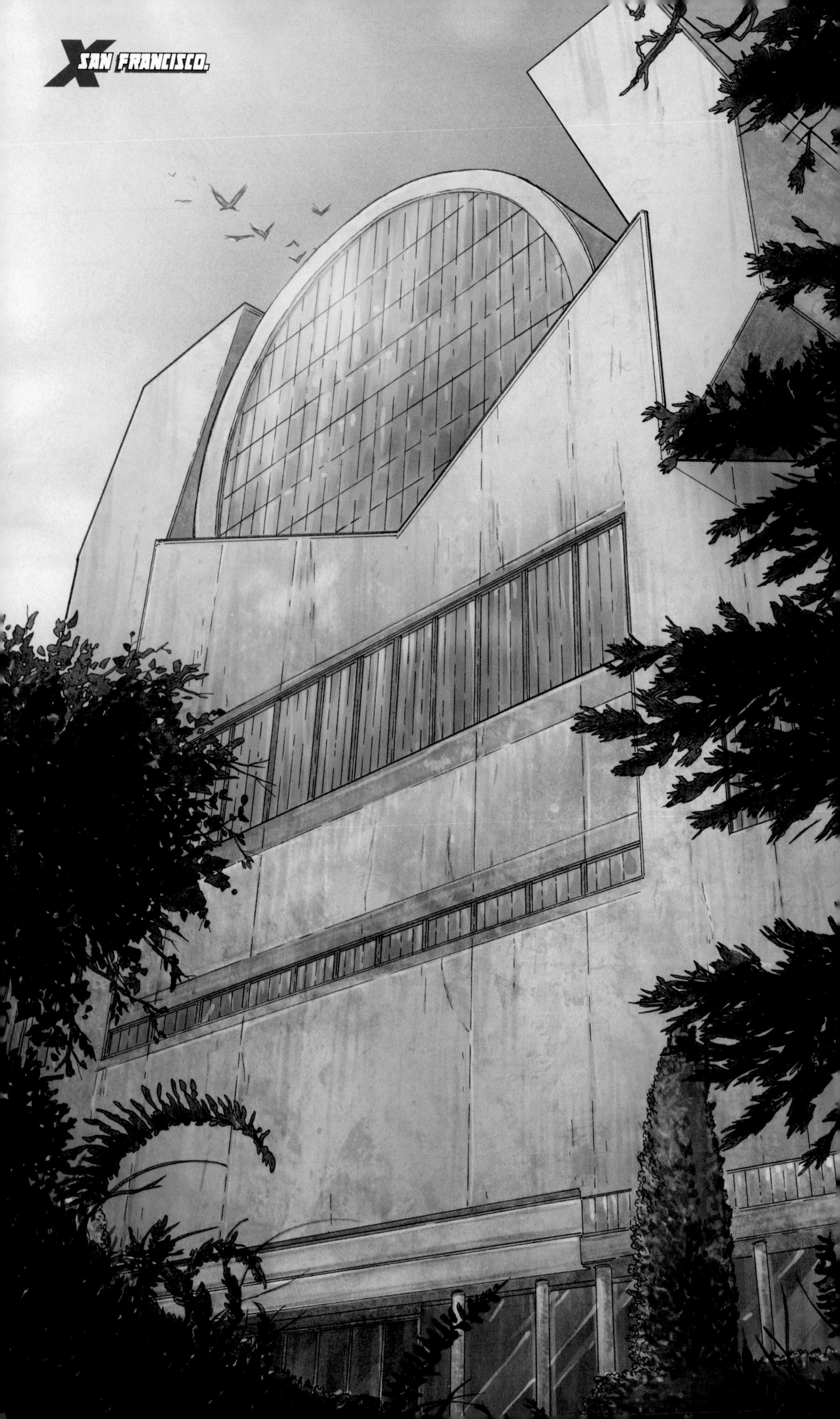
SAN FRANCISCO.

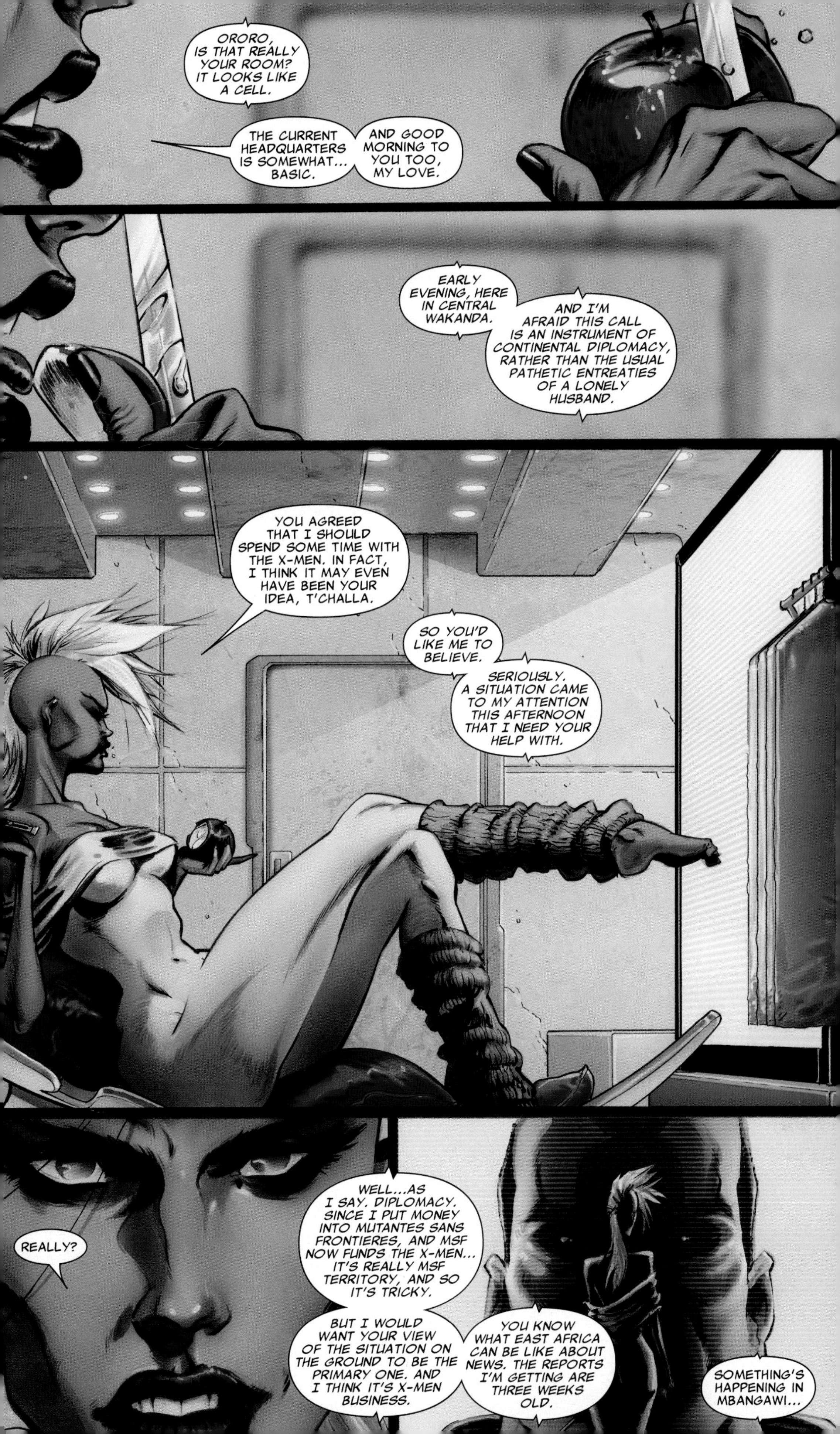
ORORO, IS THAT REALLY YOUR ROOM? IT LOOKS LIKE A CELL.
THE CURRENT HEADQUARTERS IS SOMEWHAT... BASIC.
AND GOOD MORNING TO YOU TOO, MY LOVE.
EARLY EVENING, HERE IN CENTRAL WAKANDA.
AND I'M AFRAID THIS CALL IS AN INSTRUMENT OF CONTINENTAL DIPLOMACY, RATHER THAN THE USUAL PATHETIC ENTREATIES OF A LONELY HUSBAND.
YOU AGREED THAT I SHOULD SPEND SOME TIME WITH THE X-MEN. IN FACT, I THINK IT MAY EVEN HAVE BEEN YOUR IDEA, T'CHALLA.
SO YOU'D LIKE ME TO BELIEVE.
SERIOUSLY. A SITUATION CAME TO MY ATTENTION THIS AFTERNOON THAT I NEED YOUR HELP WITH.
REALLY?
WELL...AS I SAY. DIPLOMACY. SINCE I PUT MONEY INTO MUTANTES SANS FRONTIERES, AND MSF NOW FUNDS THE X-MEN... IT'S REALLY MSF TERRITORY, AND SO IT'S TRICKY.
BUT I WOULD WANT YOUR VIEW OF THE SITUATION ON THE GROUND TO BE THE PRIMARY ONE. AND I THINK IT'S X-MEN BUSINESS.
YOU KNOW WHAT EAST AFRICA CAN BE LIKE ABOUT NEWS. THE REPORTS I'M GETTING ARE THREE WEEKS OLD.
SOMETHING'S HAPPENING IN MBANGAWI...

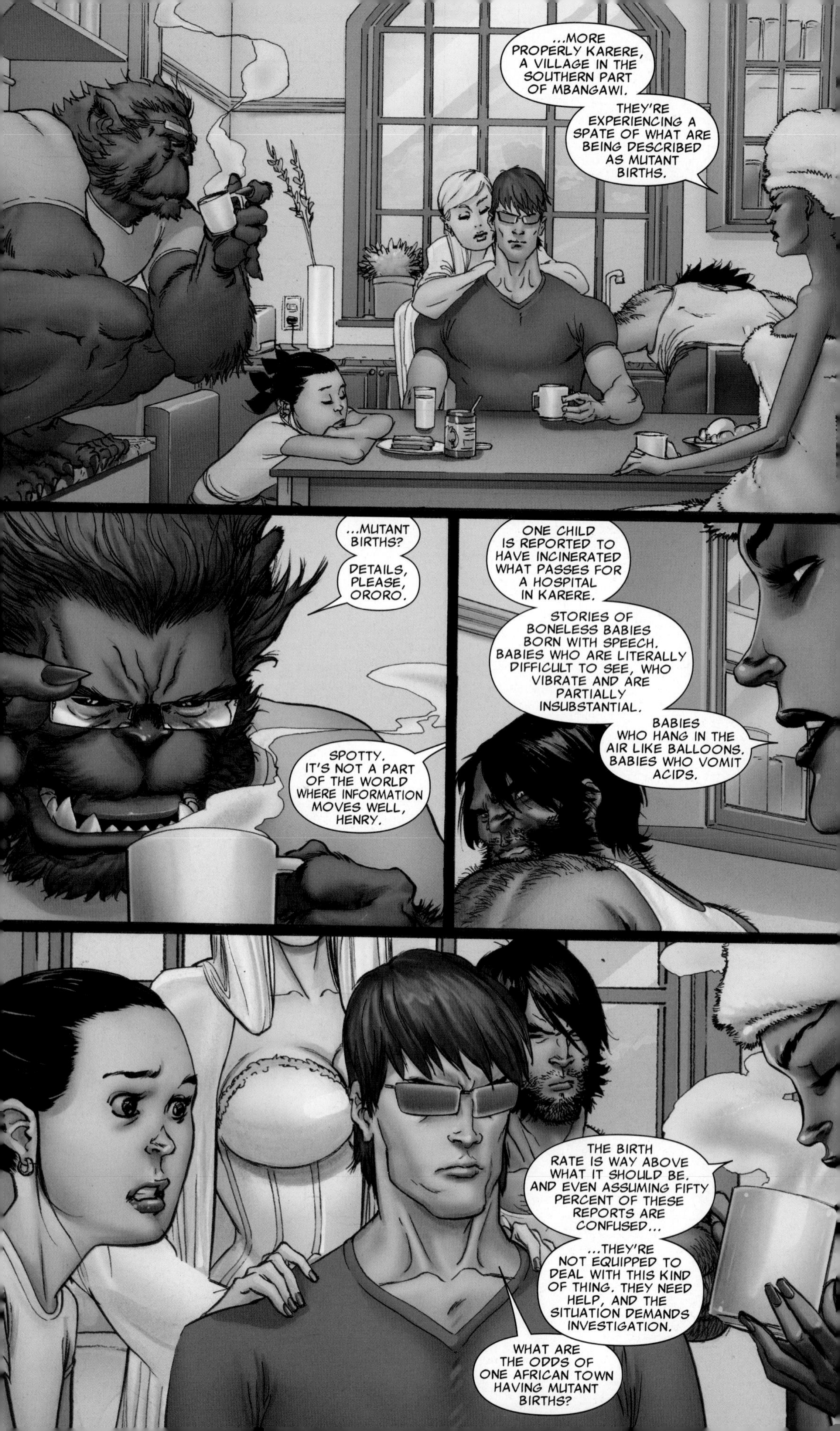
...MORE PROPERLY KARERE, A VILLAGE IN THE SOUTHERN PART OF MBANGAWI.
THEY'RE EXPERIENCING A SPATE OF WHAT ARE BEING DESCRIBED AS MUTANT BIRTHS.
...MUTANT BIRTHS?
DETAILS, PLEASE, ORORO.
SPOTTY. IT'S NOT A PART OF THE WORLD WHERE INFORMATION MOVES WELL, HENRY.
ONE CHILD IS REPORTED TO HAVE INCINERATED WHAT PASSES FOR A HOSPITAL IN KARERE.
STORIES OF BONELESS BABIES BORN WITH SPEECH. BABIES WHO ARE LITERALLY DIFFICULT TO SEE, WHO VIBRATE AND ARE PARTIALLY INSUBSTANTIAL.
BABIES WHO HANG IN THE AIR LIKE BALLOONS. BABIES WHO VOMIT ACIDS.
THE BIRTH RATE IS WAY ABOVE WHAT IT SHOULD BE. AND EVEN ASSUMING FIFTY PERCENT OF THESE REPORTS ARE CONFUSED...
...THEY'RE NOT EQUIPPED TO DEAL WITH THIS KIND OF THING. THEY NEED HELP, AND THE SITUATION DEMANDS INVESTIGATION.
WHAT ARE THE ODDS OF ONE AFRICAN TOWN HAVING MUTANT BIRTHS?

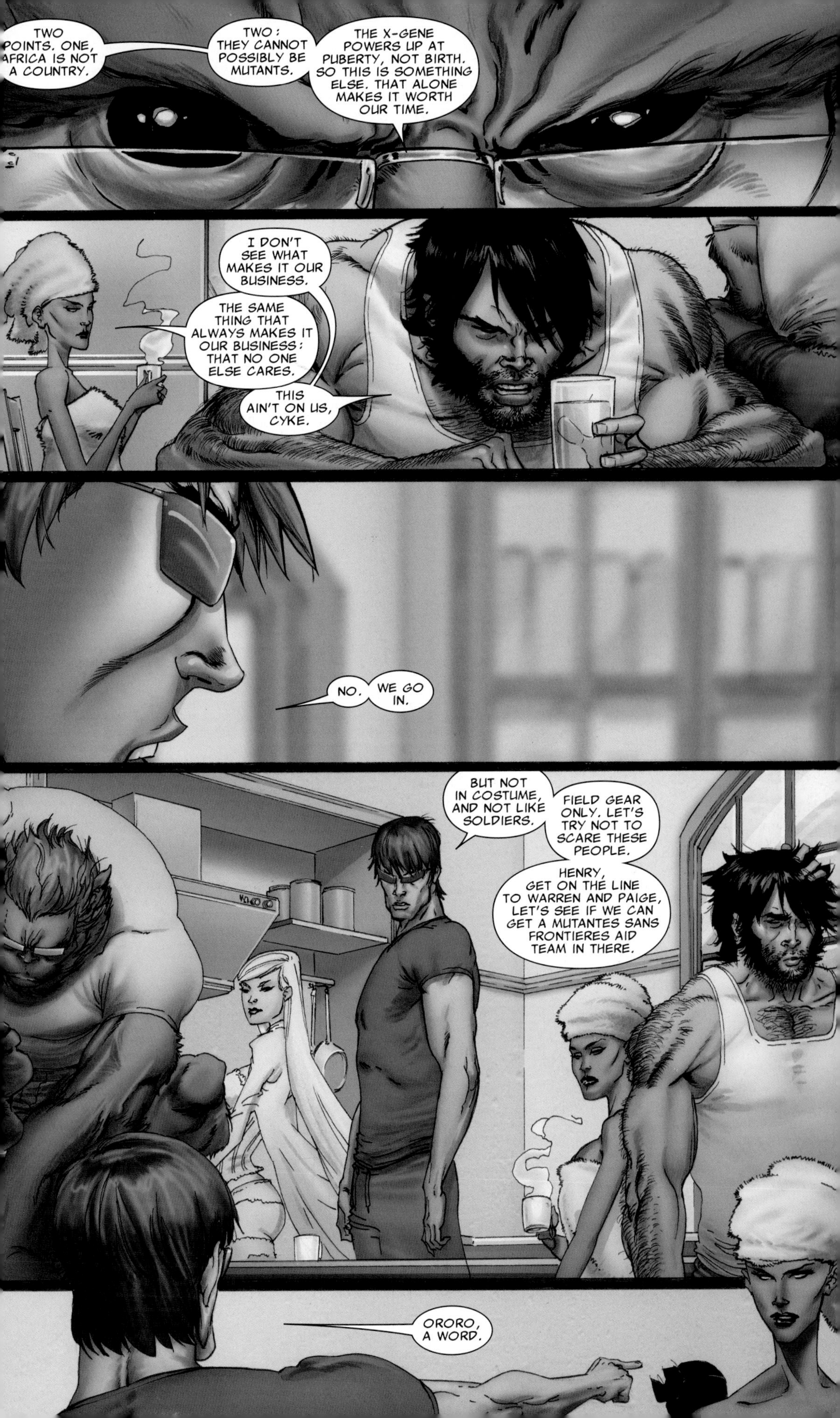
TWO POINTS. ONE, AFRICA IS NOT A COUNTRY.
TWO; THEY CANNOT POSSIBLY BE MUTANTS.
THE X-GENE POWERS UP AT PUBERTY, NOT BIRTH. SO THIS IS SOMETHING ELSE. THAT ALONE MAKES IT WORTH OUR TIME.
I DON'T SEE WHAT MAKES IT OUR BUSINESS.
THE SAME THING THAT ALWAYS MAKES IT OUR BUSINESS: THAT NO ONE ELSE CARES.
THIS AIN'T ON US, CYKE.
NO.
WE GO IN.
BUT NOT IN COSTUME, AND NOT LIKE SOLDIERS.
FIELD GEAR ONLY. LET'S TRY NOT TO SCARE THESE PEOPLE.
HENRY, GET ON THE LINE TO WARREN AND PAIGE, LET'S SEE IF WE CAN GET A MUTANTES SANS FRONTIERES AID TEAM IN THERE.
ORORO, A WORD.

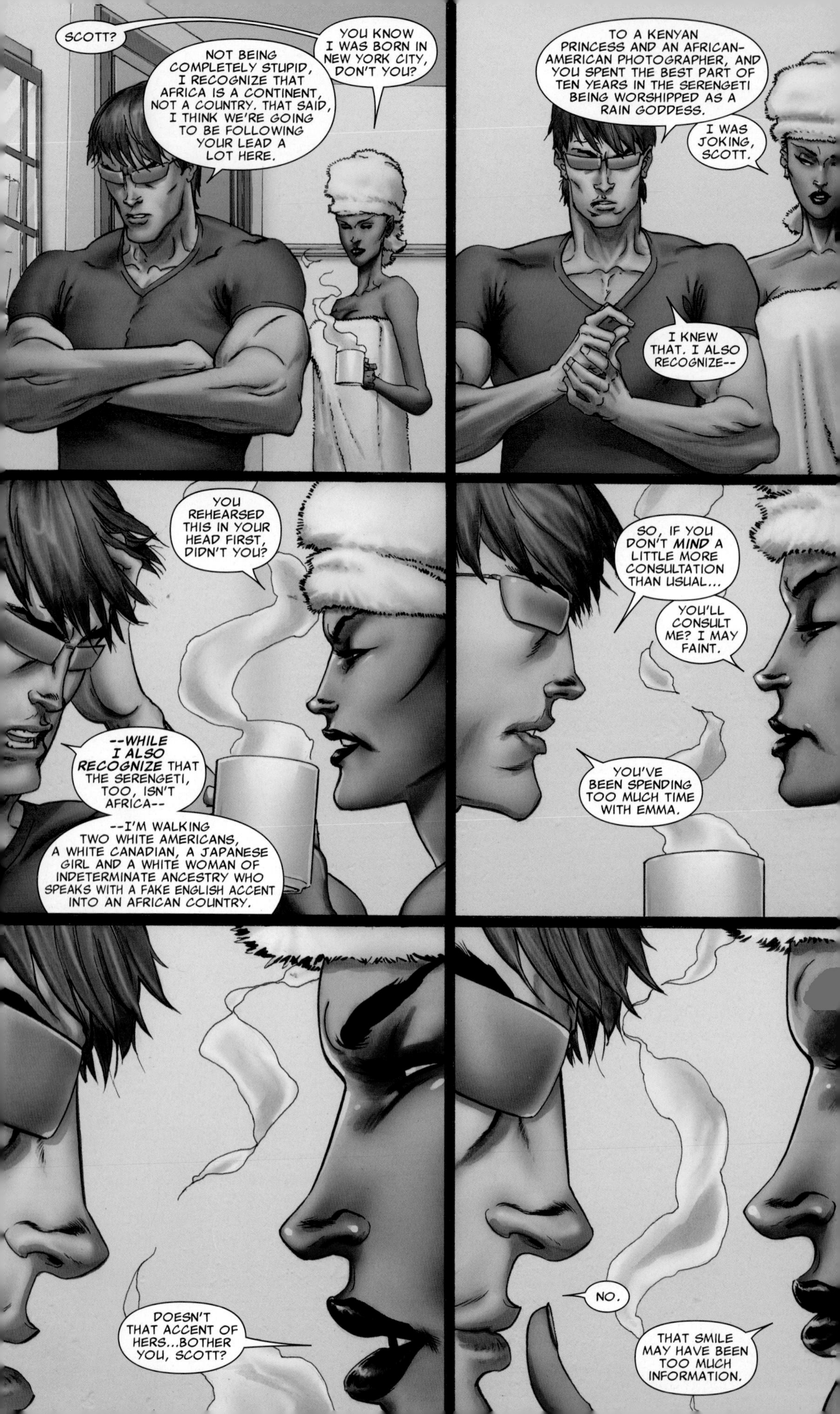
SCOTT?
YOU KNOW I WAS BORN IN NEW YORK CITY, DON'T YOU?
NOT BEING COMPLETELY STUPID, I RECOGNIZE THAT AFRICA IS A CONTINENT, NOT A COUNTRY. THAT SAID, I THINK WE'RE GOING TO BE FOLLOWING YOUR LEAD A LOT HERE.
TO A KENYAN PRINCESS AND AN AFRICAN-AMERICAN PHOTOGRAPHER, AND YOU SPENT THE BEST PART OF TEN YEARS IN THE SERENGETI BEING WORSHIPPED AS A RAIN GODDESS.
I WAS JOKING, SCOTT.
I KNEW THAT. I ALSO RECOGNIZE--
YOU REHEARSED THIS IN YOUR HEAD FIRST, DIDN'T YOU?
--WHILE I ALSO RECOGNIZE THAT THE SERENGETI, TOO, ISN'T AFRICA--
--I'M WALKING TWO WHITE AMERICANS, A WHITE CANADIAN, A JAPANESE GIRL AND A WHITE WOMAN OF INDETERMINATE ANCESTRY WHO SPEAKS WITH A FAKE ENGLISH ACCENT INTO AN AFRICAN COUNTRY.
SO, IF YOU DON'T MIND A LITTLE MORE CONSULTATION THAN USUAL...
YOU'LL CONSULT ME? I MAY FAINT.
YOU'VE BEEN SPENDING TOO MUCH TIME WITH EMMA.
DOESN'T THAT ACCENT OF HERS...BOTHER YOU, SCOTT?
NO.
THAT SMILE MAY HAVE BEEN TOO MUCH INFORMATION.

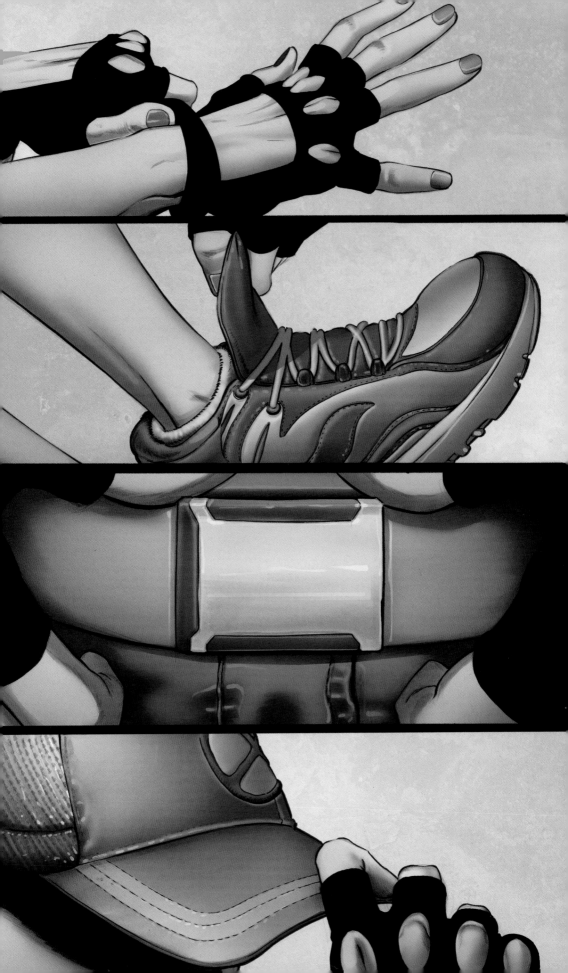

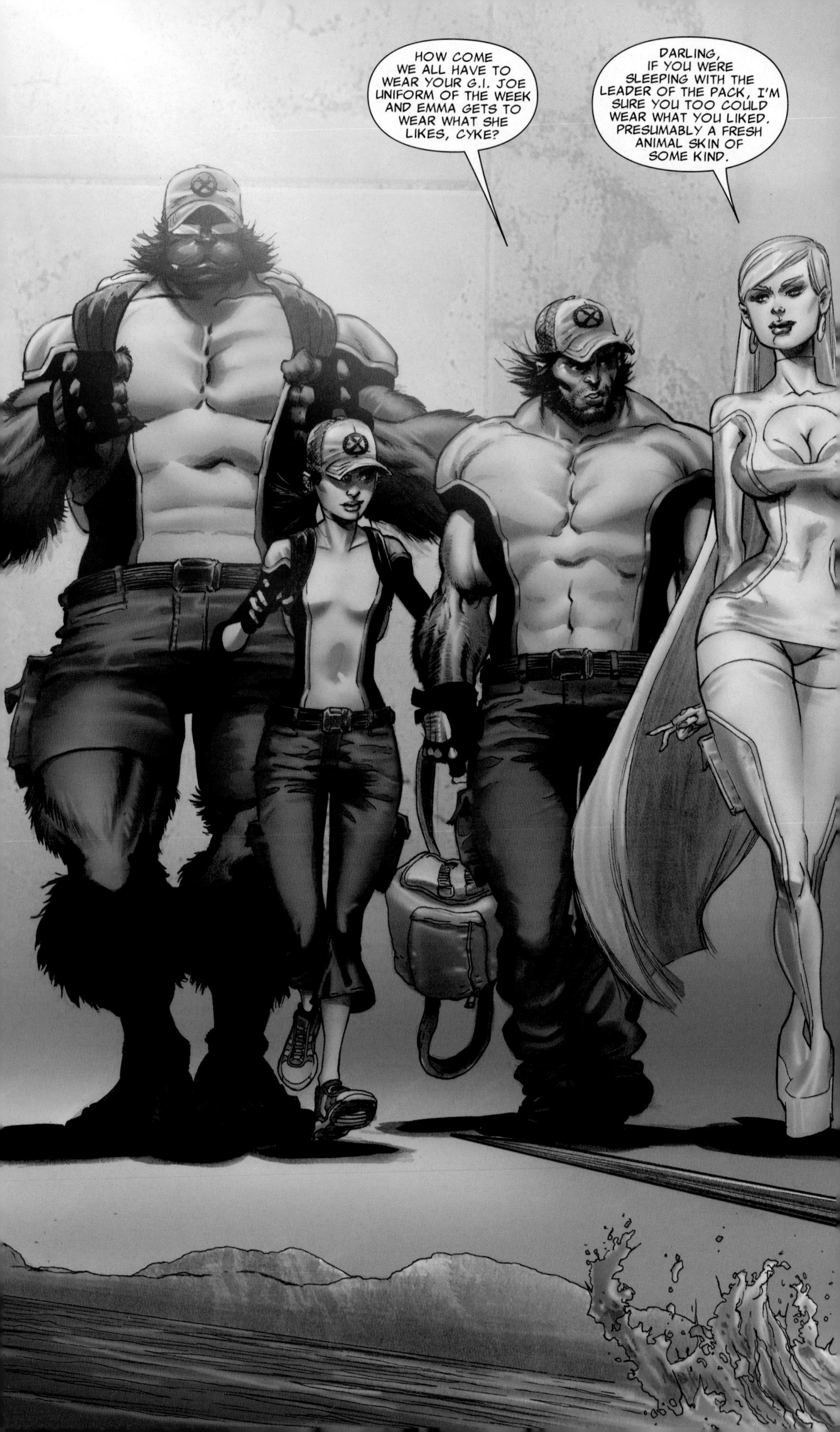
HOW COME WE ALL HAVE TO WEAR YOUR G.I. JOE UNIFORM OF THE WEEK AND EMMA GETS TO WEAR WHAT SHE LIKES, CYKE?
DARLING, IF YOU WERE SLEEPING WITH THE LEADER OF THE PACK, I'M SURE YOU TOO COULD WEAR WHAT YOU LIKED. PRESUMABLY A FRESH ANIMAL SKIN OF SOME KIND.

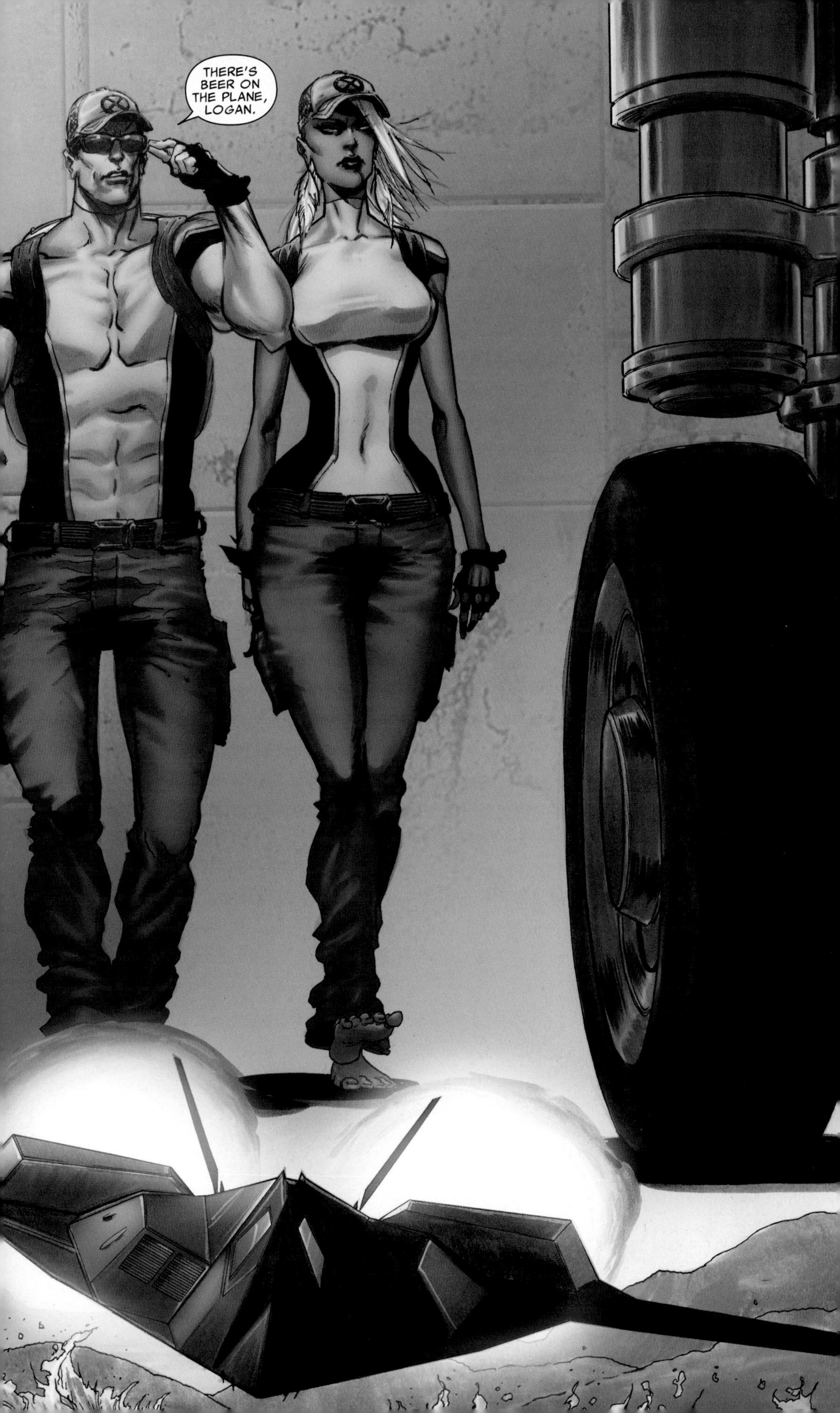
THERE'S BEER ON THE PLANE, LOGAN.

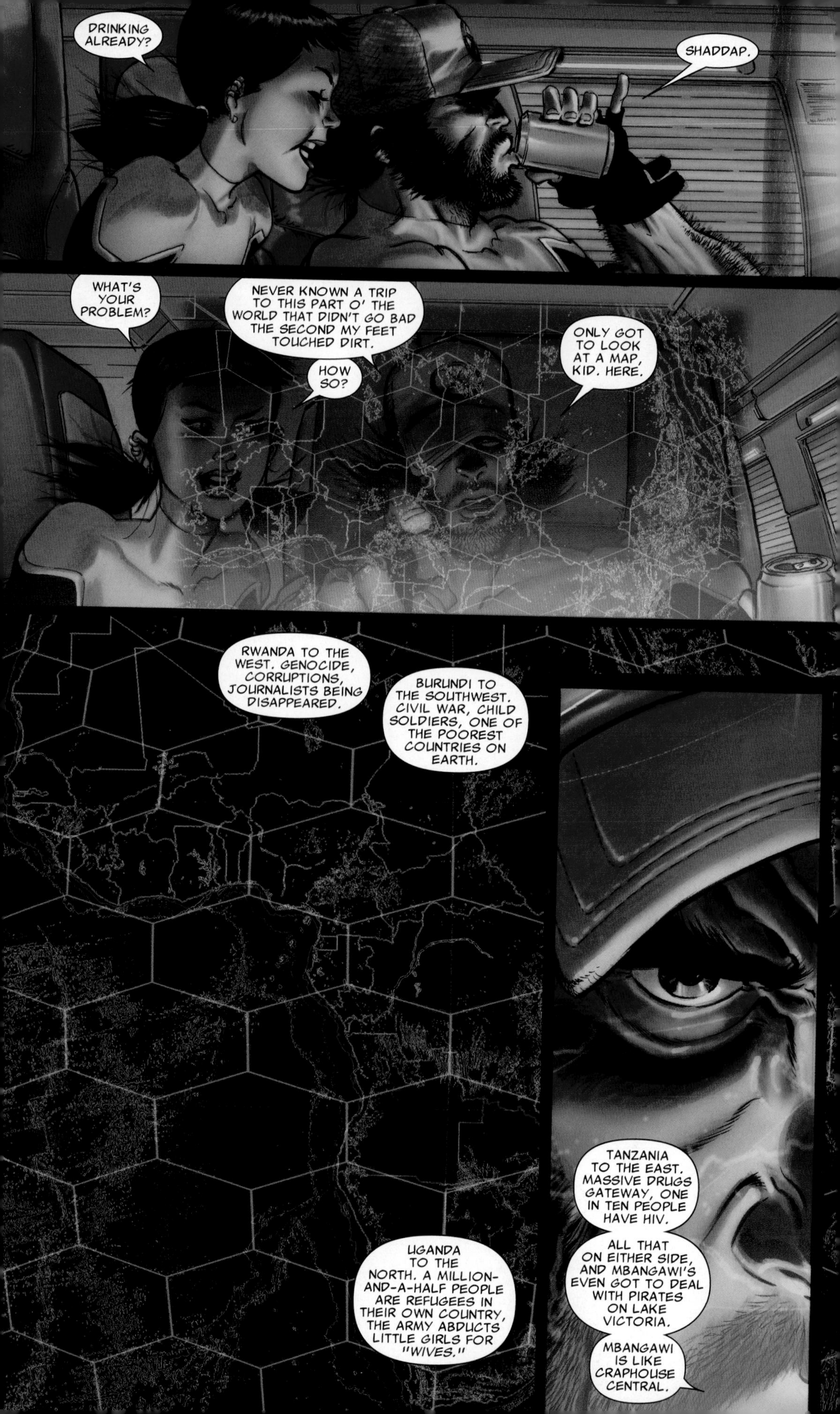
DRINKING ALREADY?
SHADDAP.
WHAT'S YOUR PROBLEM?
NEVER KNOWN A TRIP TO THIS PART O' THE WORLD THAT DIDN'T GO BAD THE SECOND MY FEET TOUCHED DIRT.
HOW SO?
ONLY GOT TO LOOK AT A MAP, KID. HERE.
RWANDA TO THE WEST. GENOCIDE, CORRUPTIONS, JOURNALISTS BEING DISAPPEARED.
BURUNDI TO THE SOUTHWEST. CIVIL WAR, CHILD SOLDIERS, ONE OF THE POOREST COUNTRIES ON EARTH.
UGANDA TO THE NORTH. A MILLION-AND-A-HALF PEOPLE ARE REFUGEES IN THEIR OWN COUNTRY, THE ARMY ABDUCTS LITTLE GIRLS FOR "WIVES."
TANZANIA TO THE EAST. MASSIVE DRUGS GATEWAY, ONE IN TEN PEOPLE HAVE HIV.
ALL THAT ON EITHER SIDE, AND MBANGAWI'S EVEN GOT TO DEAL WITH PIRATES ON LAKE VICTORIA.
MBANGAWI IS LIKE CRAPHOUSE CENTRAL.

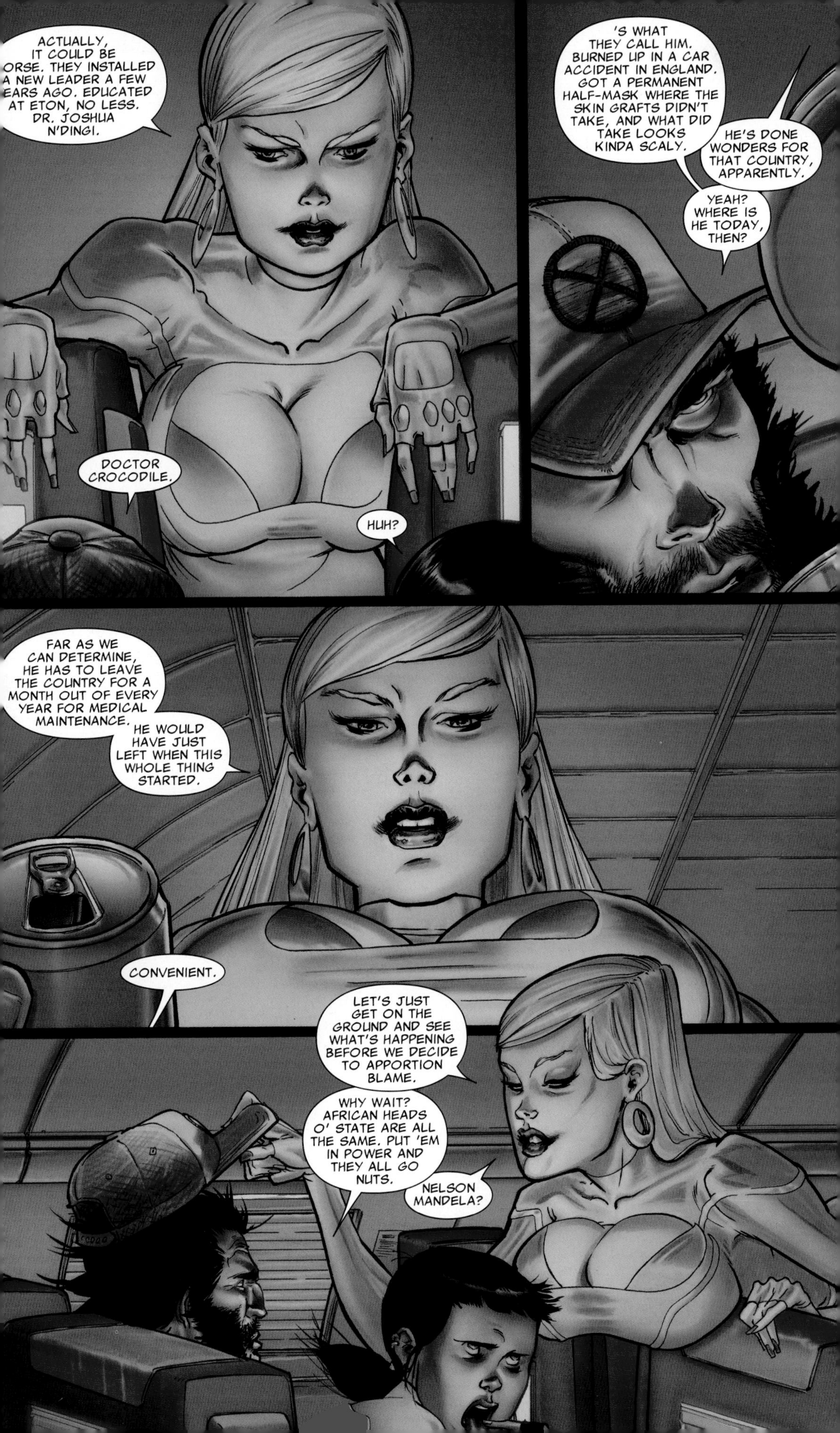
ACTUALLY, IT COULD BE ORSE. THEY INSTALLED A NEW LEADER A FEW EARS AGO. EDUCATED AT ETON, NO LESS. DR. JOSHUA N'DINGI.
DOCTOR CROCODILE.
HUH?
'S WHAT THEY CALL HIM. BURNED UP IN A CAR ACCIDENT IN ENGLAND. GOT A PERMANENT HALF-MASK WHERE THE SKIN GRAFTS DIDN'T TAKE, AND WHAT DID TAKE LOOKS KINDA SCALY.
HE'S DONE WONDERS FOR THAT COUNTRY, APPARENTLY.
YEAH? WHERE IS HE TODAY, THEN?
FAR AS WE CAN DETERMINE, HE HAS TO LEAVE THE COUNTRY FOR A MONTH OUT OF EVERY YEAR FOR MEDICAL MAINTENANCE.
HE WOULD HAVE JUST LEFT WHEN THIS WHOLE THING STARTED.
CONVENIENT.
LET'S JUST GET ON THE GROUND AND SEE WHAT'S HAPPENING BEFORE WE DECIDE TO APPORTION BLAME.
WHY WAIT? AFRICAN HEADS O' STATE ARE ALL THE SAME. PUT 'EM IN POWER AND THEY ALL GO NUTS.
NELSON MANDELA?

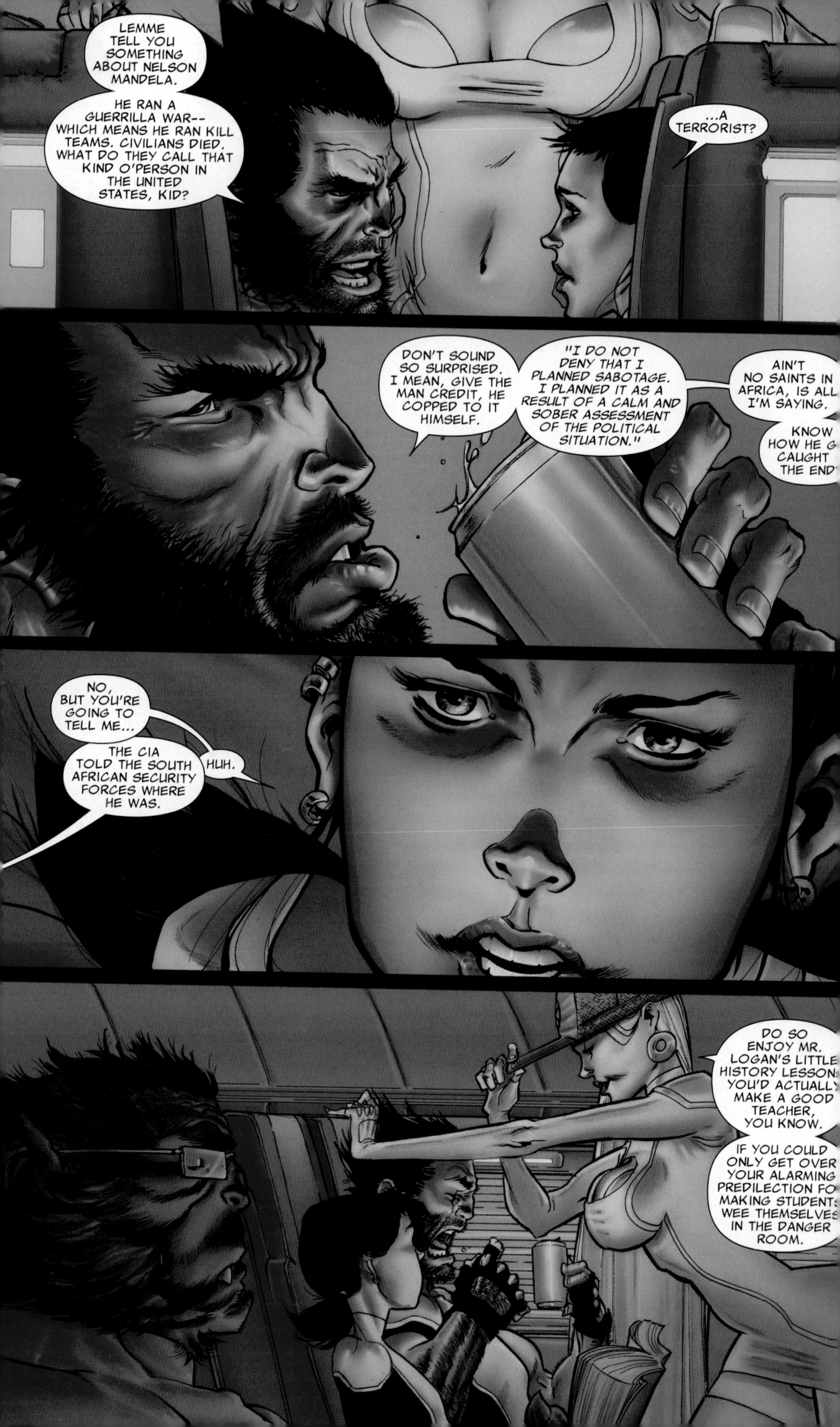
LEMME TELL YOU SOMETHING ABOUT NELSON MANDELA.
HE RAN A GUERRILLA WAR-- WHICH MEANS HE RAN KILL TEAMS. CIVILIANS DIED. WHAT DO THEY CALL THAT KIND O'PERSON IN THE UNITED STATES, KID?
...A TERRORIST?
DON'T SOUND SO SURPRISED. I MEAN, GIVE THE MAN CREDIT, HE COPPED TO IT HIMSELF.
"I DO NOT DENY THAT I PLANNED SABOTAGE. I PLANNED IT AS A RESULT OF A CALM AND SOBER ASSESSMENT OF THE POLITICAL SITUATION."
AIN'T NO SAINTS IN AFRICA, IS ALL I'M SAYING.
KNOW HOW HE G CAUGHT THE END
NO, BUT YOU'RE GOING TO TELL ME...
THE CIA TOLD THE SOUTH AFRICAN SECURITY FORCES WHERE HE WAS.
HUH.
DO SO ENJOY MR. LOGAN'S LITTLE HISTORY LESSON YOU'D ACTUALL MAKE A GOOD TEACHER, YOU KNOW.
IF YOU COULD ONLY GET OVER YOUR ALARMING PREDILECTION FO MAKING STUDENT WEE THEMSELVES IN THE DANGER ROOM.

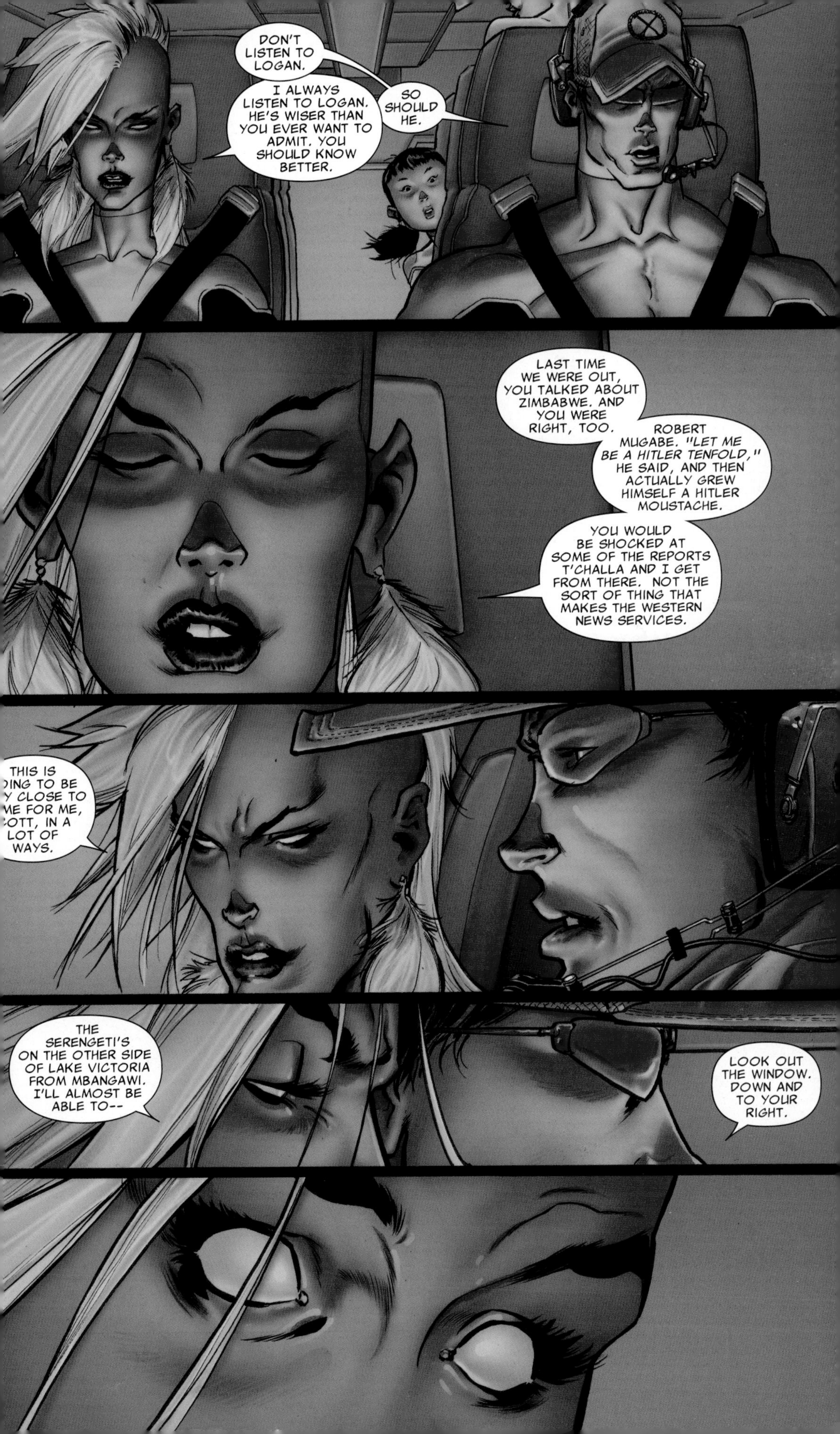

DON'T LISTEN TO LOGAN.
SO SHOULD HE.
I ALWAYS LISTEN TO LOGAN. HE'S WISER THAN YOU EVER WANT TO ADMIT. YOU SHOULD KNOW BETTER.
LAST TIME WE WERE OUT, YOU TALKED ABOUT ZIMBABWE. AND YOU WERE RIGHT, TOO.
ROBERT MUGABE. "LET ME BE A HITLER TENFOLD," HE SAID, AND THEN ACTUALLY GREW HIMSELF A HITLER MOUSTACHE.
YOU WOULD BE SHOCKED AT SOME OF THE REPORTS T'CHALLA AND I GET FROM THERE. NOT THE SORT OF THING THAT MAKES THE WESTERN NEWS SERVICES.
THIS IS
OING TO BE
Y CLOSE TO
ME FOR ME,
OTT, IN A
LOT OF
WAYS.
THE SERENGETI'S ON THE OTHER SIDE OF LAKE VICTORIA FROM MBANGAWI. I'LL ALMOST BE ABLE TO--
LOOK OUT THE WINDOW. DOWN AND TO YOUR RIGHT.

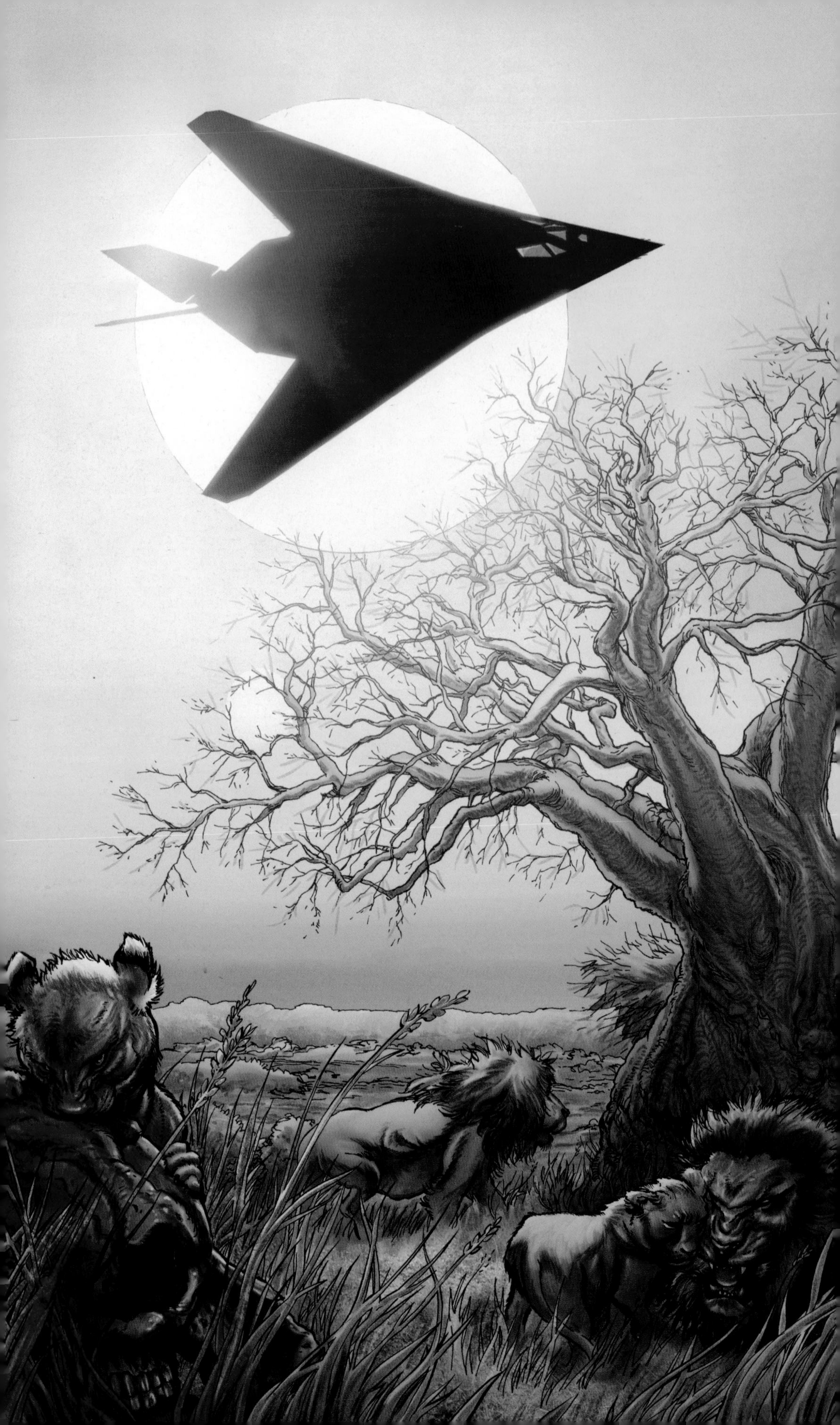

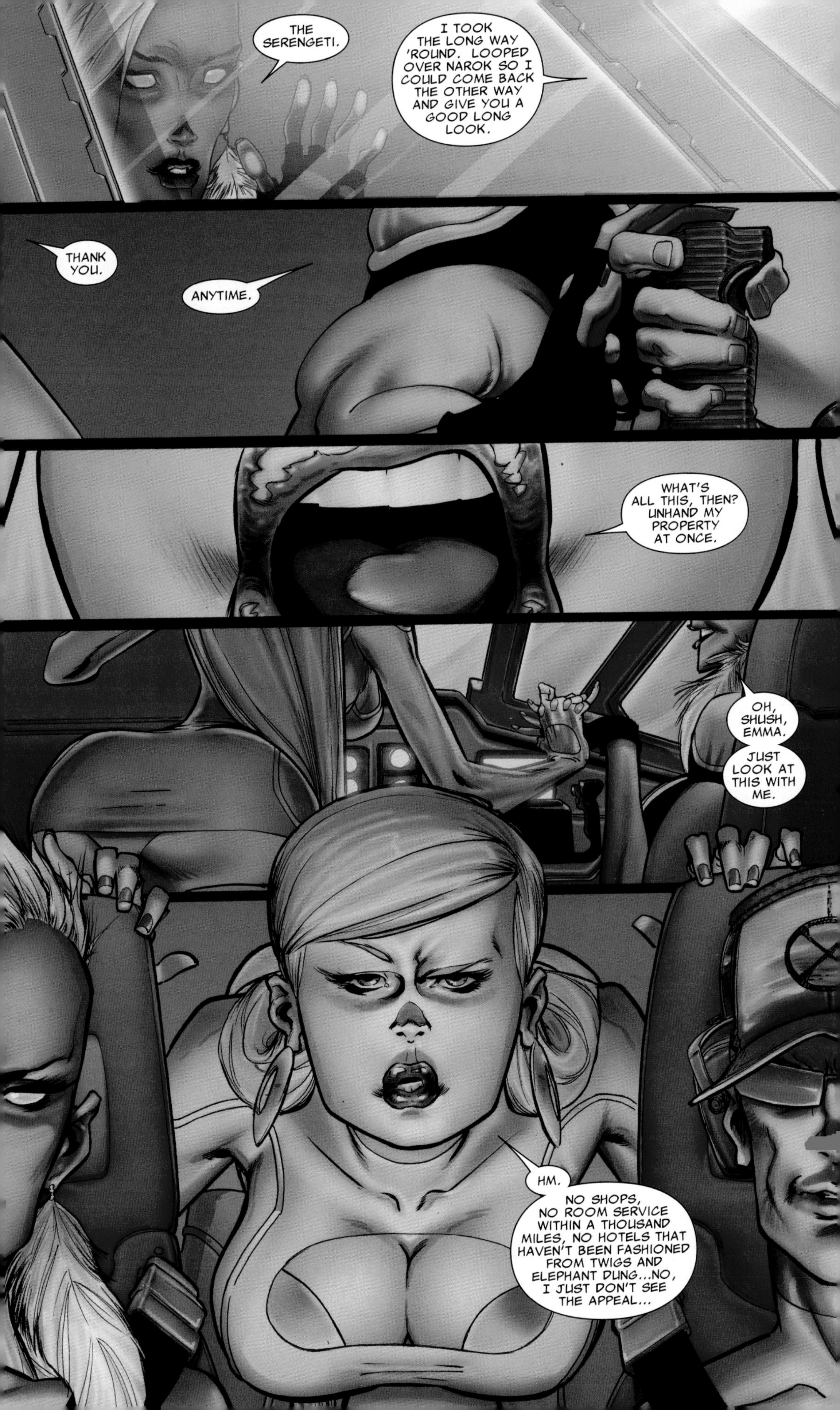
THE SERENGETI.
I TOOK THE LONG WAY 'ROUND. LOOPED OVER NAROK SO I COULD COME BACK THE OTHER WAY AND GIVE YOU A GOOD LONG LOOK.
THANK YOU.
ANYTIME.
WHAT'S ALL THIS, THEN? UNHAND MY PROPERTY AT ONCE.
OH, SHUSH, EMMA.
JUST LOOK AT THIS WITH ME.
HM.
NO SHOPS, NO ROOM SERVICE WITHIN A THOUSAND MILES, NO HOTELS THAT HAVEN'T BEEN FASHIONED FROM TWIGS AND ELEPHANT DUNG...NO, I JUST DON'T SEE THE APPEAL...

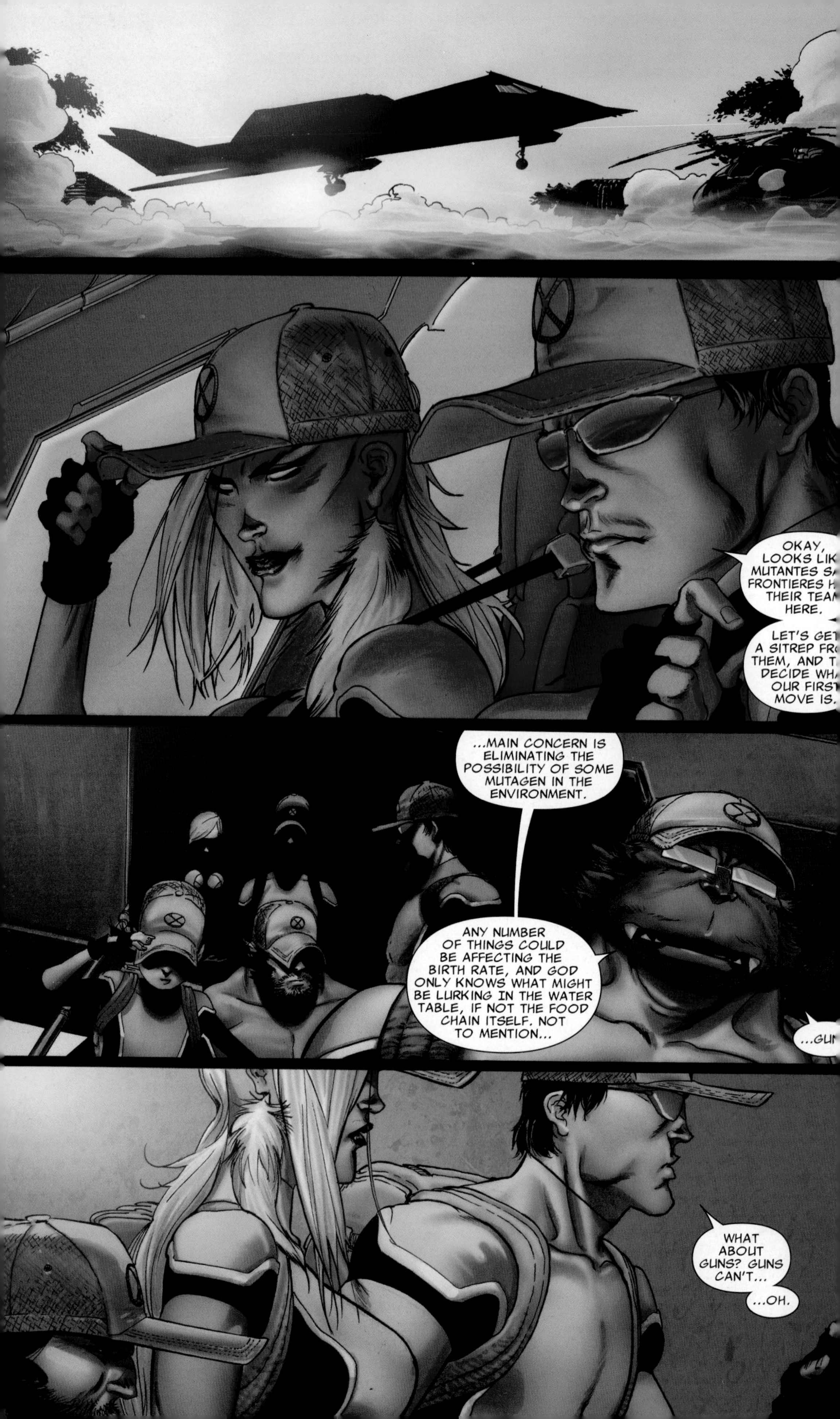

OKAY, LOOKS LIK MUTANTES S FRONTIERES H THEIR TEAM HERE.
LET'S GET A SITREP FR THEM, AND T DECIDE WHA OUR FIRST MOVE IS.
...MAIN CONCERN IS ELIMINATING THE POSSIBILITY OF SOME MUTAGEN IN THE ENVIRONMENT.
ANY NUMBER OF THINGS COULD BE AFFECTING THE BIRTH RATE, AND GOD ONLY KNOWS WHAT MIGHT BE LURKING IN THE WATER TABLE, IF NOT THE FOOD CHAIN ITSELF. NOT TO MENTION...
...GU
WHAT ABOUT GUNS? GUNS CAN'T...
...OH.

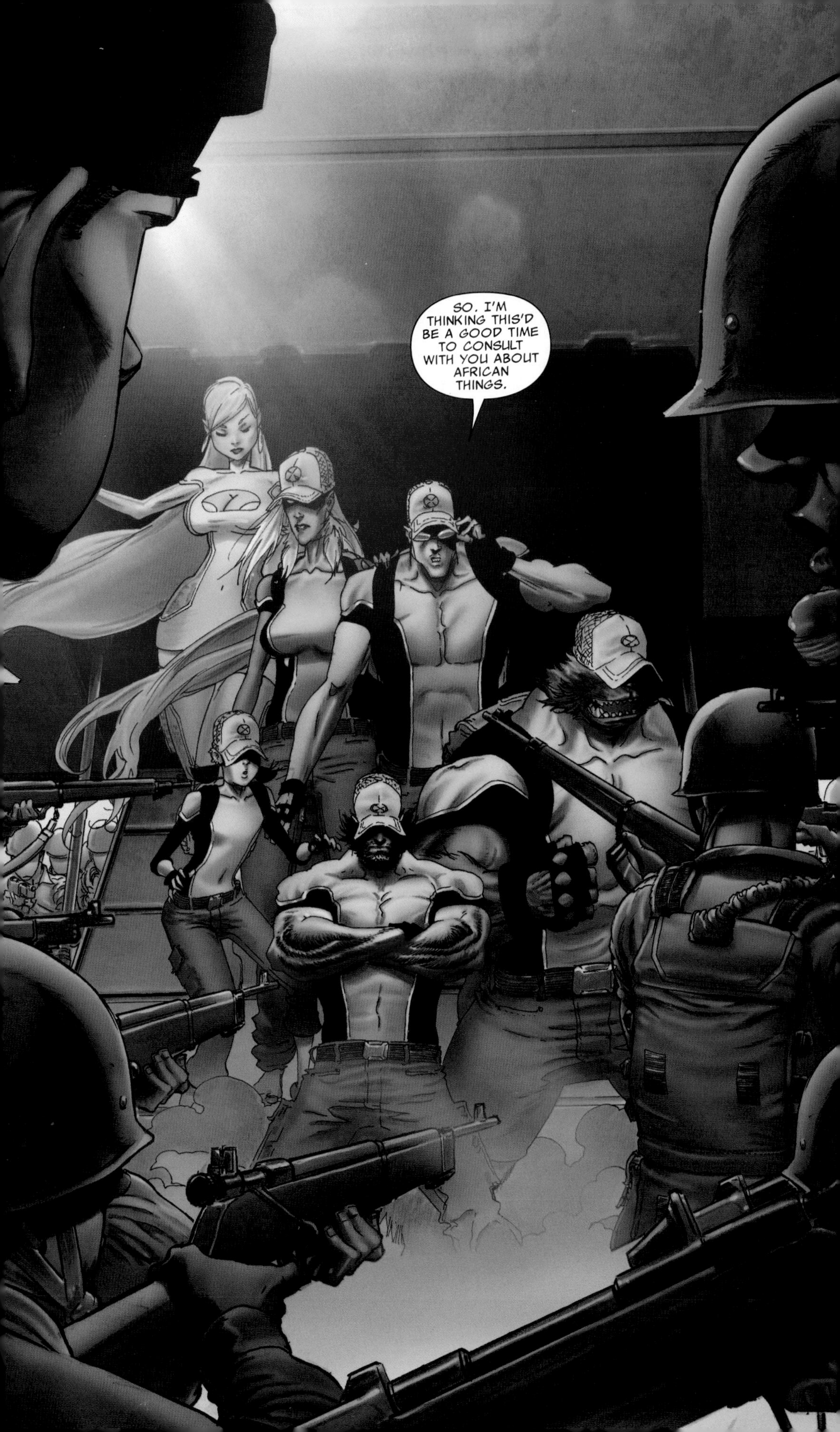
SO, I'M THINKING THIS'D BE A GOOD TIME TO CONSULT WITH YOU ABOUT AFRICAN THINGS.

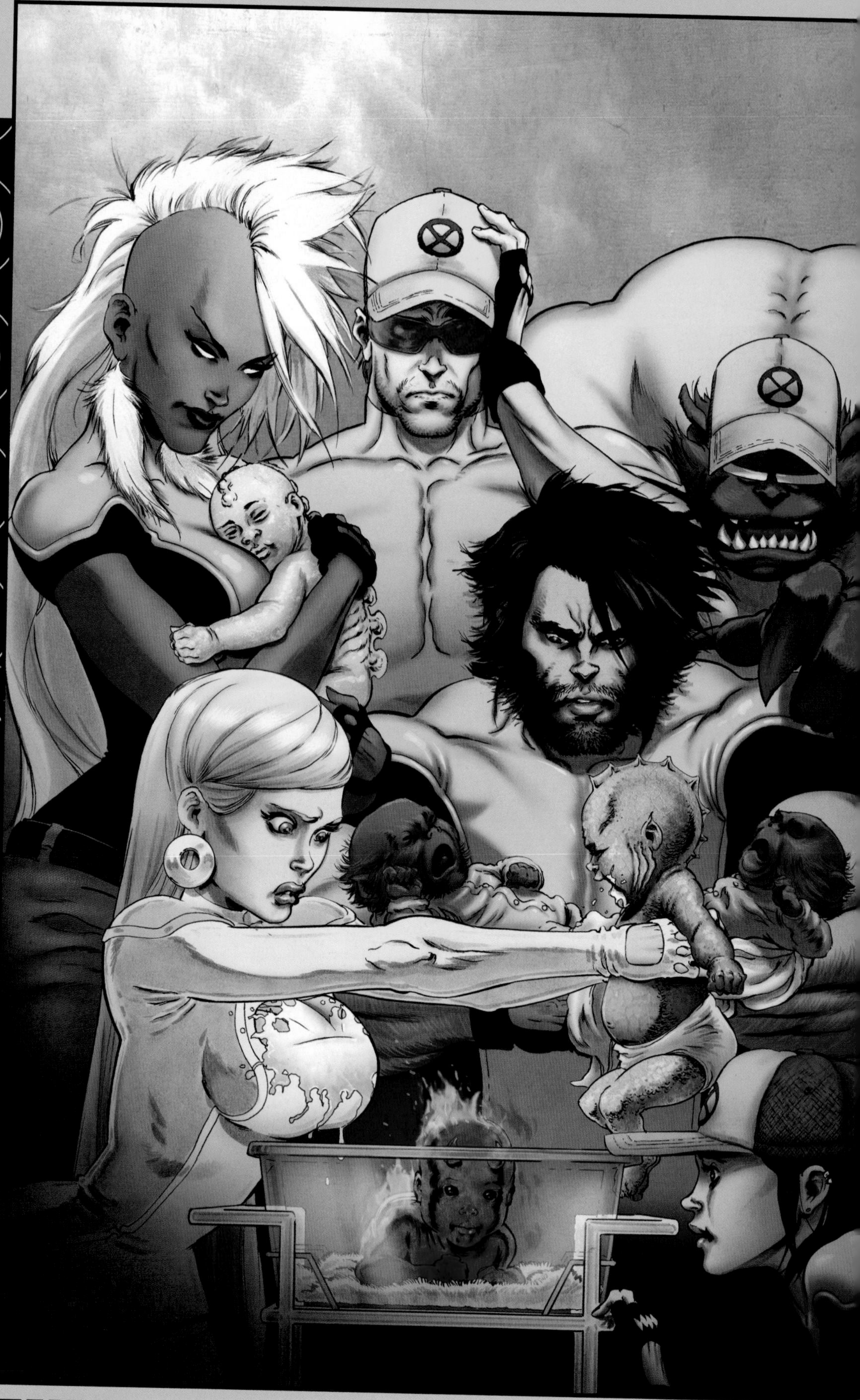

TWO

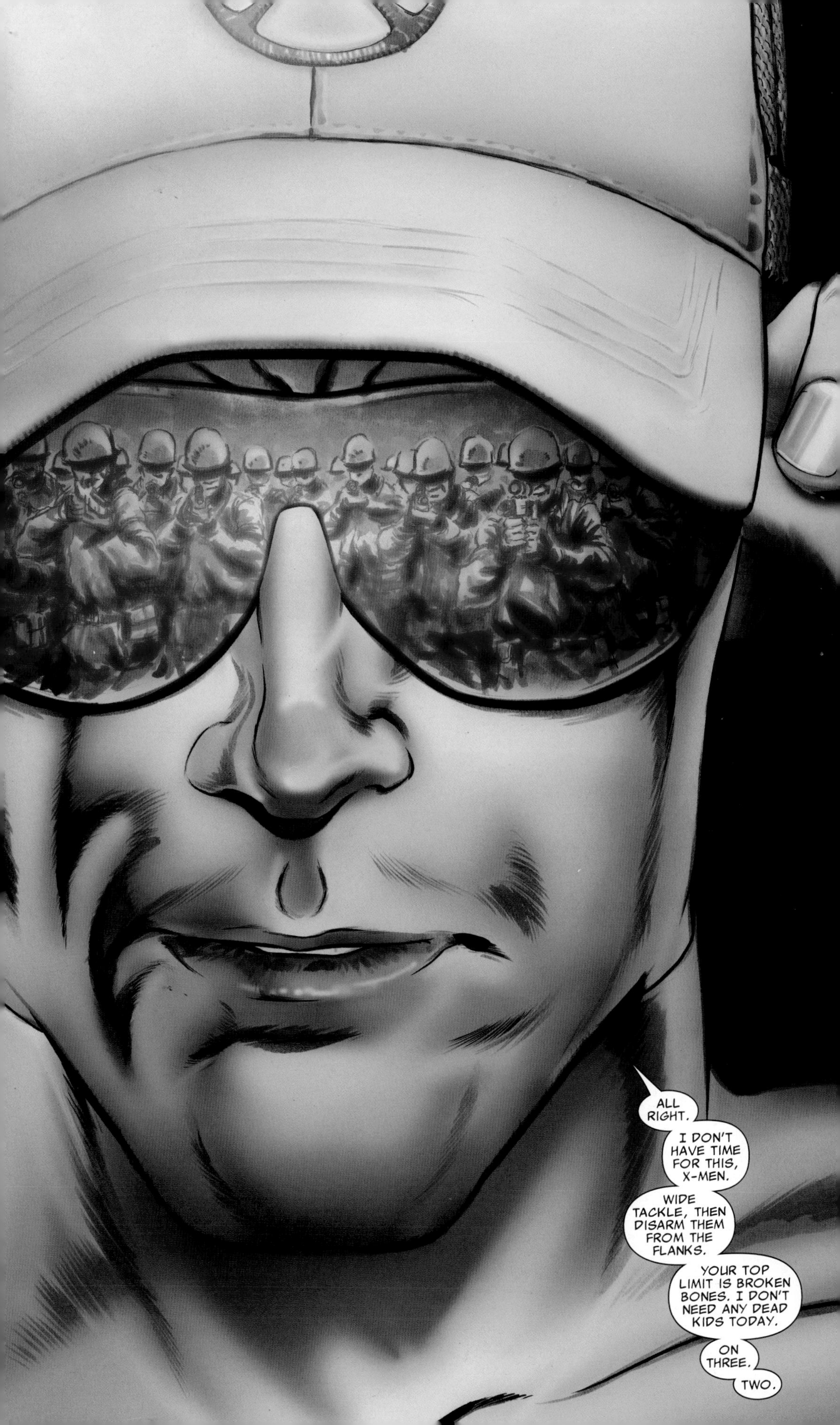
ALL RIGHT.
I DON'T HAVE TIME FOR THIS, X-MEN.
WIDE TACKLE, THEN DISARM THEM FROM THE FLANKS.
YOUR TOP LIMIT IS BROKEN BONES. I DON'T NEED ANY DEAD KIDS TODAY.
ON THREE.
TWO.

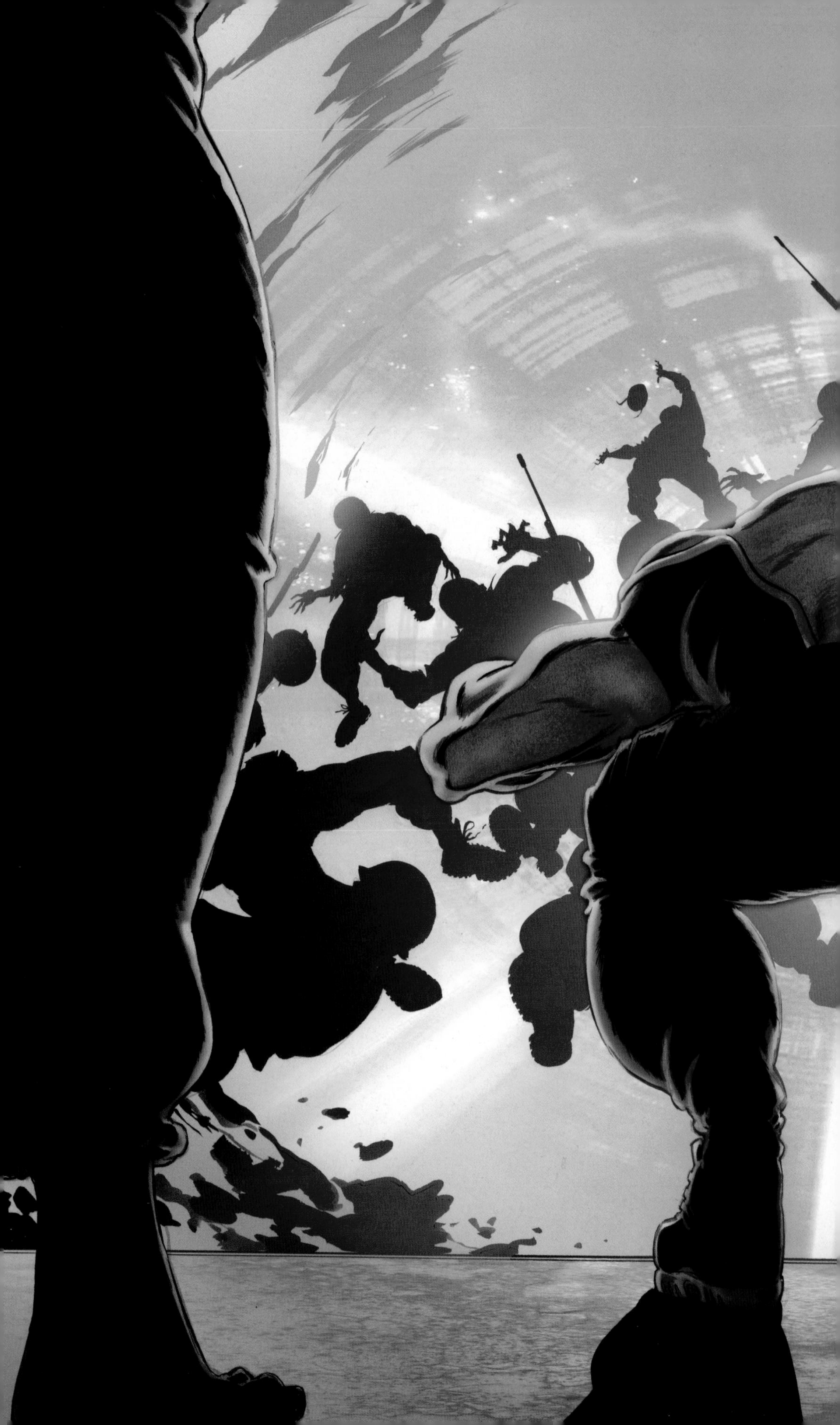

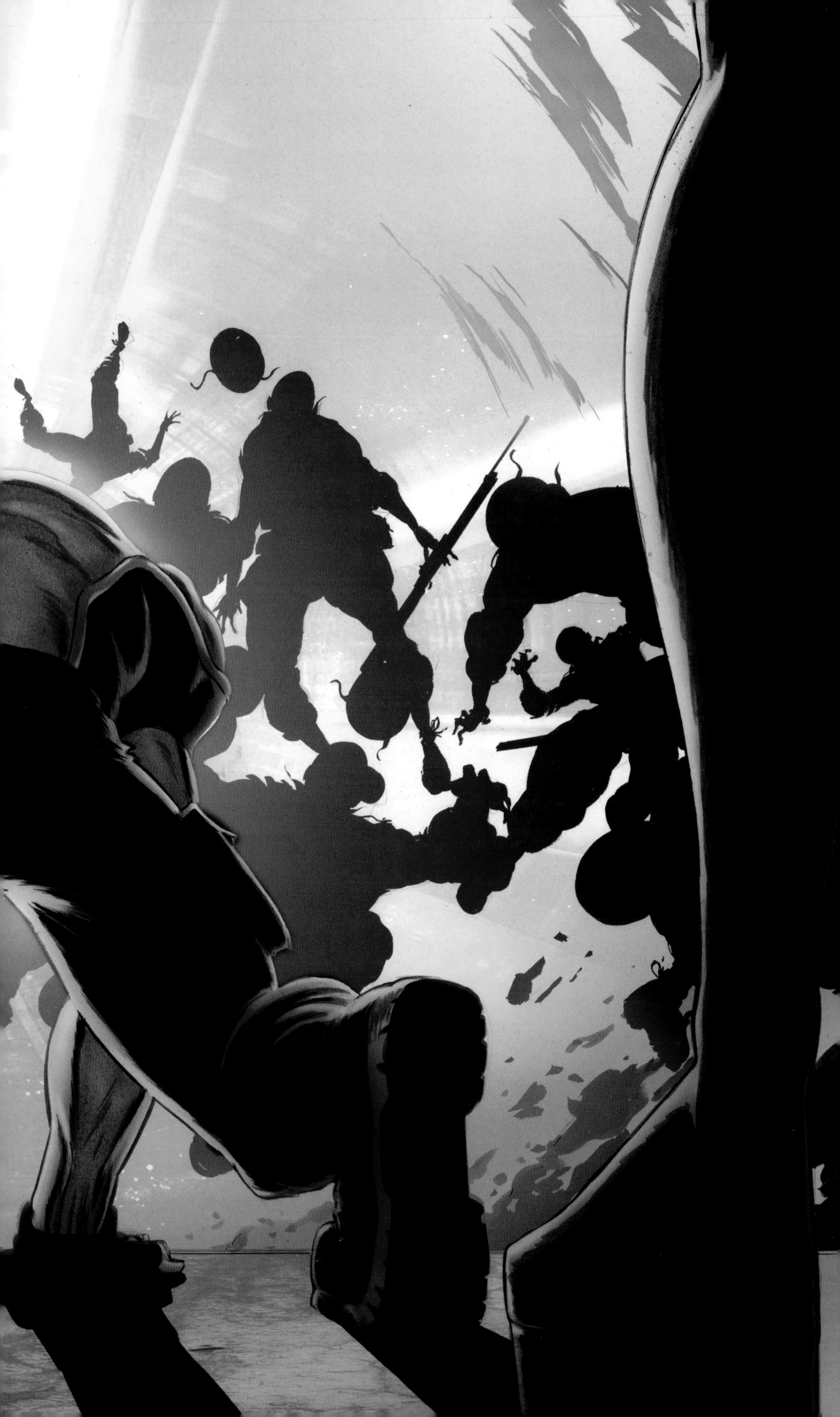

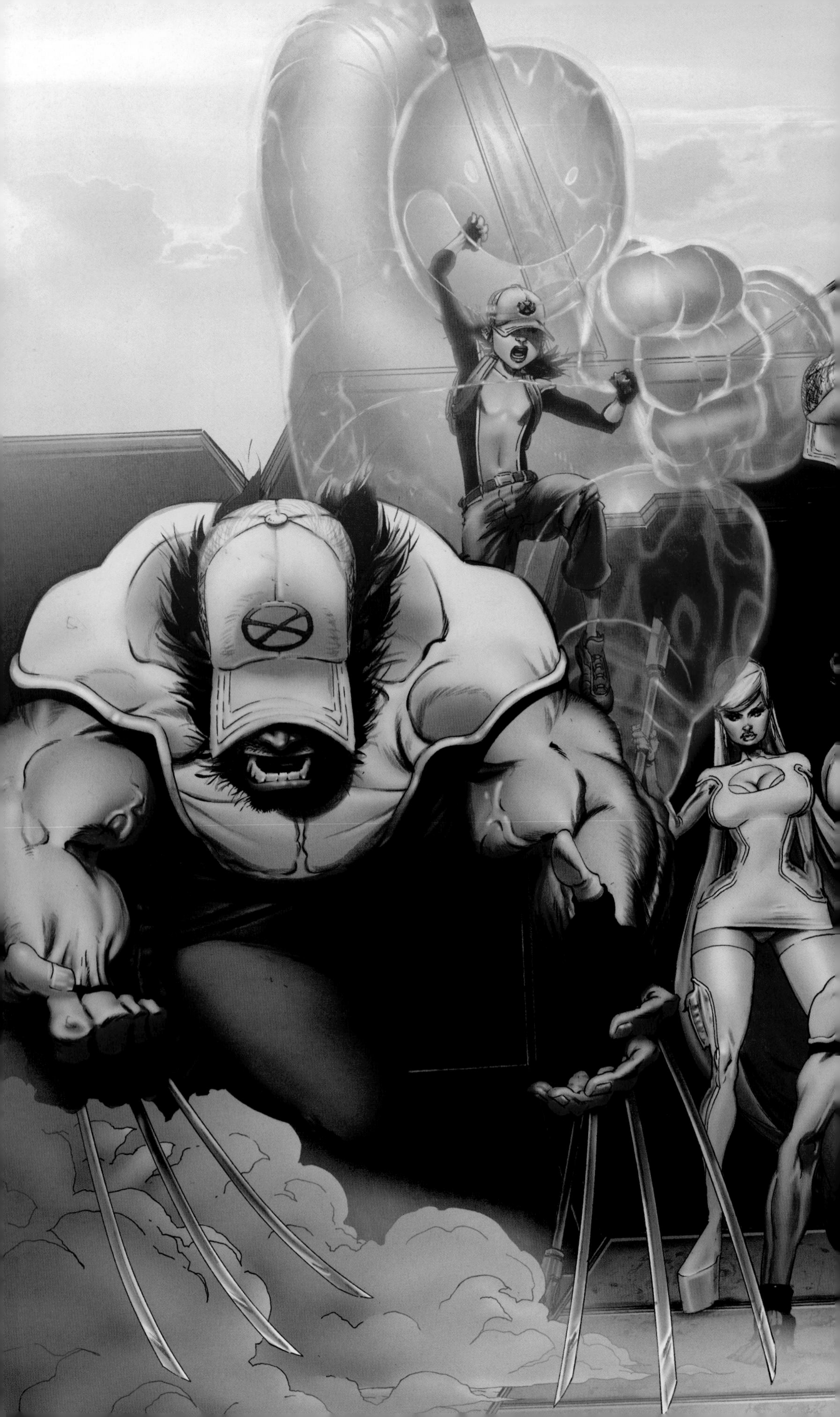

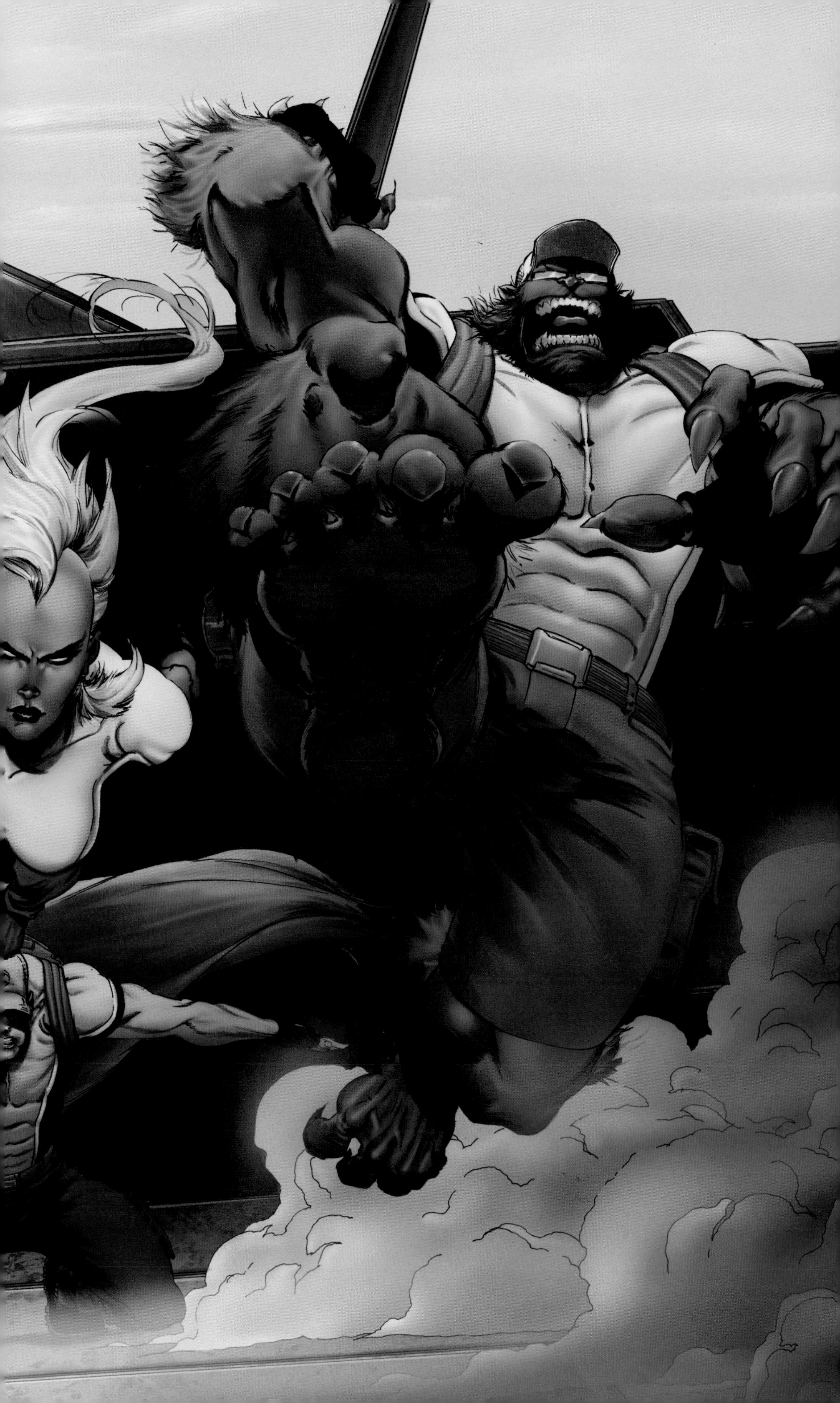

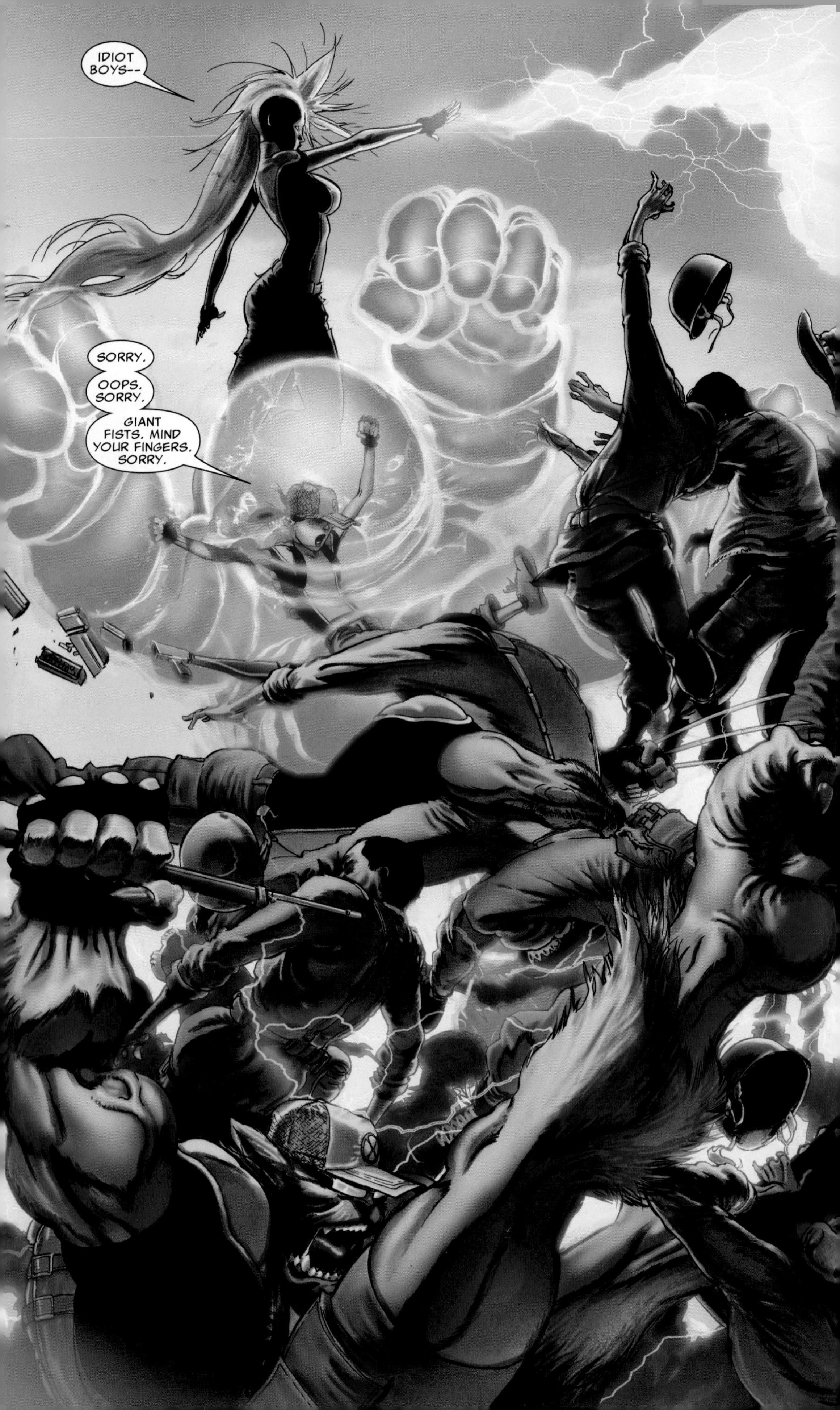
IDIOT BOYS--
SORRY.
OOPS. SORRY.
GIANT FISTS. MIND YOUR FINGERS. SORRY.

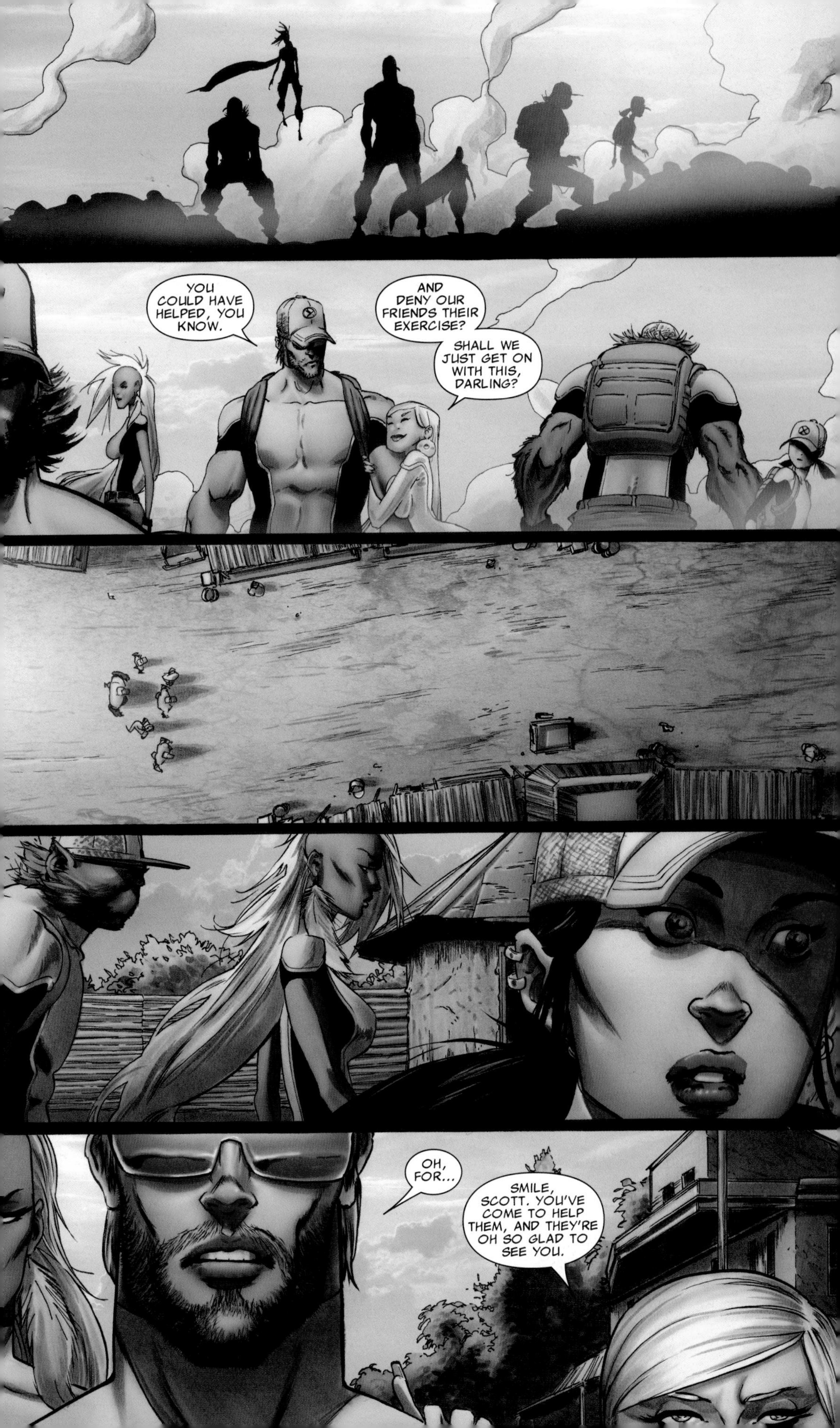
YOU COULD HAVE HELPED, YOU KNOW.
AND DENY OUR FRIENDS THEIR EXERCISE?
SHALL WE JUST GET ON WITH THIS, DARLING?
OH, FOR...
SMILE, SCOTT. YOU'VE COME TO HELP THEM, AND THEY'RE OH SO GLAD TO SEE YOU.

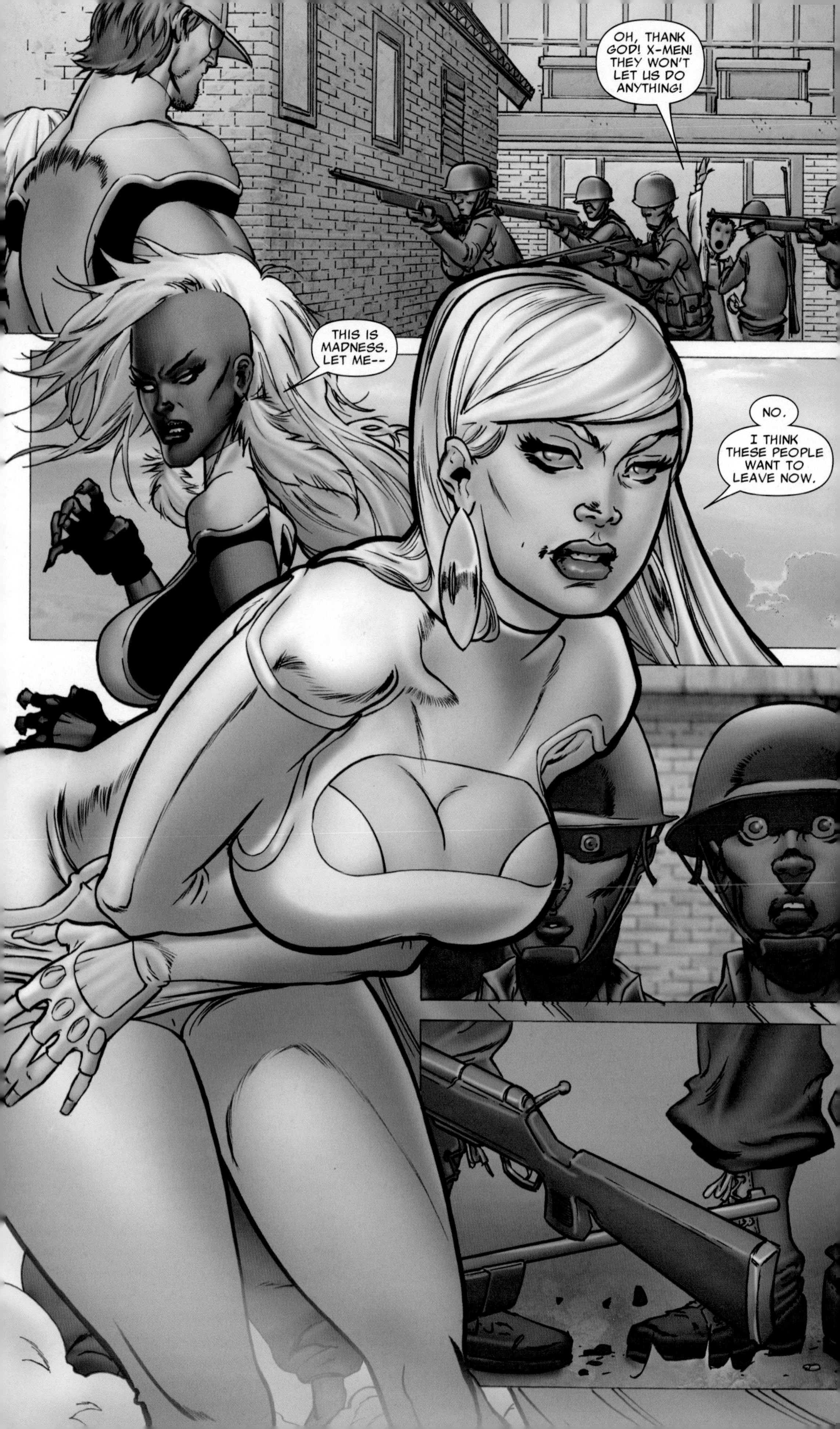
OH, THANK GOD! X-MEN! THEY WON'T LET US DO ANYTHING!
THIS IS MADNESS. LET ME--
NO.
I THINK THESE PEOPLE WANT TO LEAVE NOW.

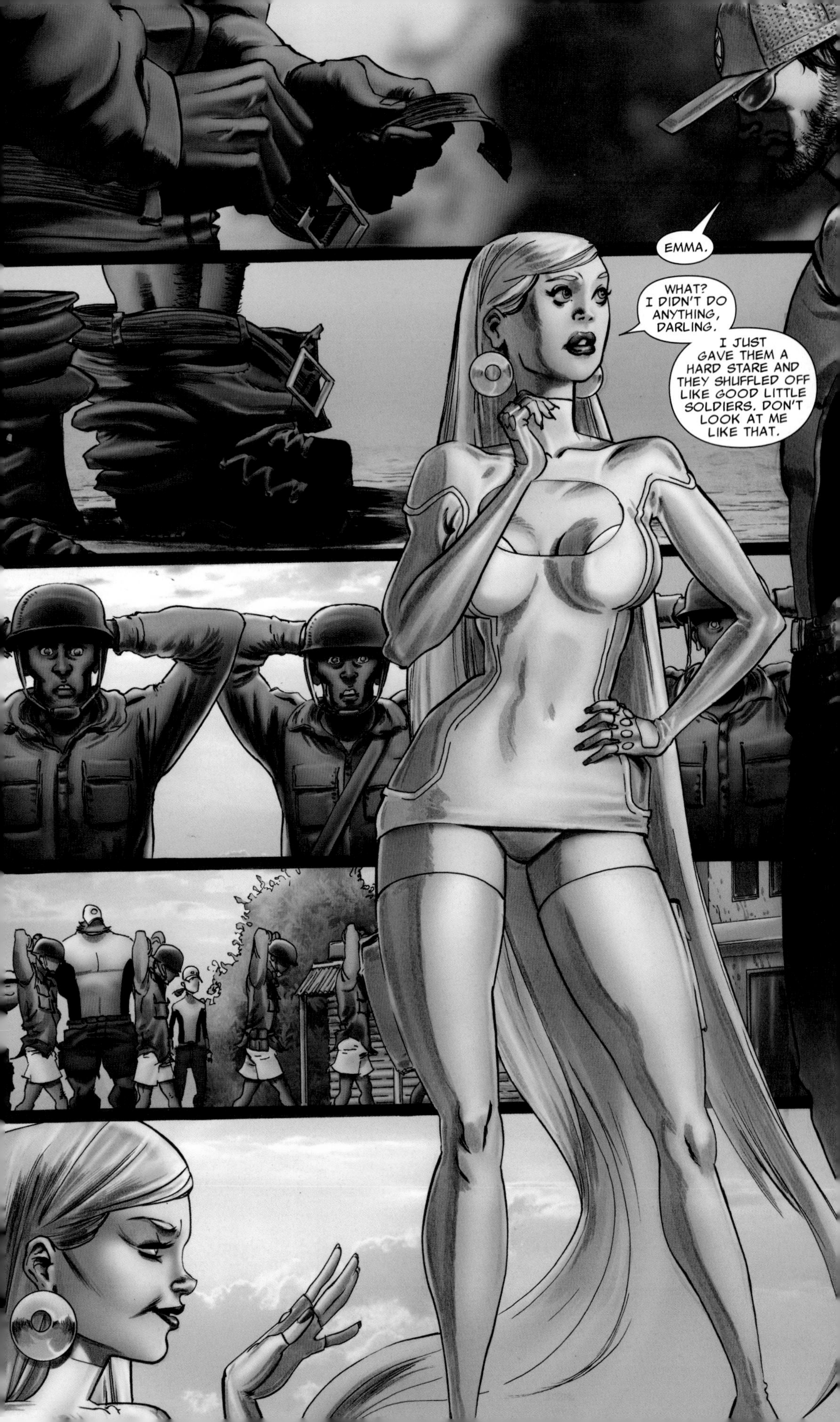
EMMA.
WHAT? I DIDN'T DO ANYTHING, DARLING.
I JUST GAVE THEM A HARD STARE AND THEY SHUFFLED OFF LIKE GOOD LITTLE SOLDIERS. DON'T LOOK AT ME LIKE THAT.

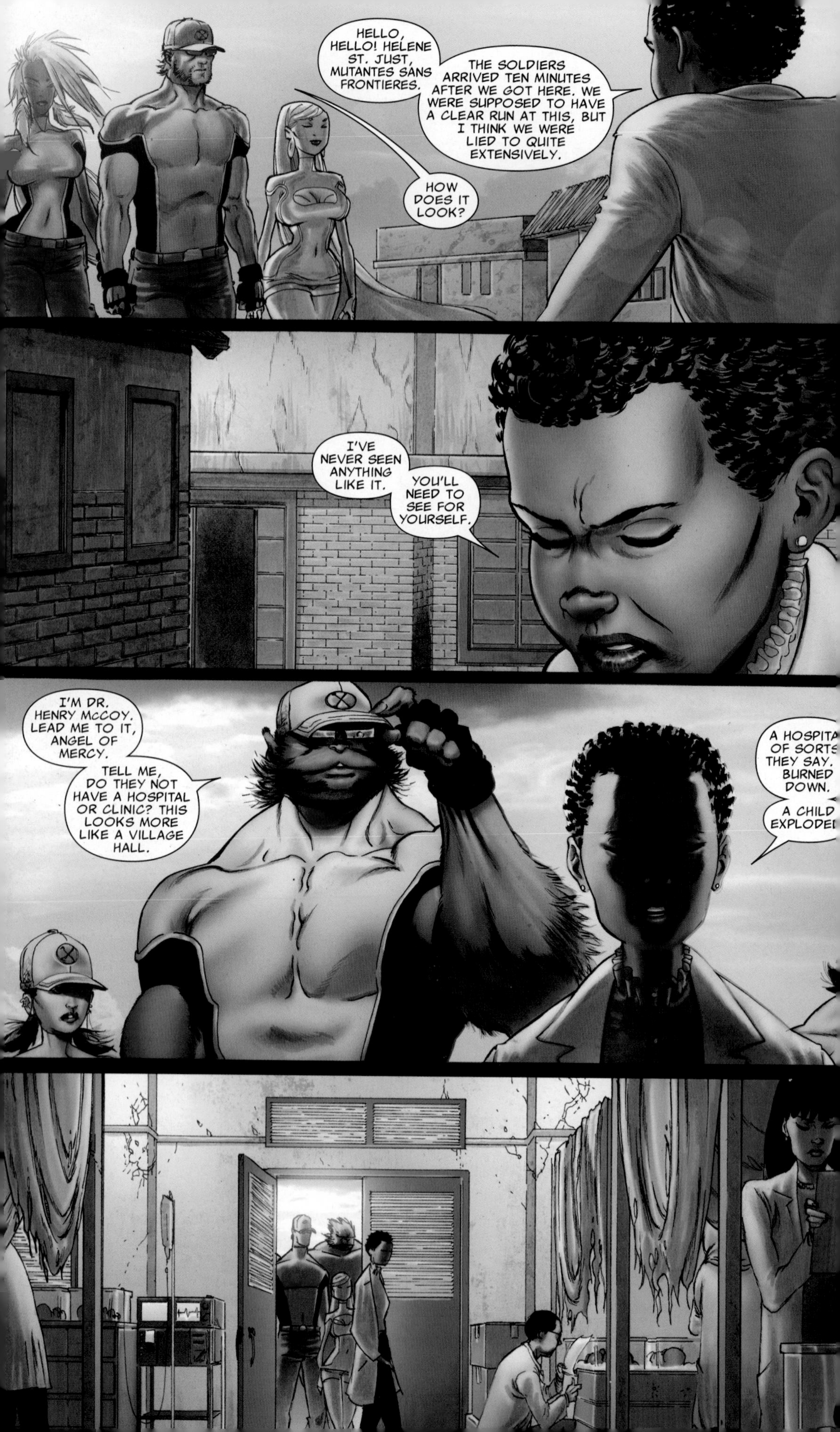
HELLO, HELLO! HELENE ST. JUST, MUTANTES SANS FRONTIERES.
THE SOLDIERS ARRIVED TEN MINUTES AFTER WE GOT HERE. WE WERE SUPPOSED TO HAVE A CLEAR RUN AT THIS, BUT I THINK WE WERE LIED TO QUITE EXTENSIVELY.
HOW DOES IT LOOK?
I'VE NEVER SEEN ANYTHING LIKE IT.
YOU'LL NEED TO SEE FOR YOURSELF.
I'M DR. HENRY McCOY. LEAD ME TO IT, ANGEL OF MERCY.
TELL ME, DO THEY NOT HAVE A HOSPITAL OR CLINIC? THIS LOOKS MORE LIKE A VILLAGE HALL.
A HOSPITA OF SORTS THEY SAY. BURNED DOWN.
A CHILD EXPLODED

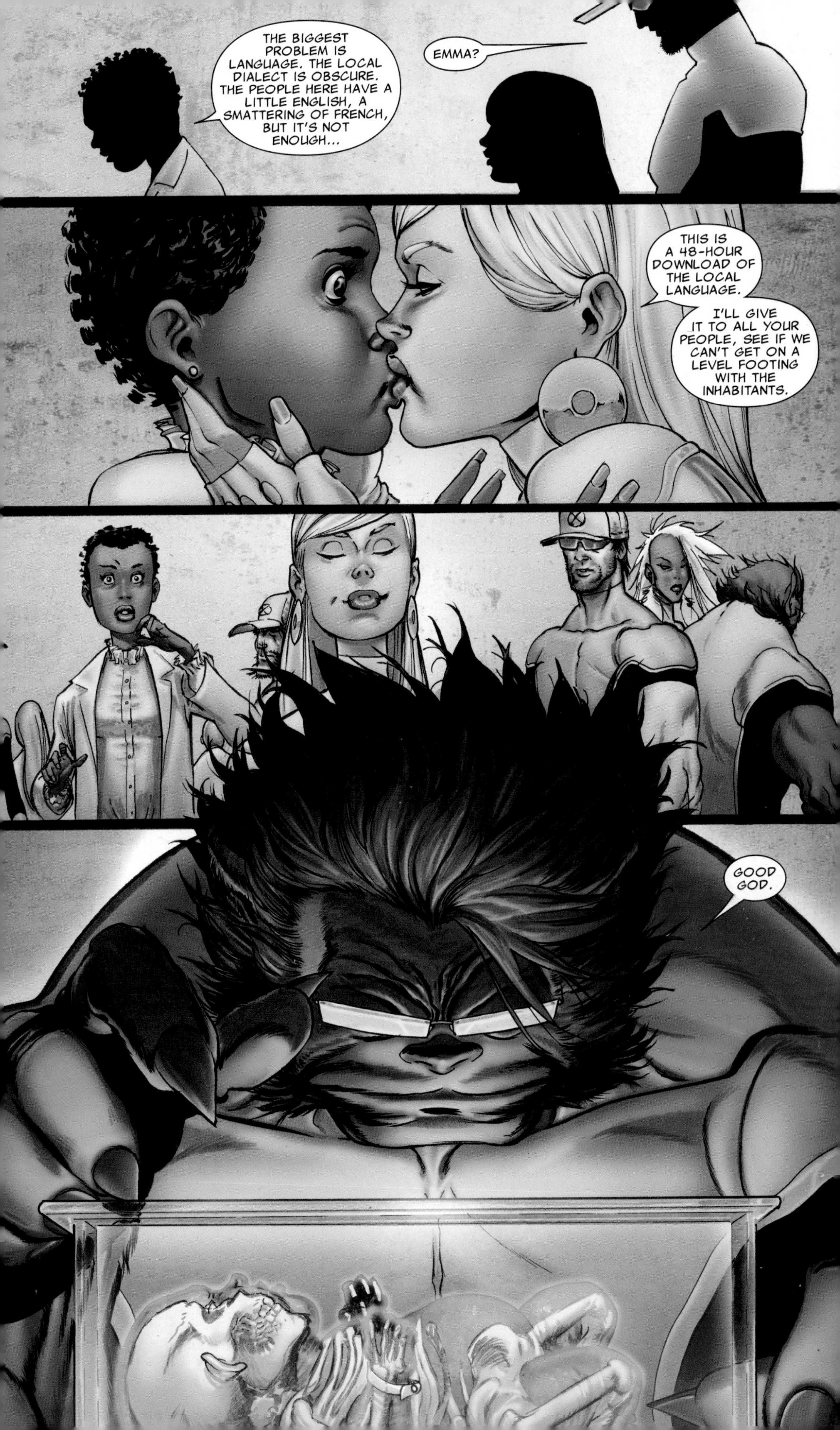
THE BIGGEST PROBLEM IS LANGUAGE. THE LOCAL DIALECT IS OBSCURE. THE PEOPLE HERE HAVE A LITTLE ENGLISH, A SMATTERING OF FRENCH, BUT IT'S NOT ENOUGH...
EMMA?
THIS IS A 48-HOUR DOWNLOAD OF THE LOCAL LANGUAGE.
I'LL GIVE IT TO ALL YOUR PEOPLE, SEE IF WE CAN'T GET ON A LEVEL FOOTING WITH THE INHABITANTS.
GOOD GOD.

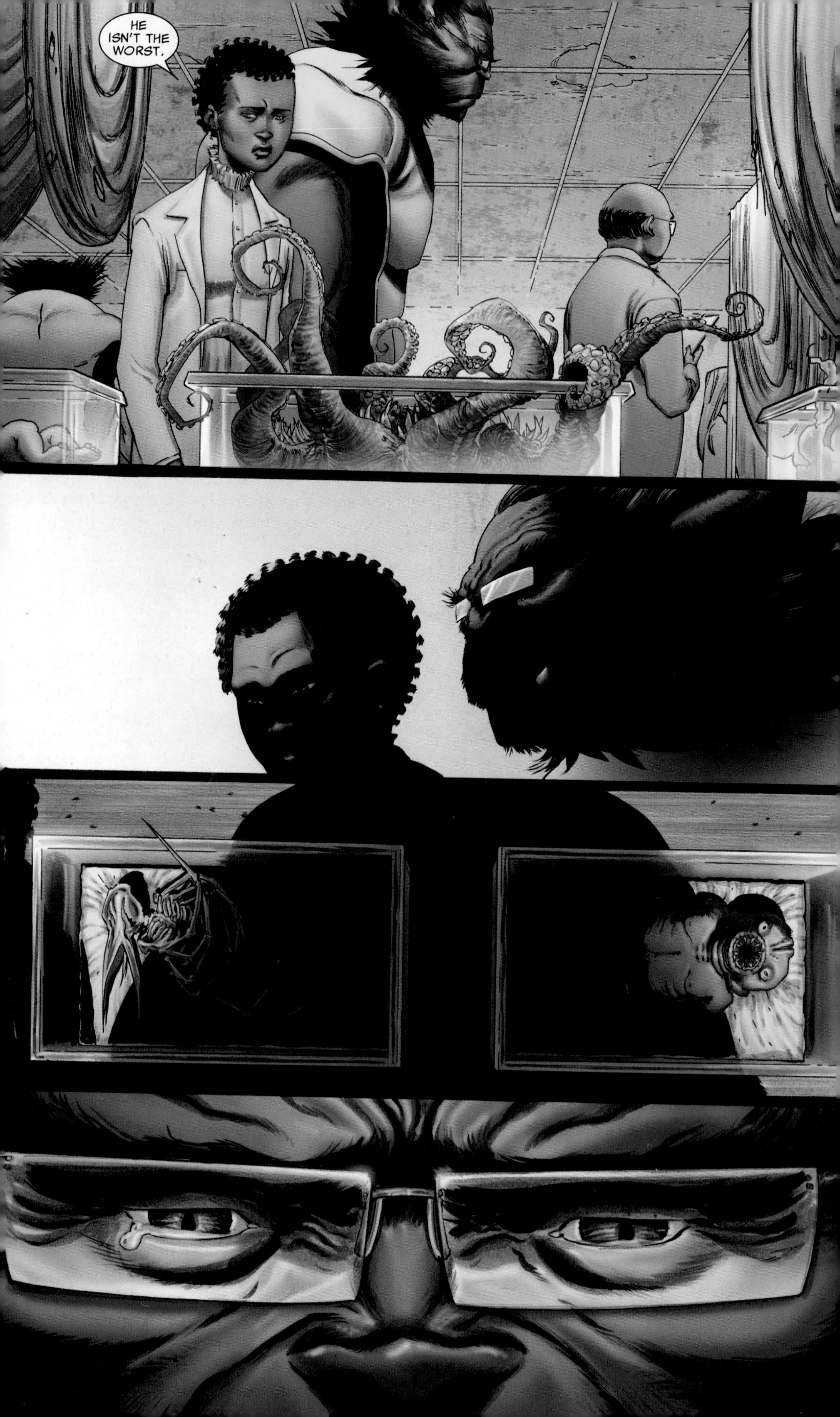
HE ISN'T THE WORST.

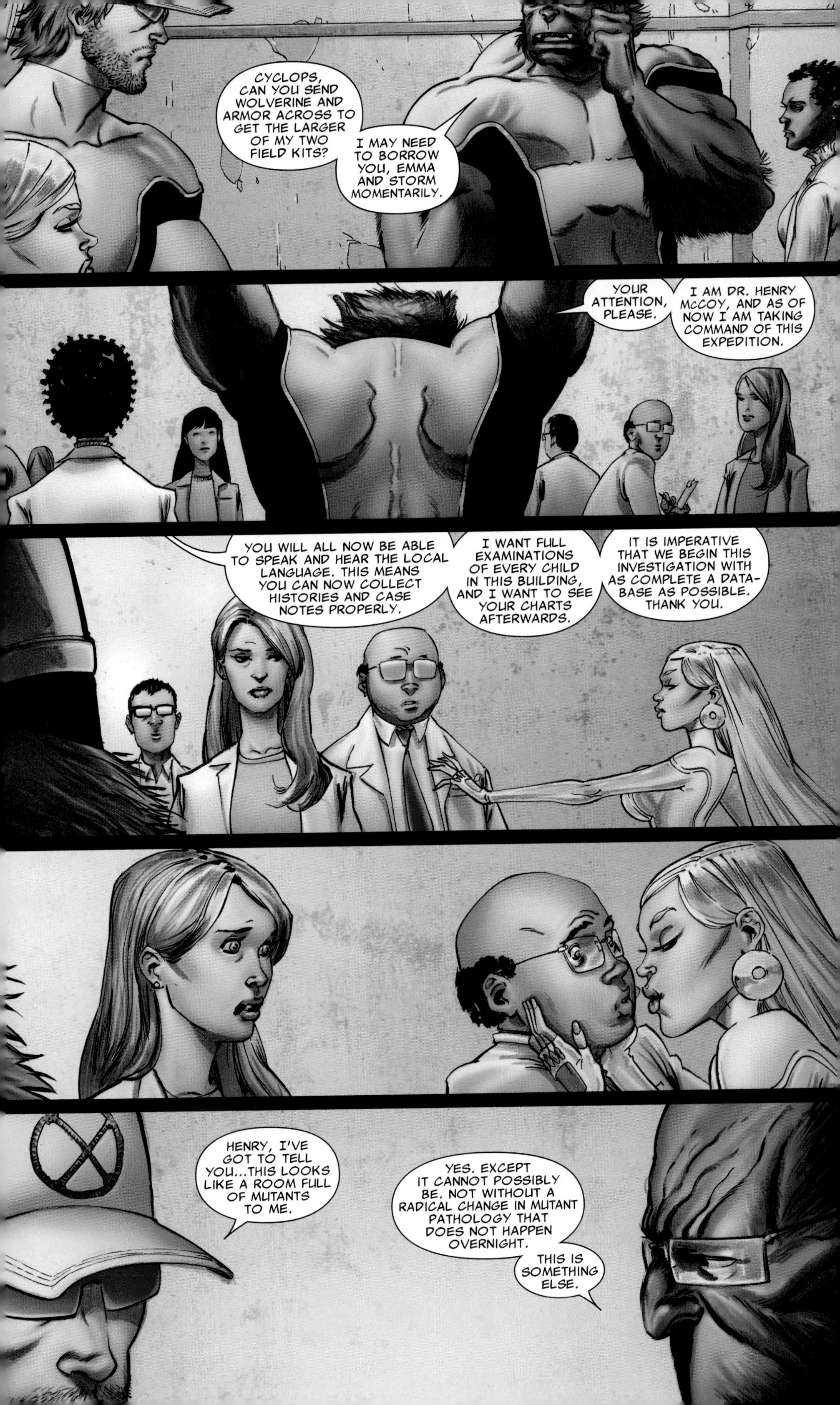
CYCLOPS, CAN YOU SEND WOLVERINE AND ARMOR ACROSS TO GET THE LARGER OF MY TWO FIELD KITS?
I MAY NEED TO BORROW YOU, EMMA AND STORM MOMENTARILY.
YOUR ATTENTION, PLEASE.
I AM DR. HENRY McCOY, AND AS OF NOW I AM TAKING COMMAND OF THIS EXPEDITION.
YOU WILL ALL NOW BE ABLE TO SPEAK AND HEAR THE LOCAL LANGUAGE. THIS MEANS YOU CAN NOW COLLECT HISTORIES AND CASE NOTES PROPERLY.
I WANT FULL EXAMINATIONS OF EVERY CHILD IN THIS BUILDING, AND I WANT TO SEE YOUR CHARTS AFTERWARDS.
IT IS IMPERATIVE THAT WE BEGIN THIS INVESTIGATION WITH AS COMPLETE A DATA-BASE AS POSSIBLE. THANK YOU.
HENRY, I'VE GOT TO TELL YOU...THIS LOOKS LIKE A ROOM FULL OF MUTANTS TO ME.
YES. EXCEPT IT CANNOT POSSIBLY BE. NOT WITHOUT A RADICAL CHANGE IN MUTANT PATHOLOGY THAT DOES NOT HAPPEN OVERNIGHT.
THIS IS SOMETHING ELSE.

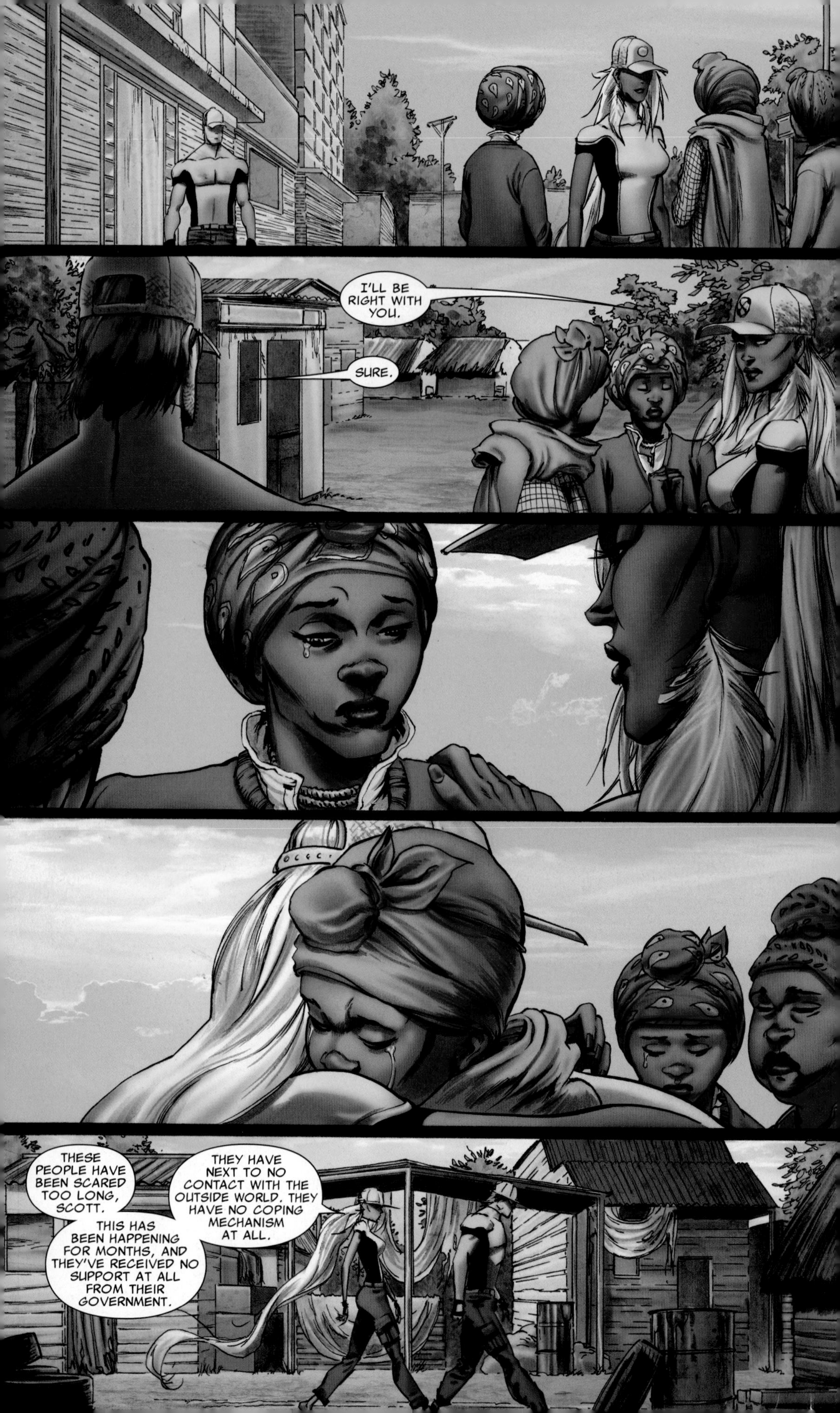
I'LL BE RIGHT WITH YOU.
SURE.
THESE PEOPLE HAVE BEEN SCARED TOO LONG, SCOTT.
THIS HAS BEEN HAPPENING FOR MONTHS, AND THEY'VE RECEIVED NO SUPPORT AT ALL FROM THEIR GOVERNMENT.
THEY HAVE NEXT TO NO CONTACT WITH THE OUTSIDE WORLD. THEY HAVE NO COPING MECHANISM AT ALL.

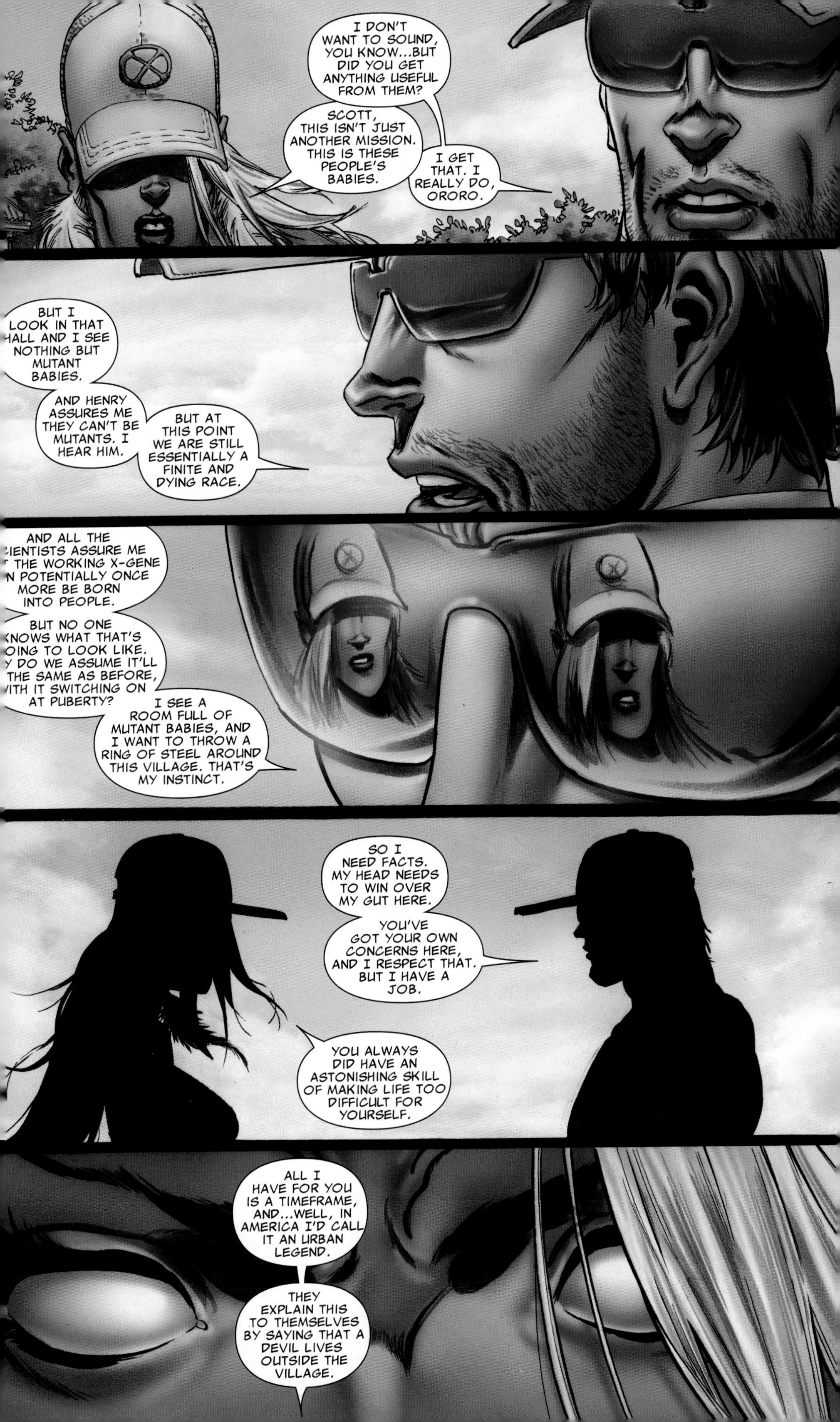
I DON'T WANT TO SOUND, YOU KNOW...BUT DID YOU GET ANYTHING USEFUL FROM THEM?
SCOTT, THIS ISN'T JUST ANOTHER MISSION. THIS IS THESE PEOPLE'S BABIES.
I GET THAT. I REALLY DO, ORORO.
BUT I LOOK IN THAT HALL AND I SEE NOTHING BUT MUTANT BABIES.
AND HENRY ASSURES ME THEY CAN'T BE MUTANTS. I HEAR HIM.
BUT AT THIS POINT WE ARE STILL ESSENTIALLY A FINITE AND DYING RACE.
AND ALL THE CIENTISTS ASSURE ME THE WORKING X-GENE N POTENTIALLY ONCE MORE BE BORN INTO PEOPLE.
BUT NO ONE KNOWS WHAT THAT'S OING TO LOOK LIKE. DO WE ASSUME IT'LL THE SAME AS BEFORE, WITH IT SWITCHING ON AT PUBERTY?
I SEE A ROOM FULL OF MUTANT BABIES, AND I WANT TO THROW A RING OF STEEL AROUND THIS VILLAGE. THAT'S MY INSTINCT.
SO I NEED FACTS. MY HEAD NEEDS TO WIN OVER MY GUT HERE.
YOU'VE GOT YOUR OWN CONCERNS HERE, AND I RESPECT THAT. BUT I HAVE A JOB.
YOU ALWAYS DID HAVE AN ASTONISHING SKILL OF MAKING LIFE TOO DIFFICULT FOR YOURSELF.
ALL I HAVE FOR YOU IS A TIMEFRAME, AND...WELL, IN AMERICA I'D CALL IT AN URBAN LEGEND.
THEY EXPLAIN THIS TO THEMSELVES BY SAYING THAT A DEVIL LIVES OUTSIDE THE VILLAGE.

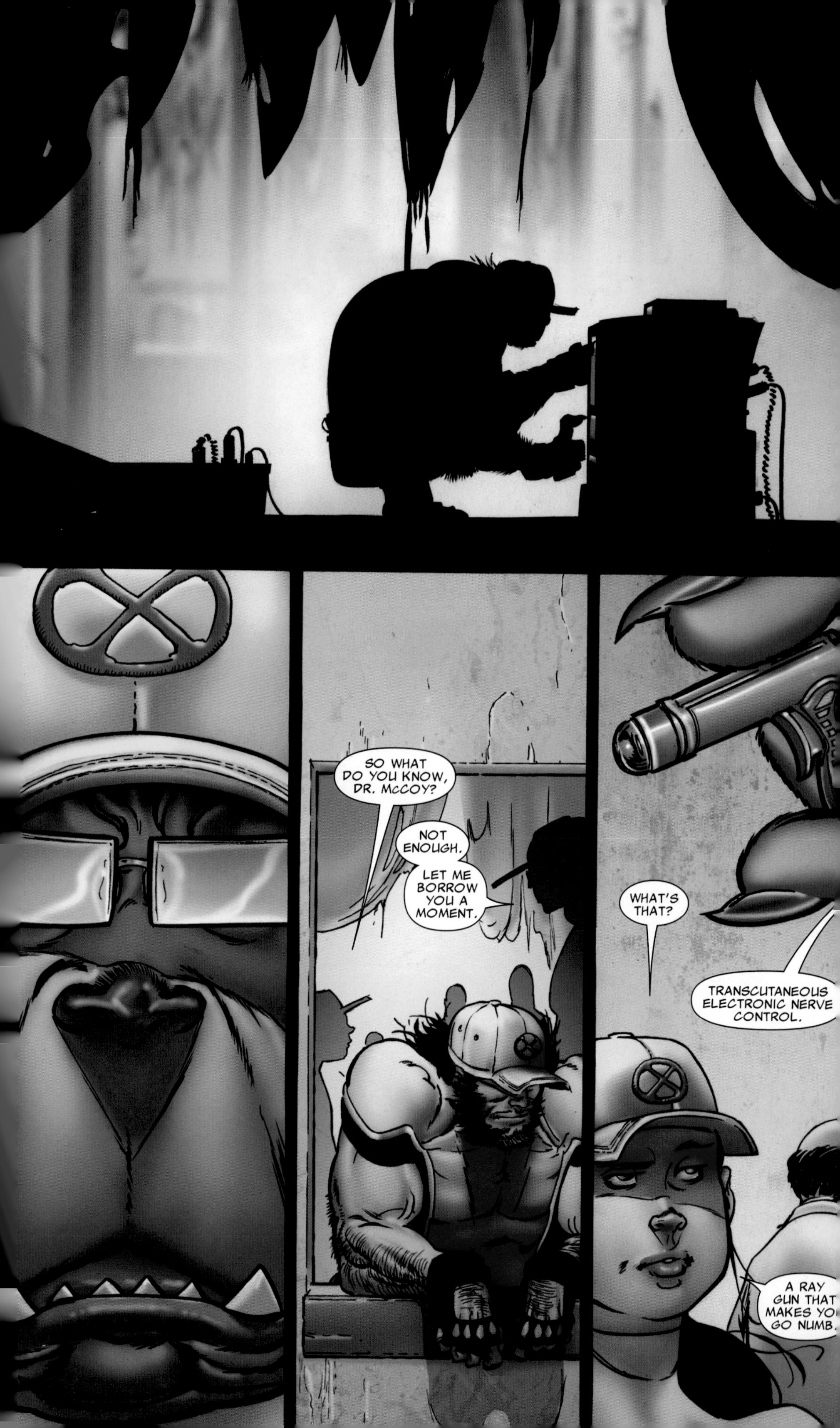
SO WHAT DO YOU KNOW, DR. McCOY?
NOT ENOUGH.
LET ME BORROW YOU A MOMENT.
WHAT'S THAT?
TRANSCUTANEOUS ELECTRONIC NERVE CONTROL.
A RAY GUN THAT MAKES YO GO NUMB.

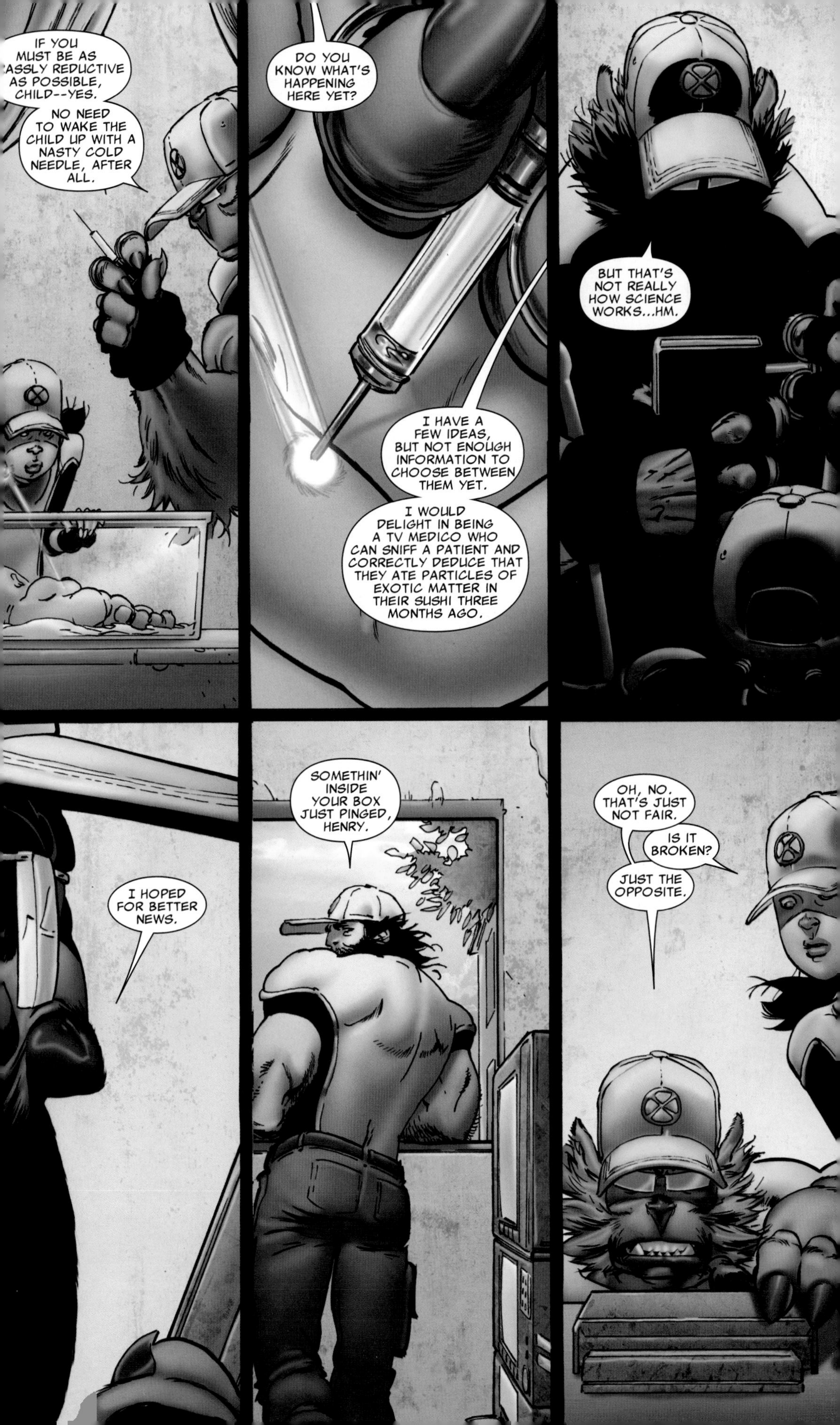
IF YOU MUST BE AS CRASSLY REDUCTIVE AS POSSIBLE, CHILD--YES.
NO NEED TO WAKE THE CHILD UP WITH A NASTY COLD NEEDLE, AFTER ALL.
DO YOU KNOW WHAT'S HAPPENING HERE YET?
I HAVE A FEW IDEAS, BUT NOT ENOUGH INFORMATION TO CHOOSE BETWEEN THEM YET.
I WOULD DELIGHT IN BEING A TV MEDICO WHO CAN SNIFF A PATIENT AND CORRECTLY DEDUCE THAT THEY ATE PARTICLES OF EXOTIC MATTER IN THEIR SUSHI THREE MONTHS AGO.
BUT THAT'S NOT REALLY HOW SCIENCE WORKS...HM.
I HOPED FOR BETTER NEWS.
SOMETHIN' INSIDE YOUR BOX JUST PINGED, HENRY.
OH, NO. THAT'S JUST NOT FAIR.
IS IT BROKEN?
JUST THE OPPOSITE.

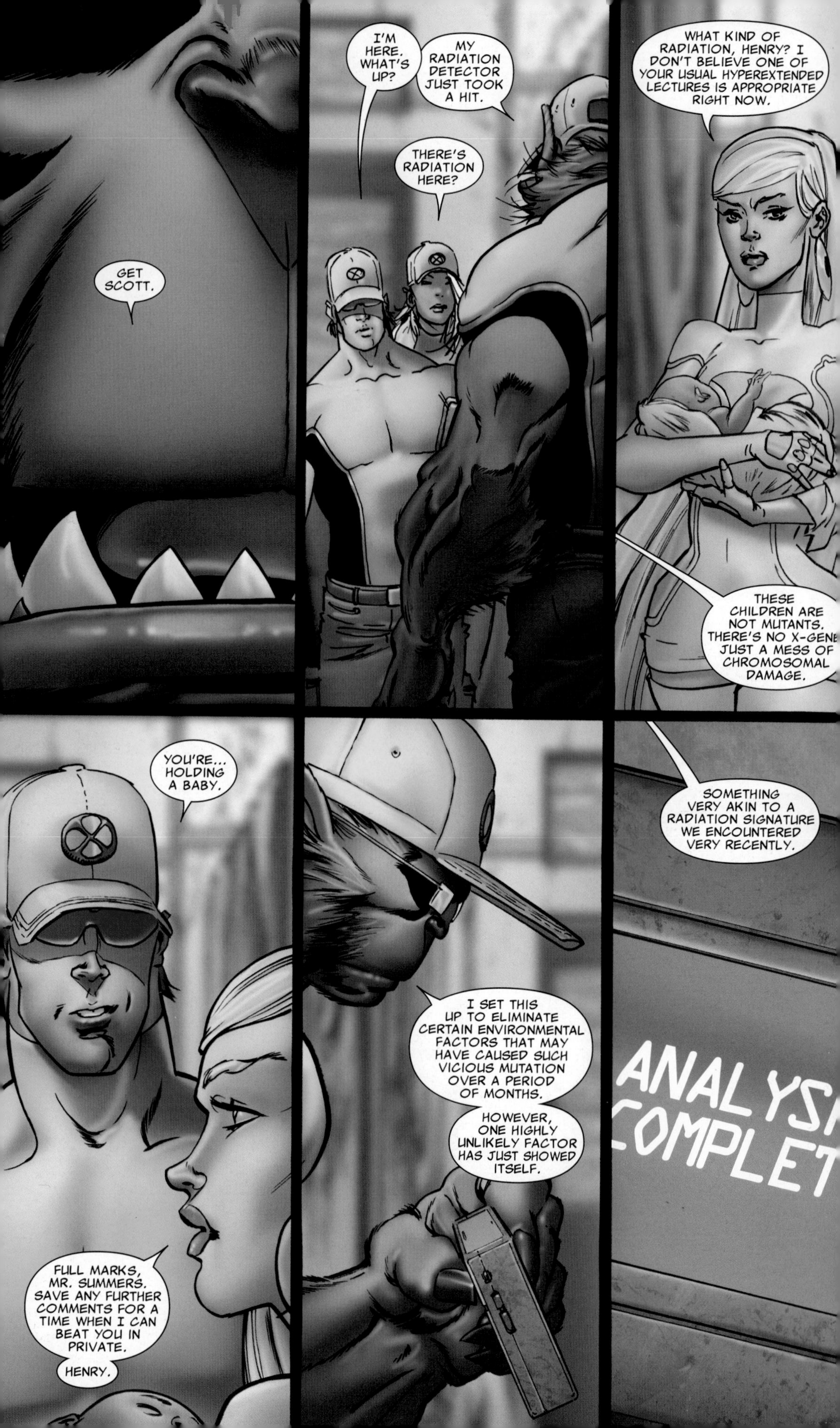
GET SCOTT.
I'M HERE. WHAT'S UP?
MY RADIATION DETECTOR JUST TOOK A HIT.
THERE'S RADIATION HERE?
WHAT KIND OF RADIATION, HENRY? I DON'T BELIEVE ONE OF YOUR USUAL HYPEREXTENDED LECTURES IS APPROPRIATE RIGHT NOW.
THESE CHILDREN ARE NOT MUTANTS. THERE'S NO X-GENE JUST A MESS OF CHROMOSOMAL DAMAGE.
SOMETHING VERY AKIN TO A RADIATION SIGNATURE WE ENCOUNTERED VERY RECENTLY.
YOU'RE... HOLDING A BABY.
FULL MARKS, MR. SUMMERS. SAVE ANY FURTHER COMMENTS FOR A TIME WHEN I CAN BEAT YOU IN PRIVATE.
HENRY.
I SET THIS UP TO ELIMINATE CERTAIN ENVIRONMENTAL FACTORS THAT MAY HAVE CAUSED SUCH VICIOUS MUTATION OVER A PERIOD OF MONTHS.
HOWEVER, ONE HIGHLY UNLIKELY FACTOR HAS JUST SHOWED ITSELF.

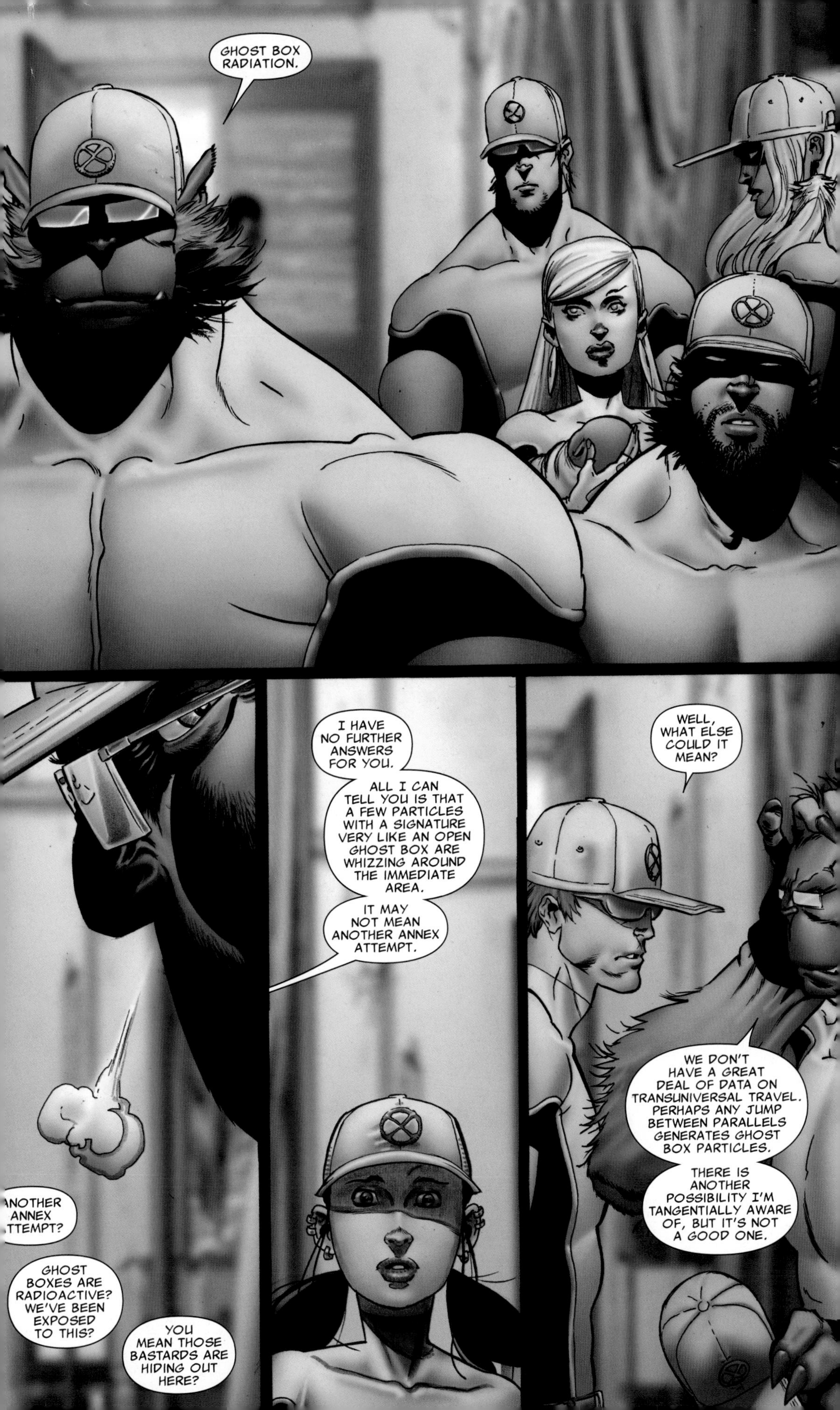
GHOST BOX RADIATION.
ANOTHER ANNEX ATTEMPT?
GHOST BOXES ARE RADIOACTIVE? WE'VE BEEN EXPOSED TO THIS?
YOU MEAN THOSE BASTARDS ARE HIDING OUT HERE?
I HAVE NO FURTHER ANSWERS FOR YOU.
ALL I CAN TELL YOU IS THAT A FEW PARTICLES WITH A SIGNATURE VERY LIKE AN OPEN GHOST BOX ARE WHIZZING AROUND THE IMMEDIATE AREA.
IT MAY NOT MEAN ANOTHER ANNEX ATTEMPT.
WELL, WHAT ELSE COULD IT MEAN?
WE DON'T HAVE A GREAT DEAL OF DATA ON TRANSUNIVERSAL TRAVEL. PERHAPS ANY JUMP BETWEEN PARALLELS GENERATES GHOST BOX PARTICLES.
THERE IS ANOTHER POSSIBILITY I'M TANGENTIALLY AWARE OF, BUT IT'S NOT A GOOD ONE.

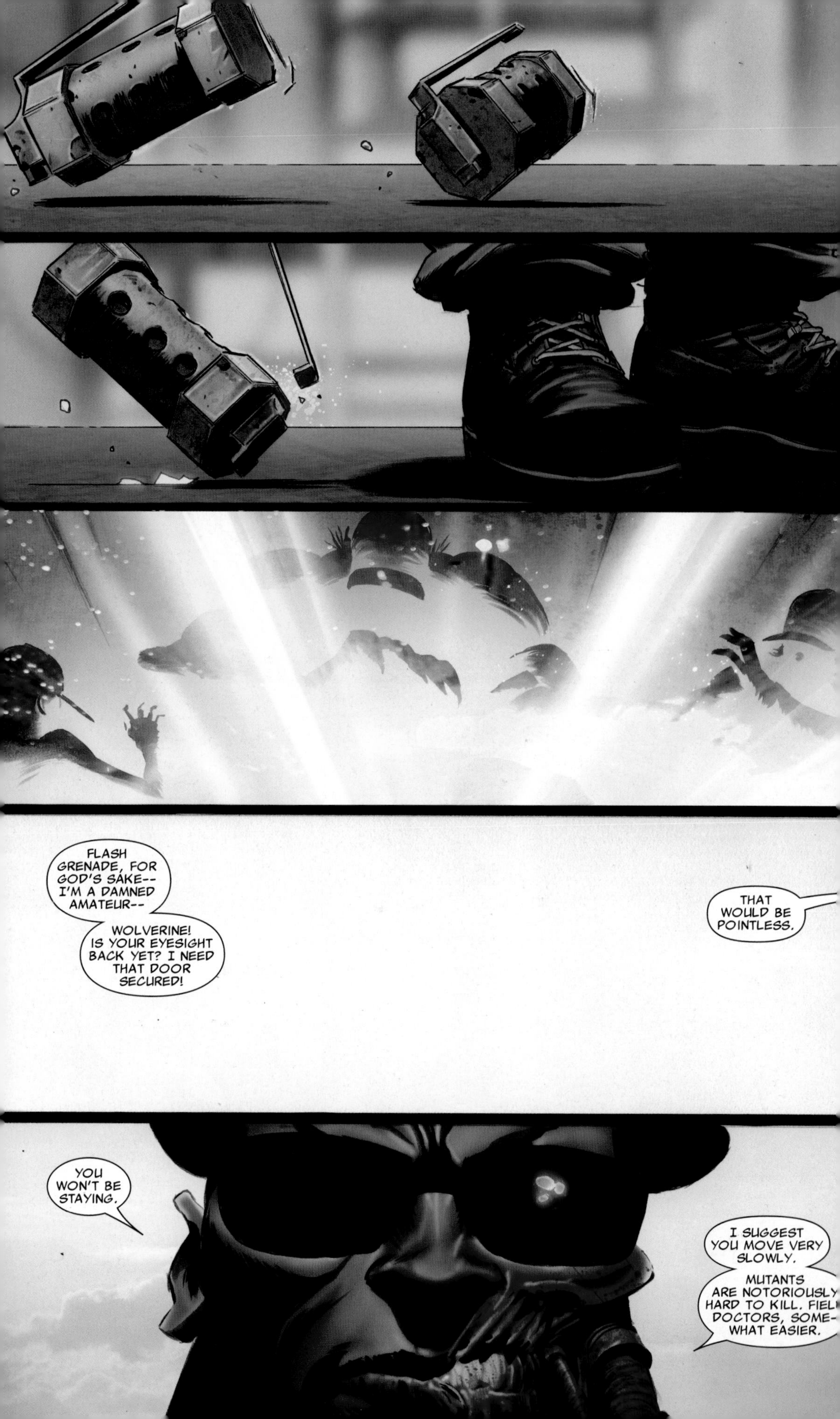
FLASH GRENADE, FOR GOD'S SAKE-- I'M A DAMNED AMATEUR--
WOLVERINE! IS YOUR EYESIGHT BACK YET? I NEED THAT DOOR SECURED!
THAT WOULD BE POINTLESS.
YOU WON'T BE STAYING.
I SUGGEST YOU MOVE VERY SLOWLY.
MUTANTS ARE NOTORIOUSLY HARD TO KILL. FIEL DOCTORS, SOME-WHAT EASIER.

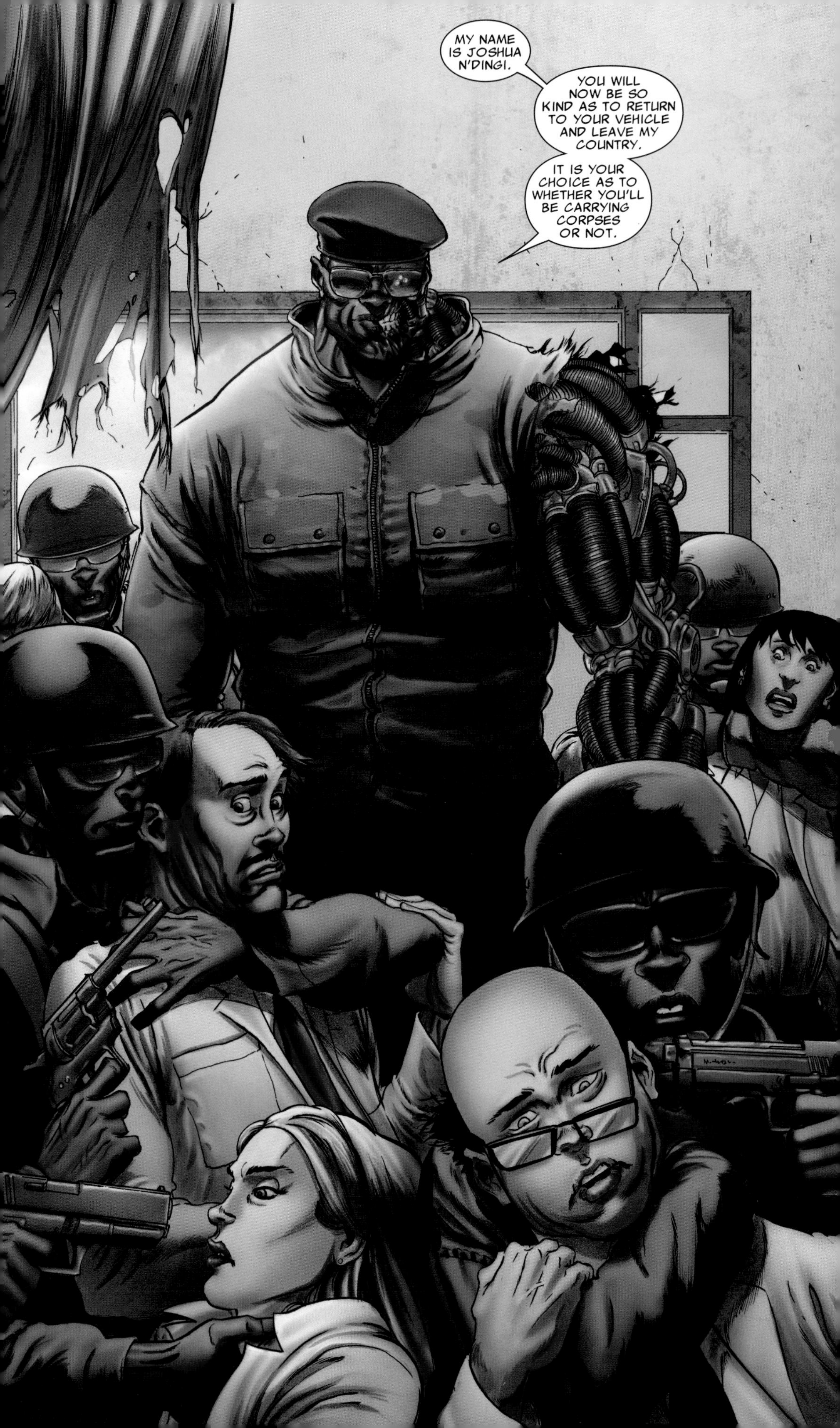
MY NAME IS JOSHUA N'DINGI.
YOU WILL NOW BE SO KIND AS TO RETURN TO YOUR VEHICLE AND LEAVE MY COUNTRY.
IT IS YOUR CHOICE AS TO WHETHER YOU'LL BE CARRYING CORPSES OR NOT.

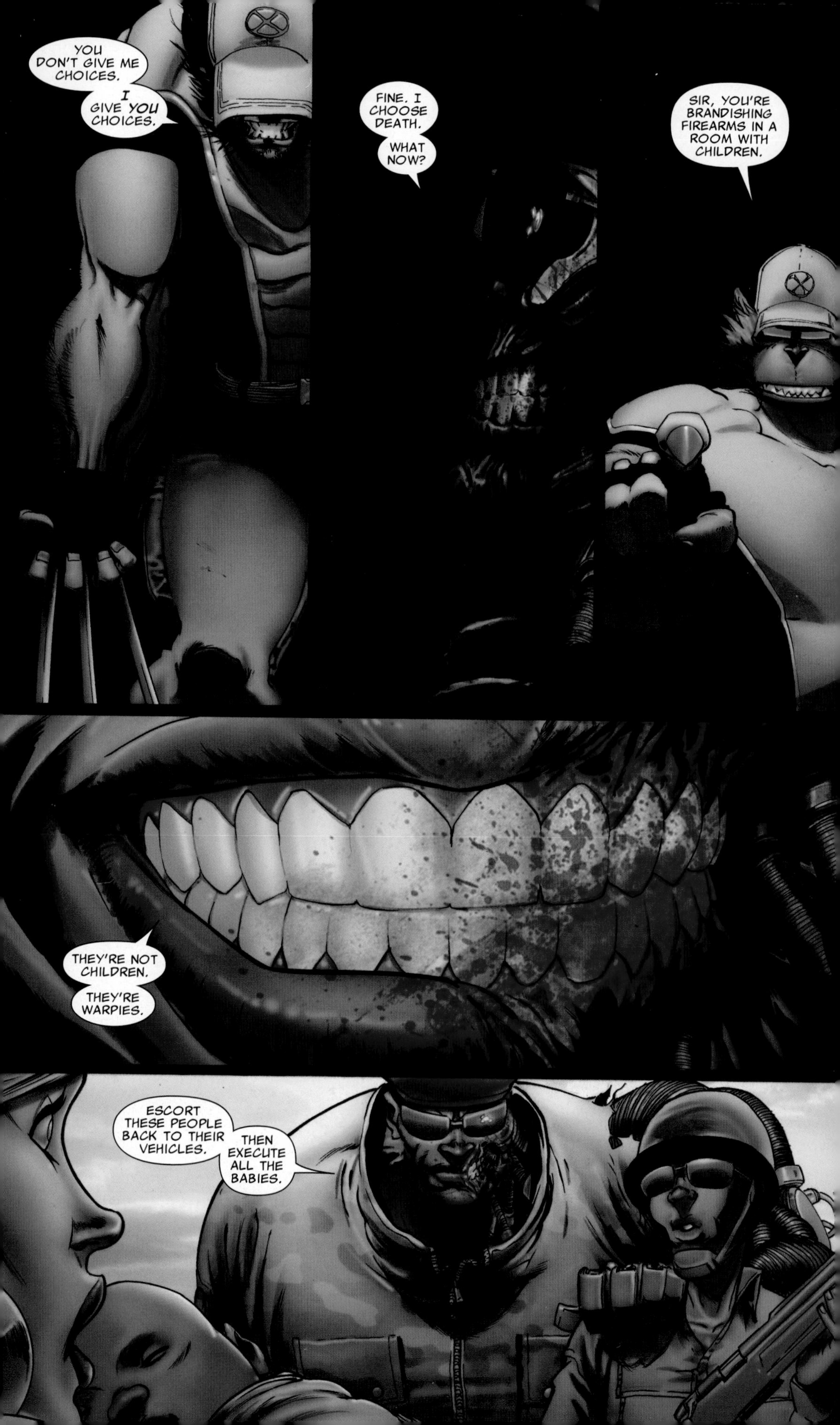
YOU DON'T GIVE ME CHOICES.
I GIVE YOU CHOICES.
FINE. I CHOOSE DEATH.
WHAT NOW?
SIR, YOU'RE BRANDISHING FIREARMS IN A ROOM WITH CHILDREN.
THEY'RE NOT CHILDREN.
THEY'RE WARPIES.
ESCORT THESE PEOPLE BACK TO THEIR VEHICLES.
THEN EXECUTE ALL THE BABIES.

THREE

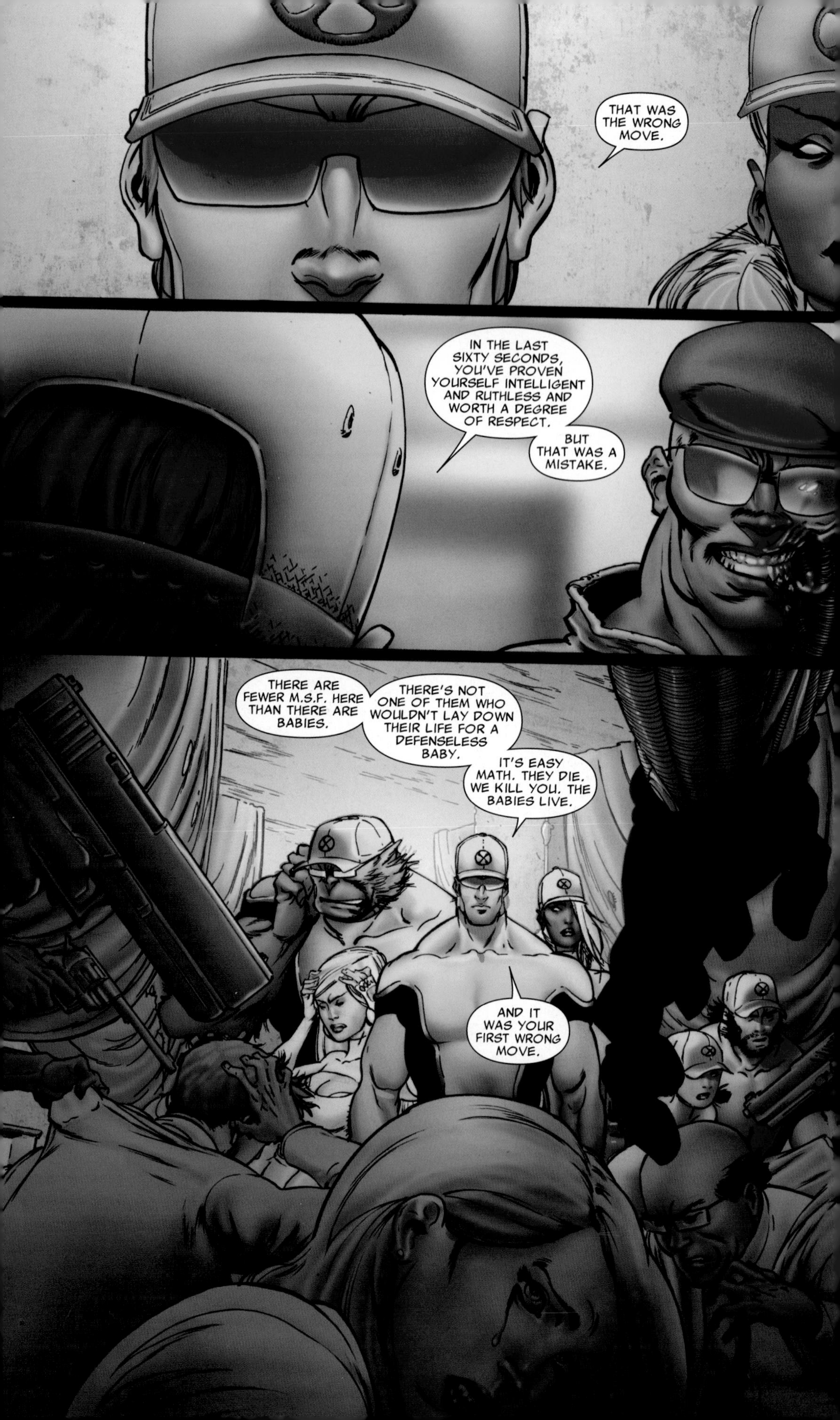
THAT WAS THE WRONG MOVE.
IN THE LAST SIXTY SECONDS, YOU'VE PROVEN YOURSELF INTELLIGENT AND RUTHLESS AND WORTH A DEGREE OF RESPECT.
BUT THAT WAS A MISTAKE.
THERE ARE FEWER M.S.F. HERE THAN THERE ARE BABIES.
THERE'S NOT ONE OF THEM WHO WOULDN'T LAY DOWN THEIR LIFE FOR A DEFENSELESS BABY.
IT'S EASY MATH. THEY DIE. WE KILL YOU. THE BABIES LIVE.
AND IT WAS YOUR FIRST WRONG MOVE.

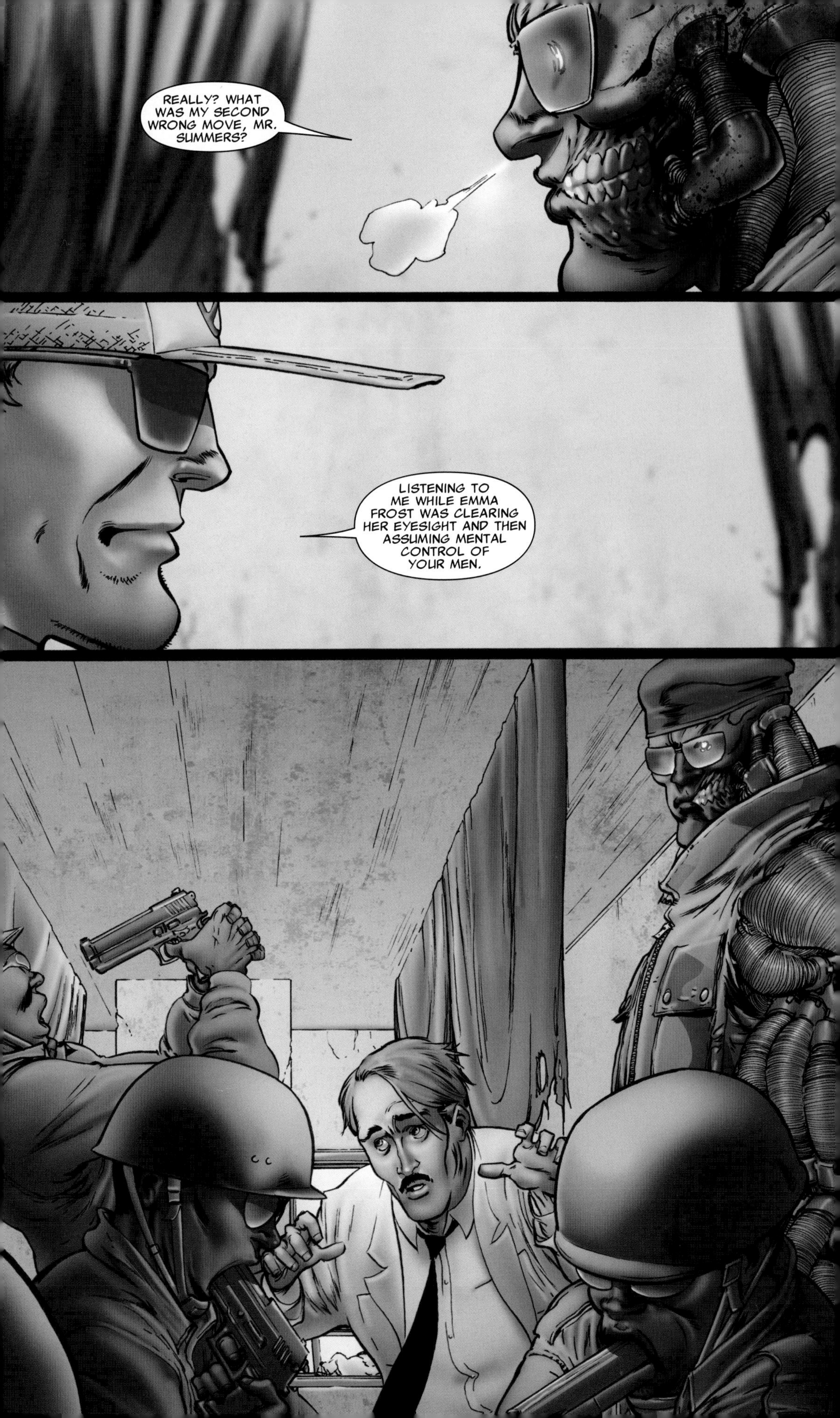
REALLY? WHAT WAS MY SECOND WRONG MOVE, MR. SUMMERS?
LISTENING TO ME WHILE EMMA FROST WAS CLEARING HER EYESIGHT AND THEN ASSUMING MENTAL CONTROL OF YOUR MEN.

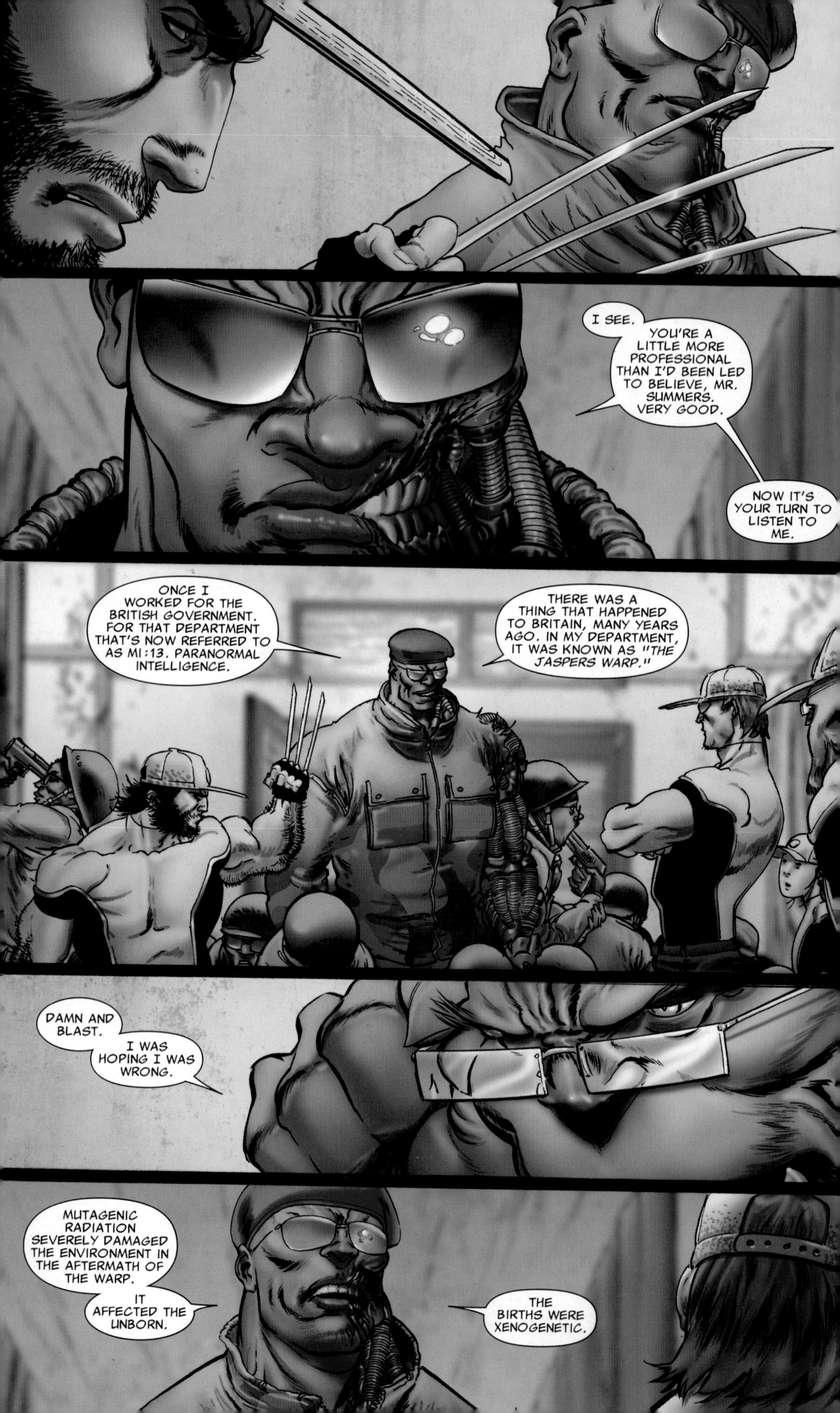
I SEE.
YOU'RE A LITTLE MORE PROFESSIONAL THAN I'D BEEN LED TO BELIEVE, MR. SUMMERS. VERY GOOD.
NOW IT'S YOUR TURN TO LISTEN TO ME.
ONCE I WORKED FOR THE BRITISH GOVERNMENT. FOR THAT DEPARTMENT THAT'S NOW REFERRED TO AS MI:13. PARANORMAL INTELLIGENCE.
THERE WAS A THING THAT HAPPENED TO BRITAIN, MANY YEARS AGO. IN MY DEPARTMENT, IT WAS KNOWN AS "THE JASPERS WARP."
DAMN AND BLAST.
I WAS HOPING I WAS WRONG.
MUTAGENIC RADIATION SEVERELY DAMAGED THE ENVIRONMENT IN THE AFTERMATH OF THE WARP.
IT AFFECTED THE UNBORN.
THE BIRTHS WERE XENOGENETIC.

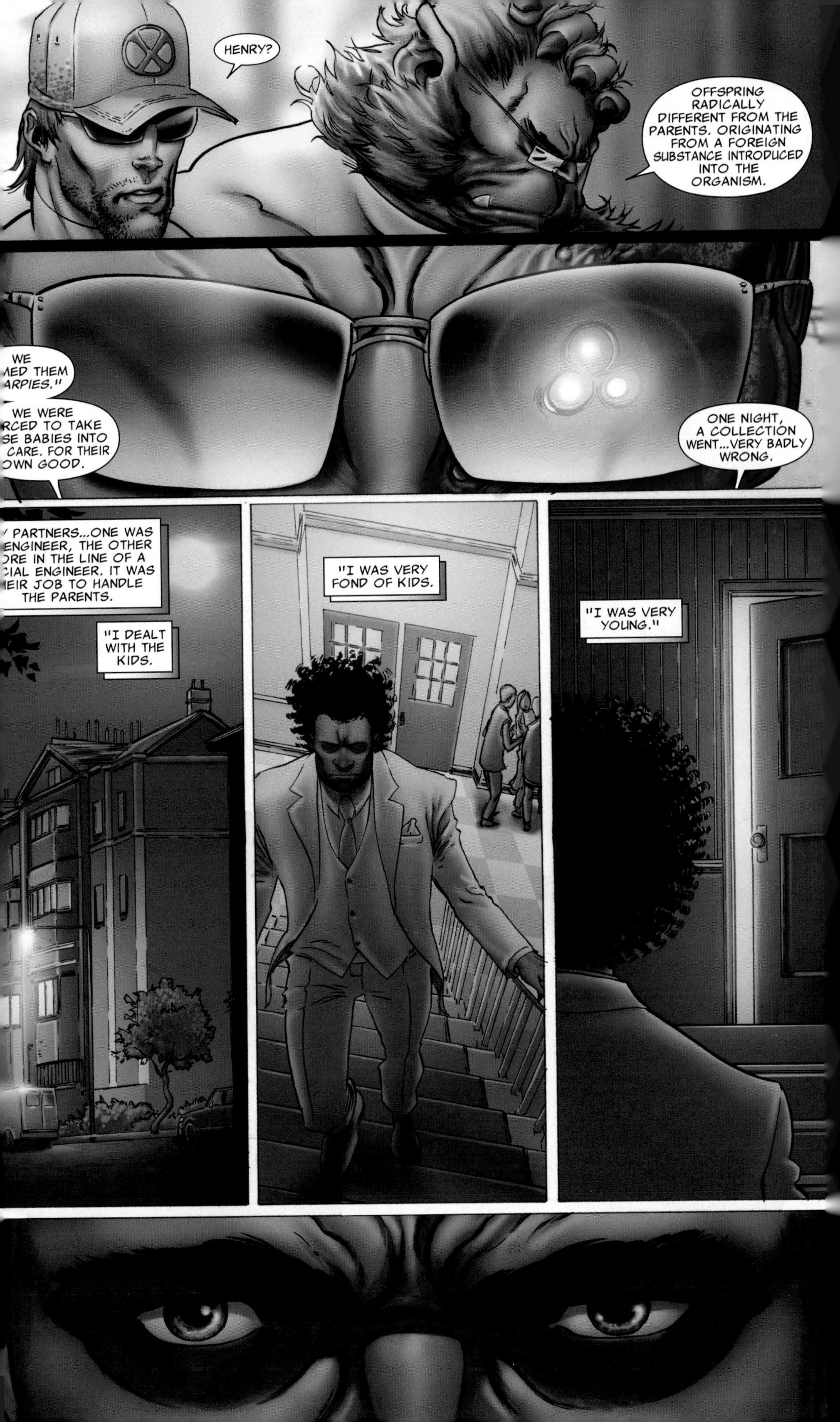

HENRY?
OFFSPRING RADICALLY DIFFERENT FROM THE PARENTS. ORIGINATING FROM A FOREIGN SUBSTANCE INTRODUCED INTO THE ORGANISM.
WE MED THEM ARPIES."
WE WERE RCED TO TAKE SE BABIES INTO CARE. FOR THEIR OWN GOOD.
ONE NIGHT, A COLLECTION WENT...VERY BADLY WRONG.
PARTNERS...ONE WAS ENGINEER, THE OTHER ORE IN THE LINE OF A CIAL ENGINEER. IT WAS EIR JOB TO HANDLE THE PARENTS.
"I DEALT WITH THE KIDS.
"I WAS VERY FOND OF KIDS.
"I WAS VERY YOUNG."

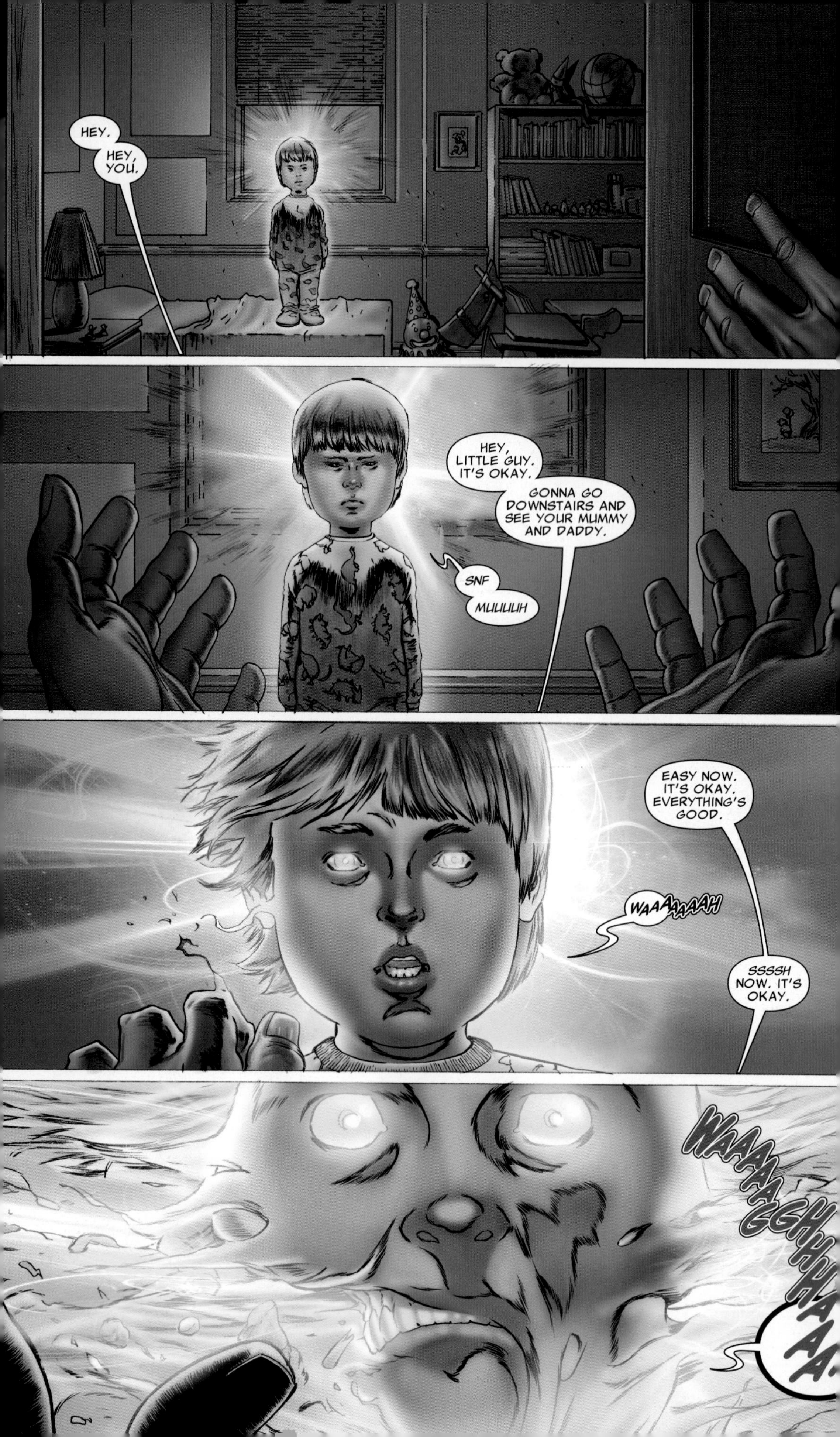
HEY.
HEY, YOU.
HEY, LITTLE GUY. IT'S OKAY.
GONNA GO DOWNSTAIRS AND SEE YOUR MUMMY AND DADDY.
SNF
MUUUUH
EASY NOW. IT'S OKAY. EVERYTHING'S GOOD.
WAAAAAAAH
SSSSH NOW. IT'S OKAY.
WAAAAAAGGHHHHAAAA

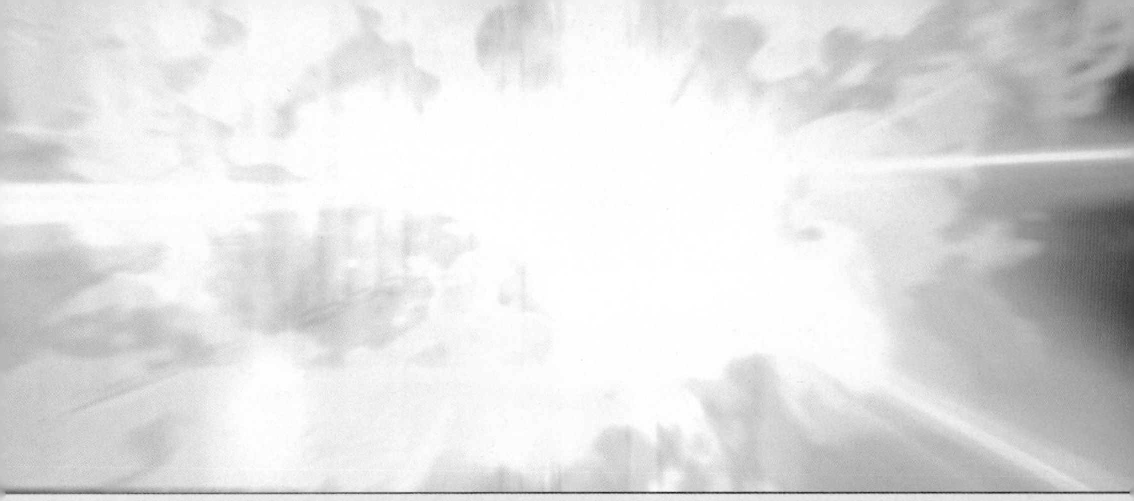

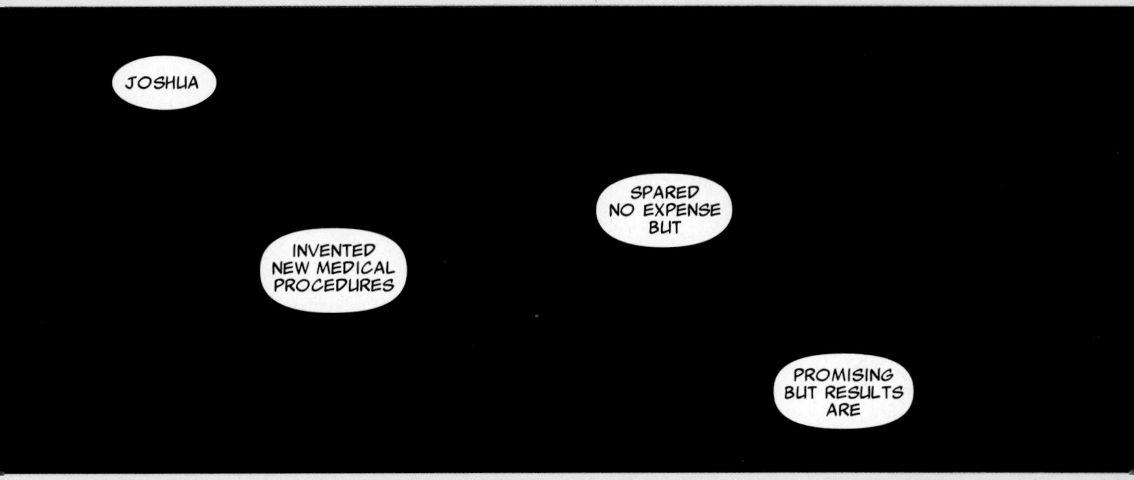
JOSHUA
SPARED NO EXPENSE BUT
INVENTED NEW MEDICAL PROCEDURES
PROMISING BUT RESULTS ARE

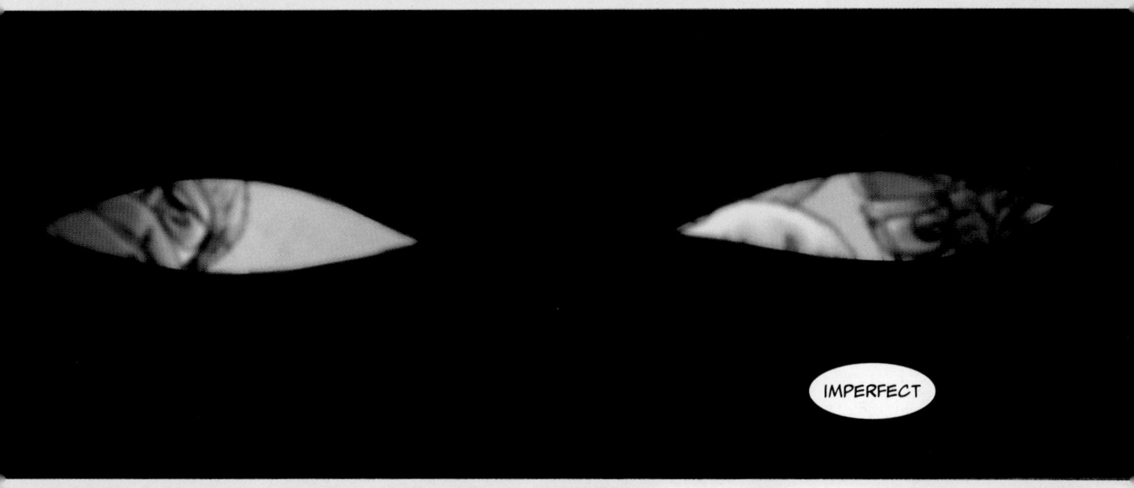
IMPERFECT

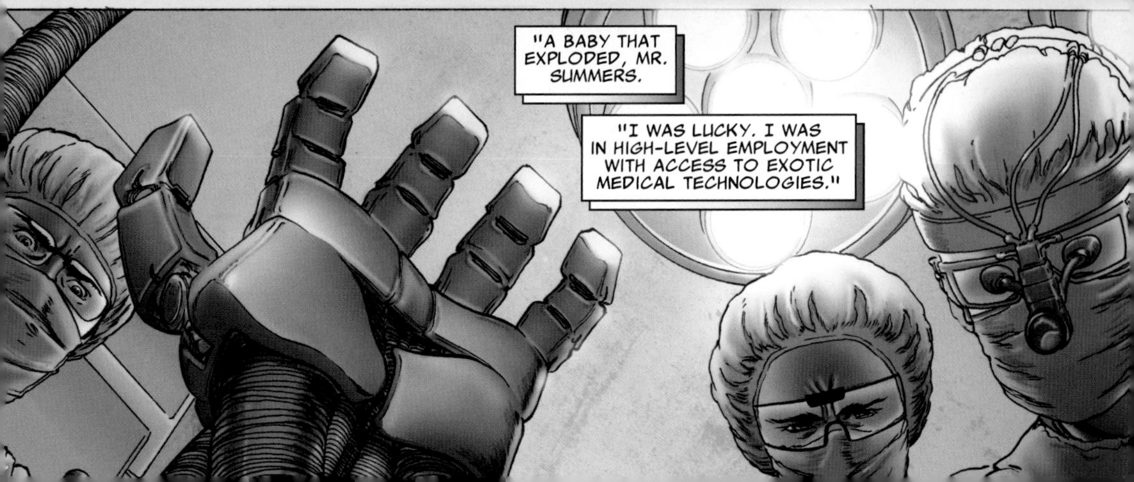
"A BABY THAT EXPLODED, MR. SUMMERS.
"I WAS LUCKY. I WAS IN HIGH-LEVEL EMPLOYMENT WITH ACCESS TO EXOTIC MEDICAL TECHNOLOGIES."

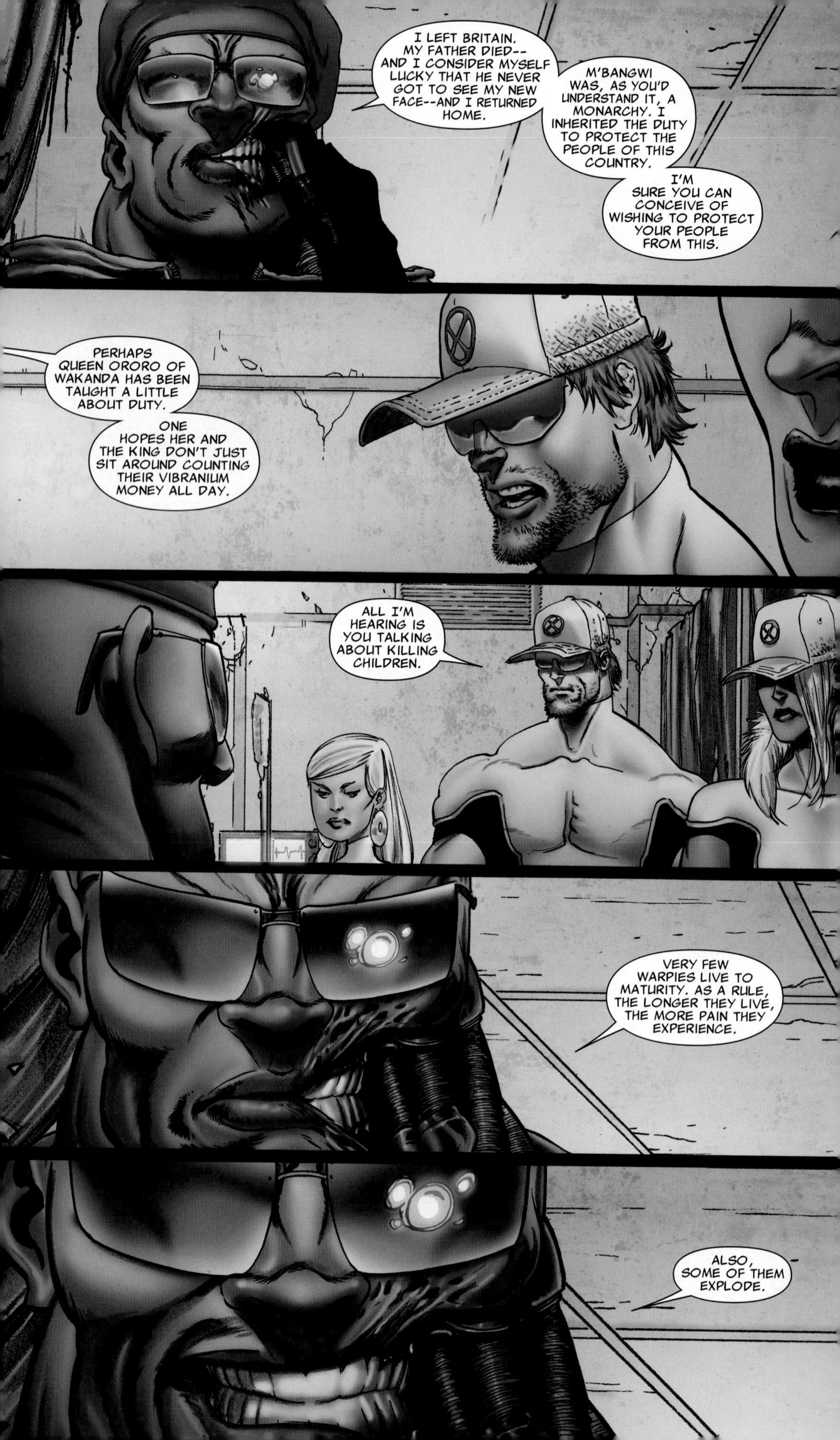
I LEFT BRITAIN. MY FATHER DIED-- AND I CONSIDER MYSELF LUCKY THAT HE NEVER GOT TO SEE MY NEW FACE--AND I RETURNED HOME.
M'BANGWI WAS, AS YOU'D UNDERSTAND IT, A MONARCHY. I INHERITED THE DUTY TO PROTECT THE PEOPLE OF THIS COUNTRY.
I'M SURE YOU CAN CONCEIVE OF WISHING TO PROTECT YOUR PEOPLE FROM THIS.
PERHAPS QUEEN ORORO OF WAKANDA HAS BEEN TAUGHT A LITTLE ABOUT DUTY.
ONE HOPES HER AND THE KING DON'T JUST SIT AROUND COUNTING THEIR VIBRANIUM MONEY ALL DAY.
ALL I'M HEARING IS YOU TALKING ABOUT KILLING CHILDREN.
VERY FEW WARPIES LIVE TO MATURITY. AS A RULE, THE LONGER THEY LIVE, THE MORE PAIN THEY EXPERIENCE.
ALSO, SOME OF THEM EXPLODE.

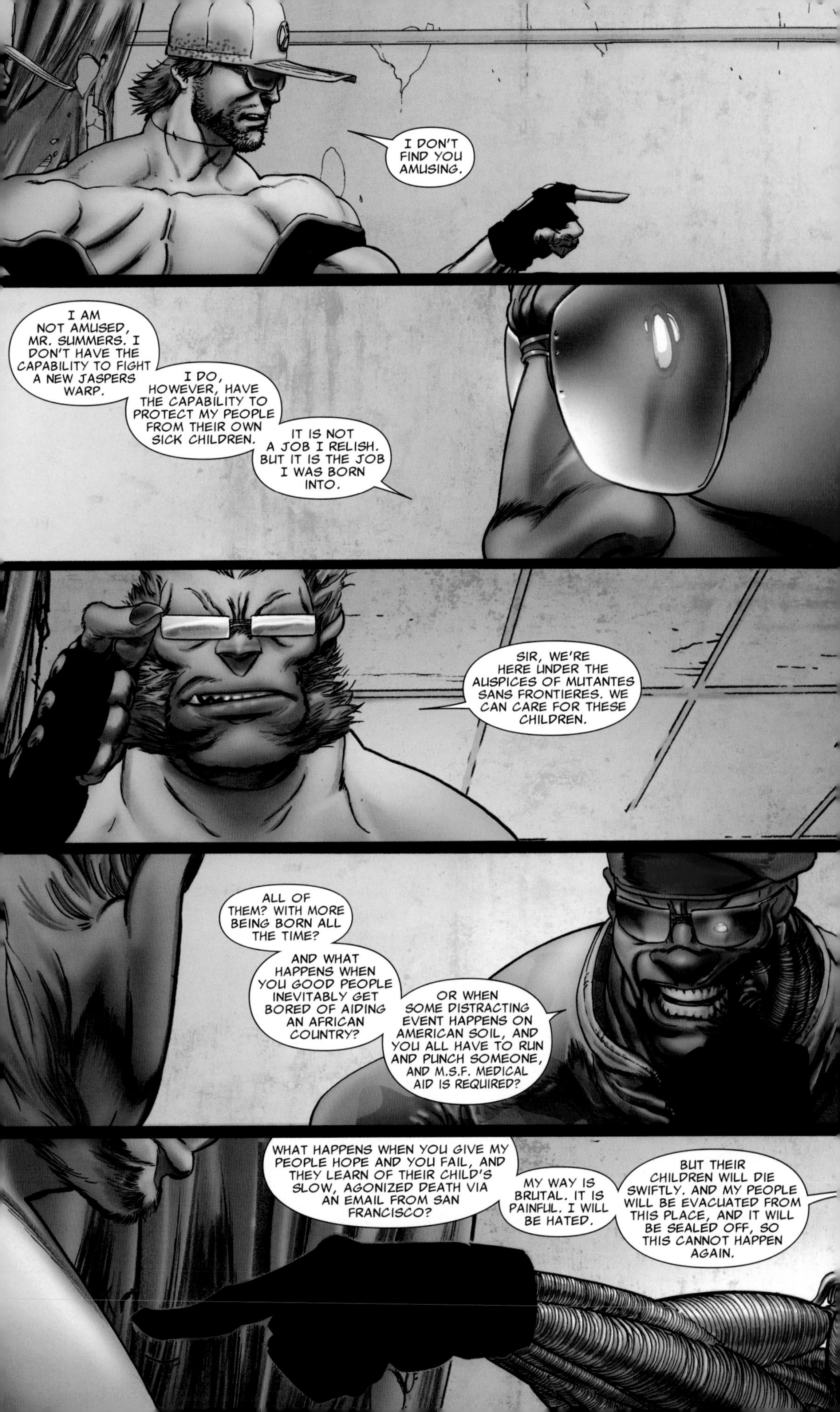
I DON'T FIND YOU AMUSING.
I AM NOT AMUSED, MR. SUMMERS. I DON'T HAVE THE CAPABILITY TO FIGHT A NEW JASPERS WARP.
I DO, HOWEVER, HAVE THE CAPABILITY TO PROTECT MY PEOPLE FROM THEIR OWN SICK CHILDREN.
IT IS NOT A JOB I RELISH. BUT IT IS THE JOB I WAS BORN INTO.
SIR, WE'RE HERE UNDER THE AUSPICES OF MUTANTES SANS FRONTIERES. WE CAN CARE FOR THESE CHILDREN.
ALL OF THEM? WITH MORE BEING BORN ALL THE TIME?
AND WHAT HAPPENS WHEN YOU GOOD PEOPLE INEVITABLY GET BORED OF AIDING AN AFRICAN COUNTRY?
OR WHEN SOME DISTRACTING EVENT HAPPENS ON AMERICAN SOIL, AND YOU ALL HAVE TO RUN AND PUNCH SOMEONE, AND M.S.F. MEDICAL AID IS REQUIRED?
WHAT HAPPENS WHEN YOU GIVE MY PEOPLE HOPE AND YOU FAIL, AND THEY LEARN OF THEIR CHILD'S SLOW, AGONIZED DEATH VIA AN EMAIL FROM SAN FRANCISCO?
MY WAY IS BRUTAL. IT IS PAINFUL. I WILL BE HATED.
BUT THEIR CHILDREN WILL DIE SWIFTLY. AND MY PEOPLE WILL BE EVACUATED FROM THIS PLACE, AND IT WILL BE SEALED OFF, SO THIS CANNOT HAPPEN AGAIN.

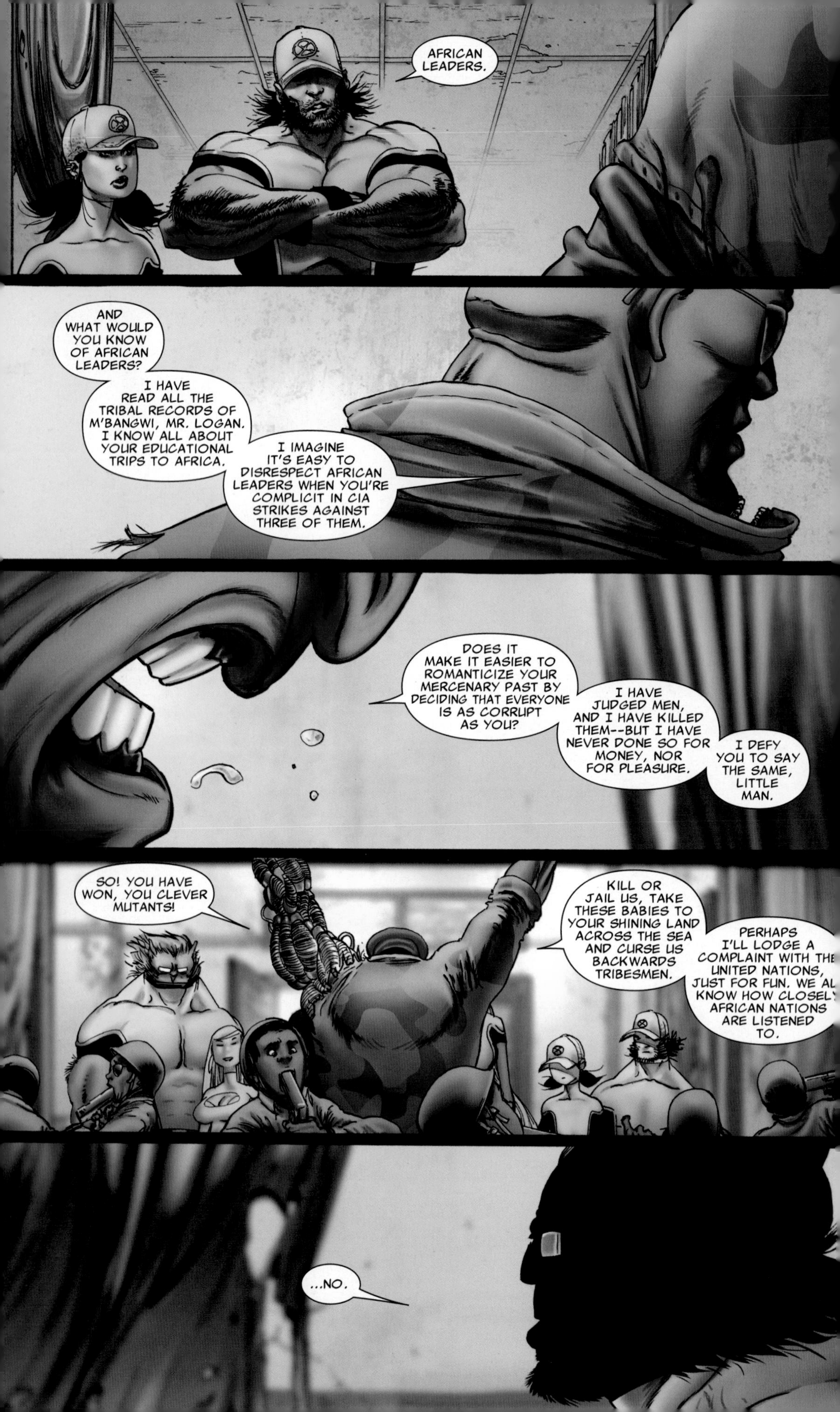
AFRICAN LEADERS.
AND WHAT WOULD YOU KNOW OF AFRICAN LEADERS?
I HAVE READ ALL THE TRIBAL RECORDS OF M'BANGWI, MR. LOGAN. I KNOW ALL ABOUT YOUR EDUCATIONAL TRIPS TO AFRICA.
I IMAGINE IT'S EASY TO DISRESPECT AFRICAN LEADERS WHEN YOU'RE COMPLICIT IN CIA STRIKES AGAINST THREE OF THEM.
DOES IT MAKE IT EASIER TO ROMANTICIZE YOUR MERCENARY PAST BY DECIDING THAT EVERYONE IS AS CORRUPT AS YOU?
I HAVE JUDGED MEN, AND I HAVE KILLED THEM--BUT I HAVE NEVER DONE SO FOR MONEY, NOR FOR PLEASURE.
I DEFY YOU TO SAY THE SAME, LITTLE MAN.
SO! YOU HAVE WON, YOU CLEVER MUTANTS!
KILL OR JAIL US, TAKE THESE BABIES TO YOUR SHINING LAND ACROSS THE SEA AND CURSE US BACKWARDS TRIBESMEN.
PERHAPS I'LL LODGE A COMPLAINT WITH THE UNITED NATIONS, JUST FOR FUN. WE AL KNOW HOW CLOSELY AFRICAN NATIONS ARE LISTENED TO.
...NO.

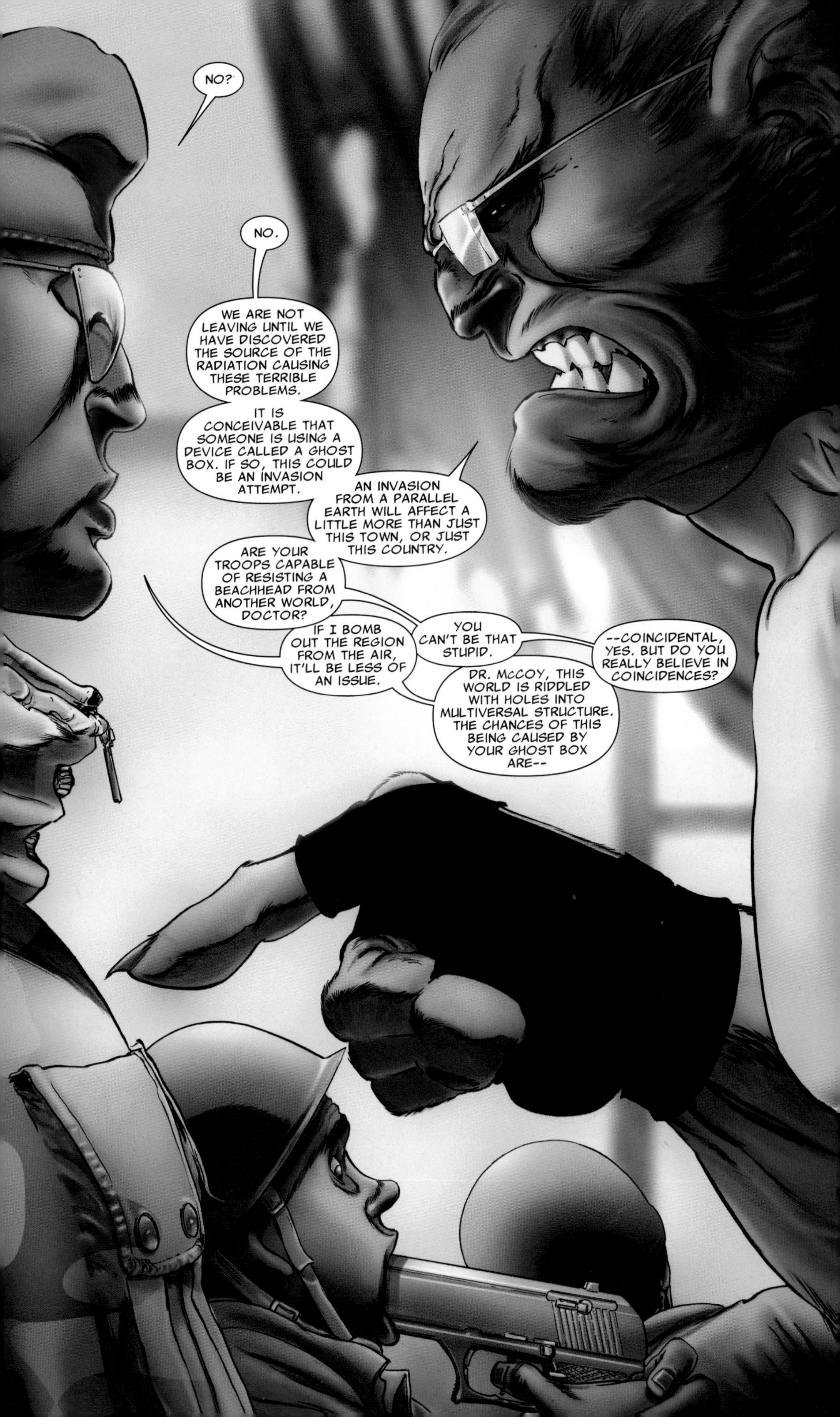
NO?
NO.
WE ARE NOT LEAVING UNTIL WE HAVE DISCOVERED THE SOURCE OF THE RADIATION CAUSING THESE TERRIBLE PROBLEMS.
IT IS CONCEIVABLE THAT SOMEONE IS USING A DEVICE CALLED A GHOST BOX. IF SO, THIS COULD BE AN INVASION ATTEMPT.
AN INVASION FROM A PARALLEL EARTH WILL AFFECT A LITTLE MORE THAN JUST THIS TOWN, OR JUST THIS COUNTRY.
ARE YOUR TROOPS CAPABLE OF RESISTING A BEACHHEAD FROM ANOTHER WORLD, DOCTOR?
IF I BOMB OUT THE REGION FROM THE AIR, IT'LL BE LESS OF AN ISSUE.
YOU CAN'T BE THAT STUPID.
DR. McCOY, THIS WORLD IS RIDDLED WITH HOLES INTO MULTIVERSAL STRUCTURE. THE CHANCES OF THIS BEING CAUSED BY YOUR GHOST BOX ARE--
--COINCIDENTAL, YES. BUT DO YOU REALLY BELIEVE IN COINCIDENCES?

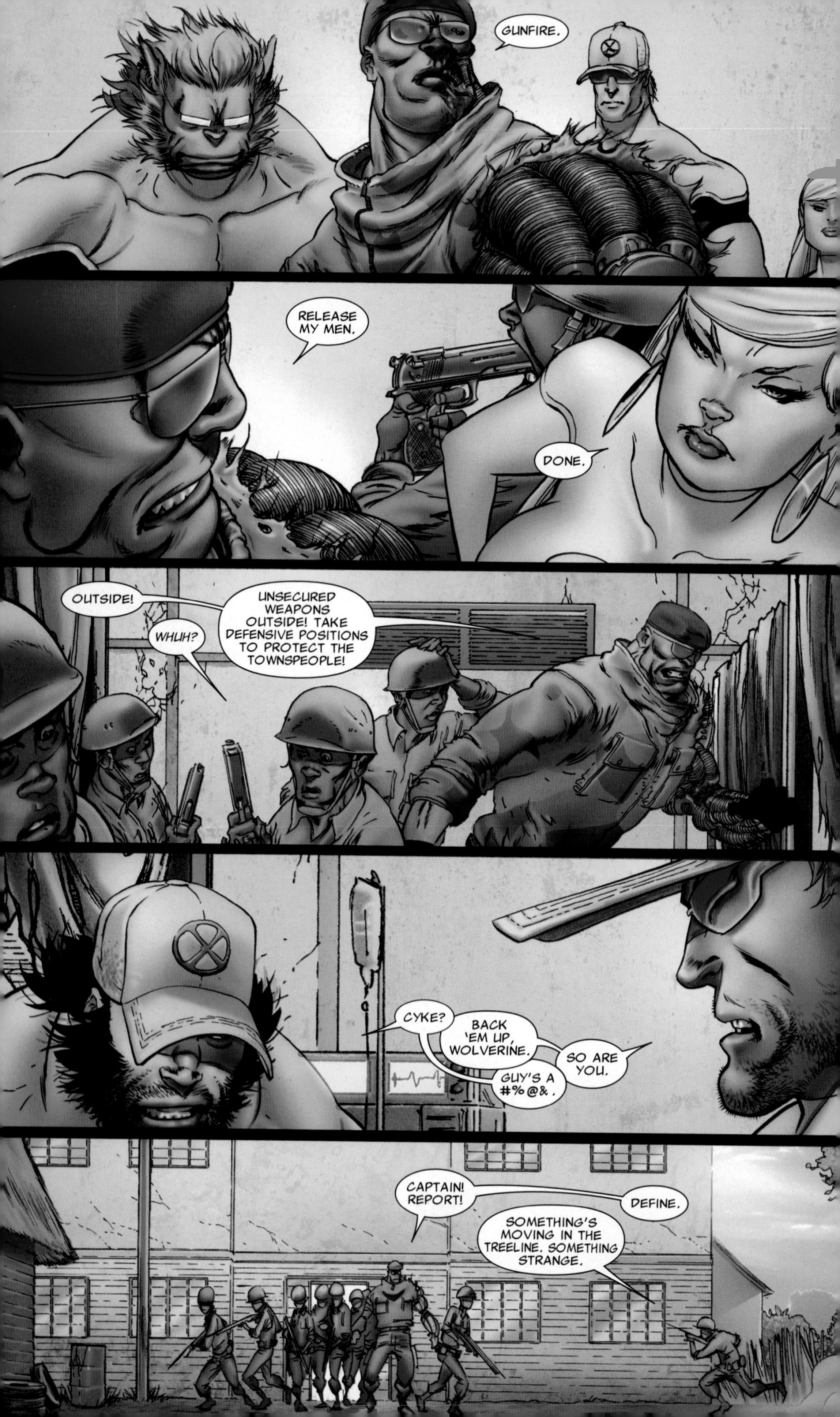
GUNFIRE.
RELEASE MY MEN.
DONE.
OUTSIDE!
WHUH?
UNSECURED WEAPONS OUTSIDE! TAKE DEFENSIVE POSITIONS TO PROTECT THE TOWNSPEOPLE!
CYKE?
BACK 'EM UP, WOLVERINE.
GUY'S A #%@&.
SO ARE YOU.
CAPTAIN! REPORT!
DEFINE.
SOMETHING'S MOVING IN THE TREELINE. SOMETHING STRANGE.

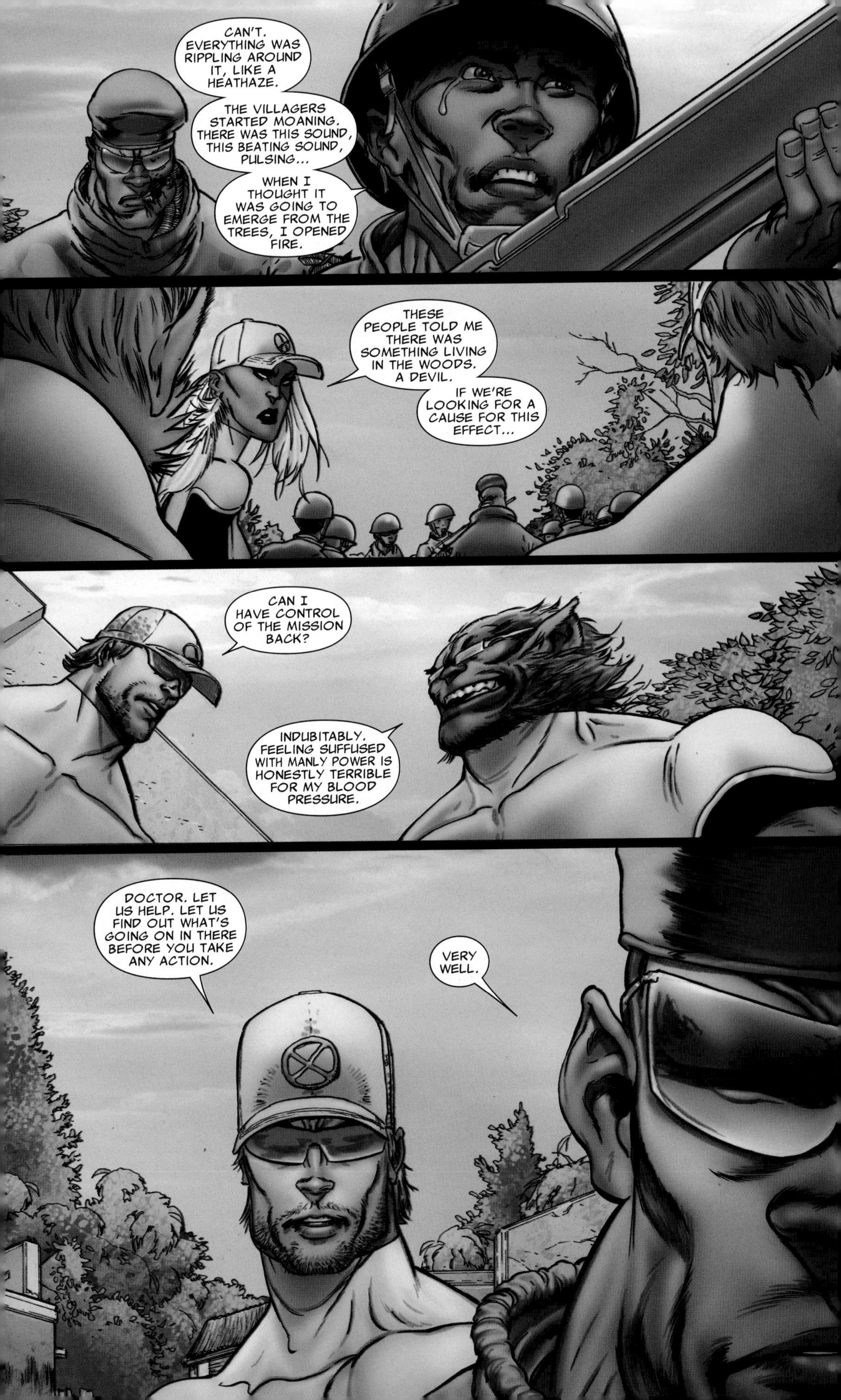
CAN'T. EVERYTHING WAS RIPPLING AROUND IT, LIKE A HEATHAZE.
THE VILLAGERS STARTED MOANING. THERE WAS THIS SOUND, THIS BEATING SOUND, PULSING...
WHEN I THOUGHT IT WAS GOING TO EMERGE FROM THE TREES, I OPENED FIRE.
THESE PEOPLE TOLD ME THERE WAS SOMETHING LIVING IN THE WOODS. A DEVIL.
IF WE'RE LOOKING FOR A CAUSE FOR THIS EFFECT...
CAN I HAVE CONTROL OF THE MISSION BACK?
INDUBITABLY. FEELING SUFFUSED WITH MANLY POWER IS HONESTLY TERRIBLE FOR MY BLOOD PRESSURE.
DOCTOR. LET US HELP. LET US FIND OUT WHAT'S GOING ON IN THERE BEFORE YOU TAKE ANY ACTION.
VERY WELL.

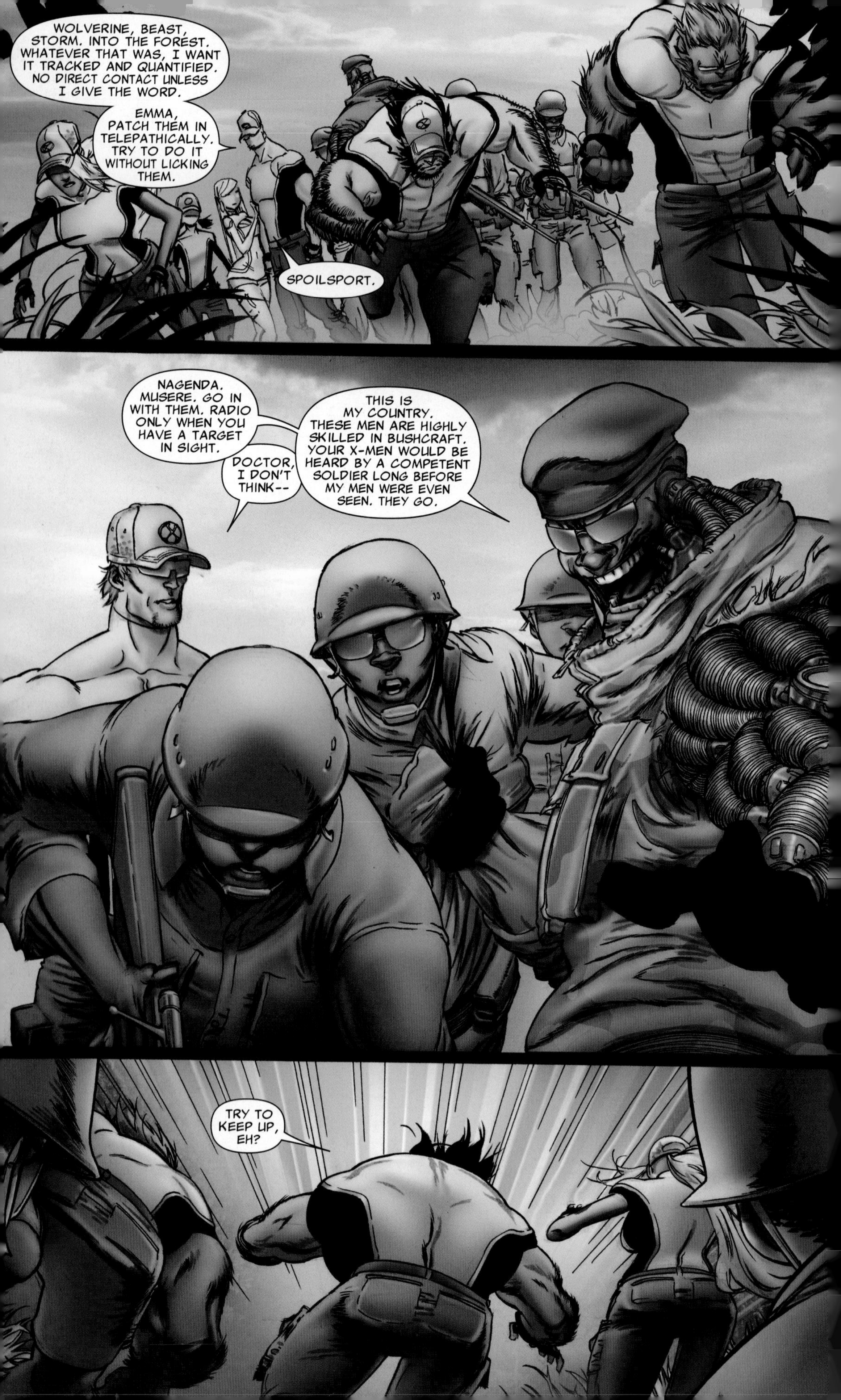
WOLVERINE, BEAST, STORM. INTO THE FOREST. WHATEVER THAT WAS, I WANT IT TRACKED AND QUANTIFIED. NO DIRECT CONTACT UNLESS I GIVE THE WORD.
EMMA, PATCH THEM IN TELEPATHICALLY. TRY TO DO IT WITHOUT LICKING THEM.
SPOILSPORT.
NAGENDA. MUSERE. GO IN WITH THEM. RADIO ONLY WHEN YOU HAVE A TARGET IN SIGHT.
DOCTOR, I DON'T THINK--
THIS IS MY COUNTRY. THESE MEN ARE HIGHLY SKILLED IN BUSHCRAFT. YOUR X-MEN WOULD BE HEARD BY A COMPETENT SOLDIER LONG BEFORE MY MEN WERE EVEN SEEN. THEY GO.
TRY TO KEEP UP, EH?

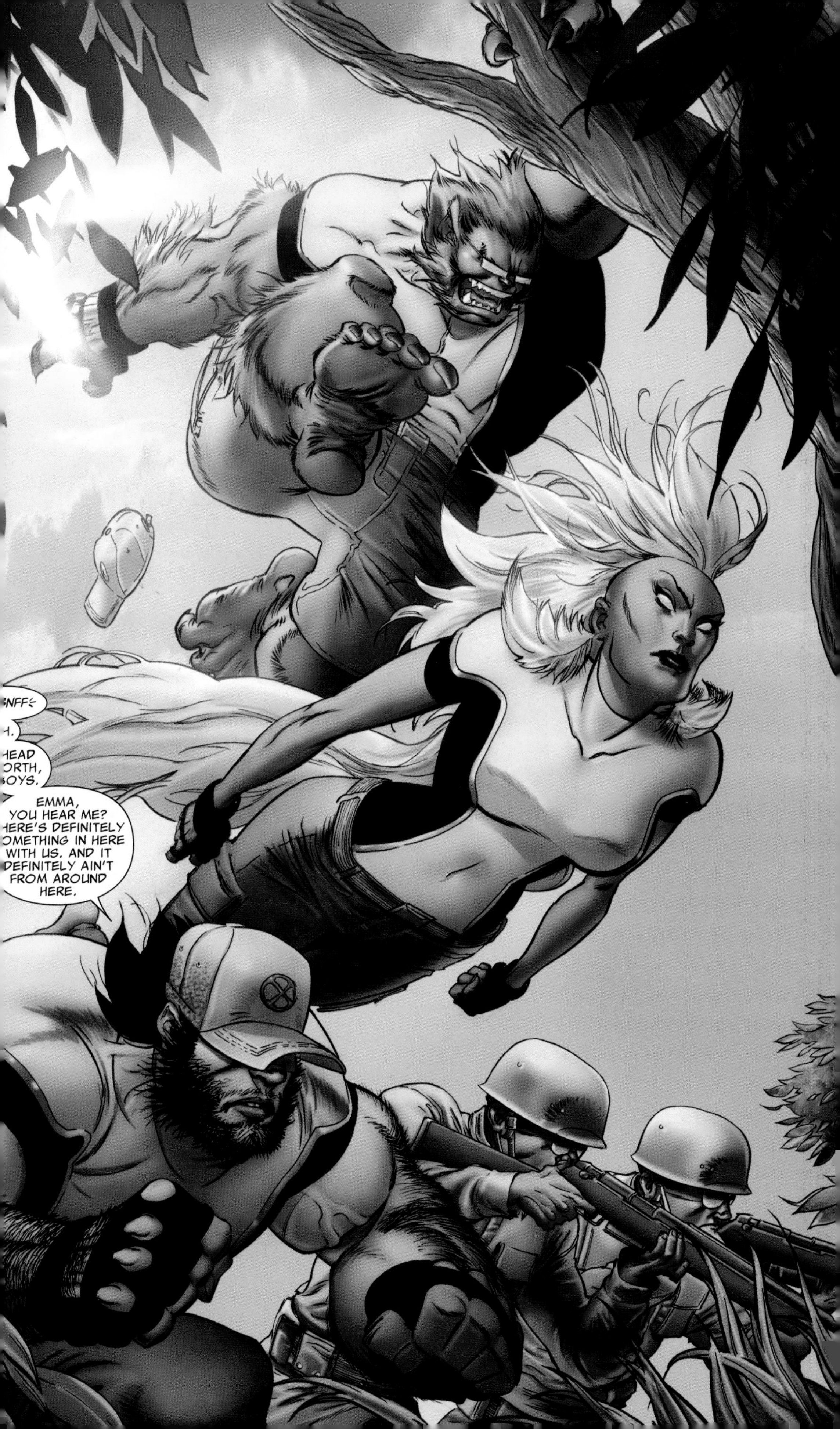
NFF
HEAD ORTH, OYS.
EMMA, YOU HEAR ME? HERE'S DEFINITELY OMETHING IN HERE WITH US. AND IT DEFINITELY AIN'T FROM AROUND HERE.

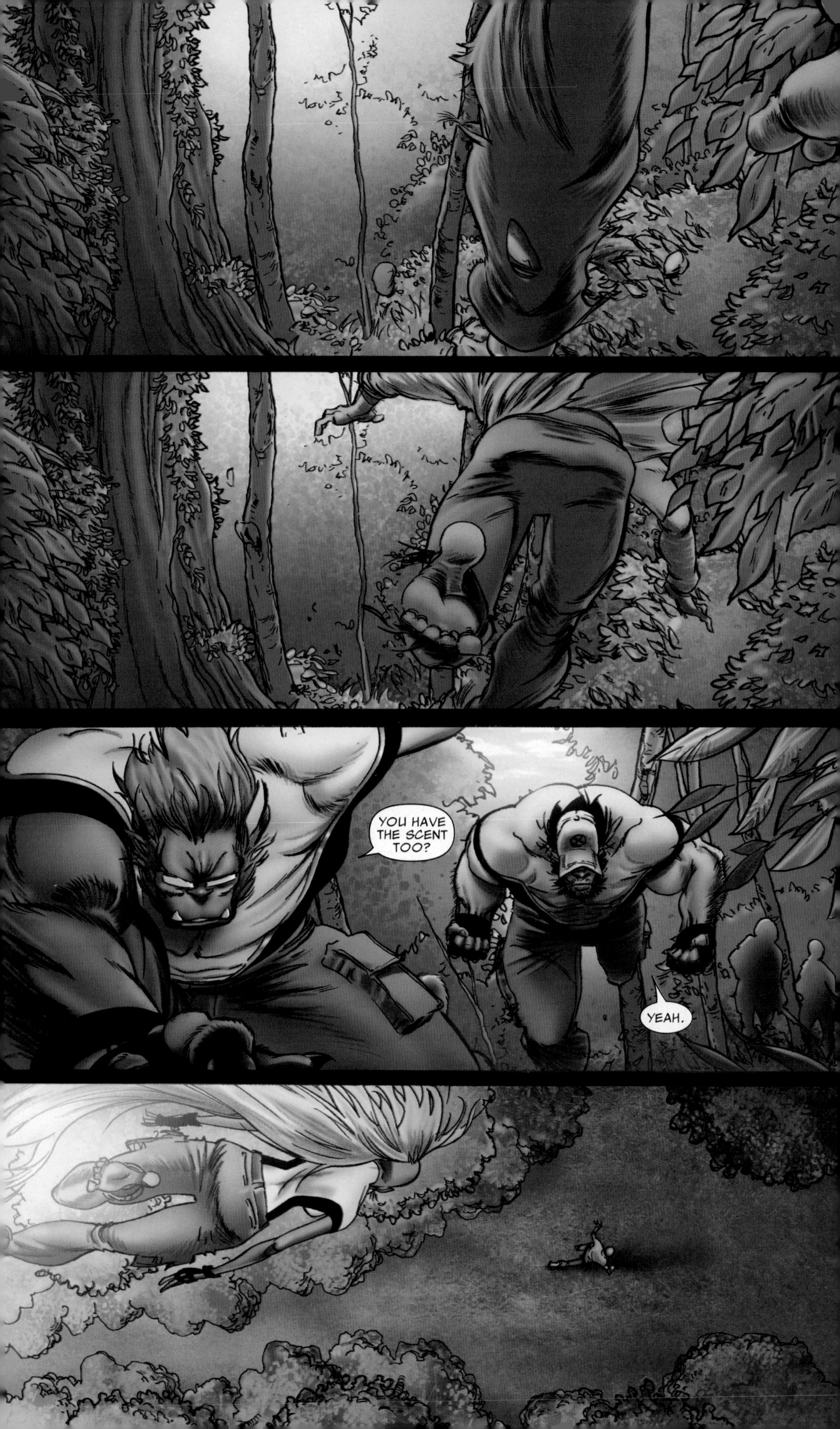
YOU HAVE THE SCENT TOO?
YEAH.

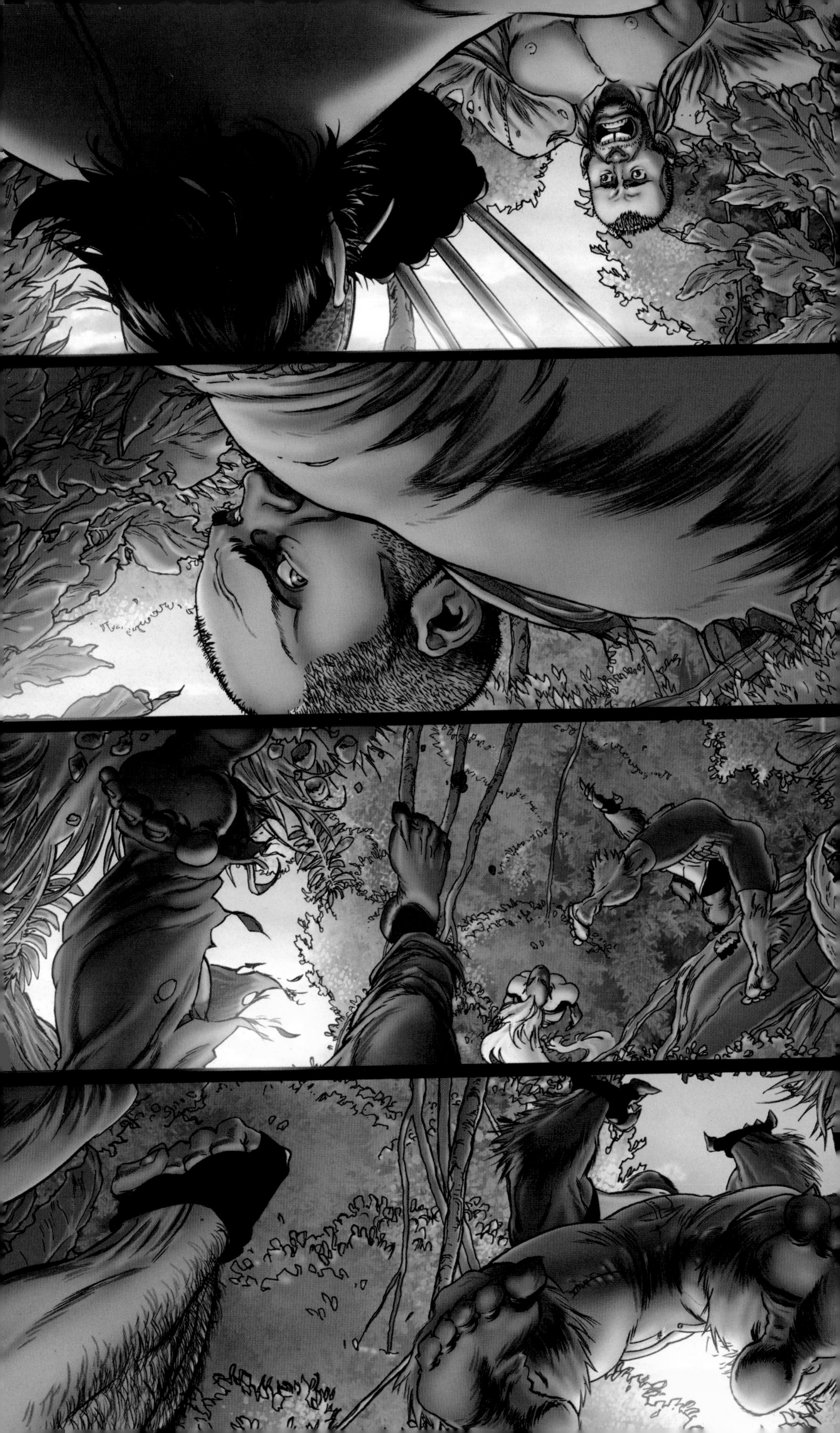

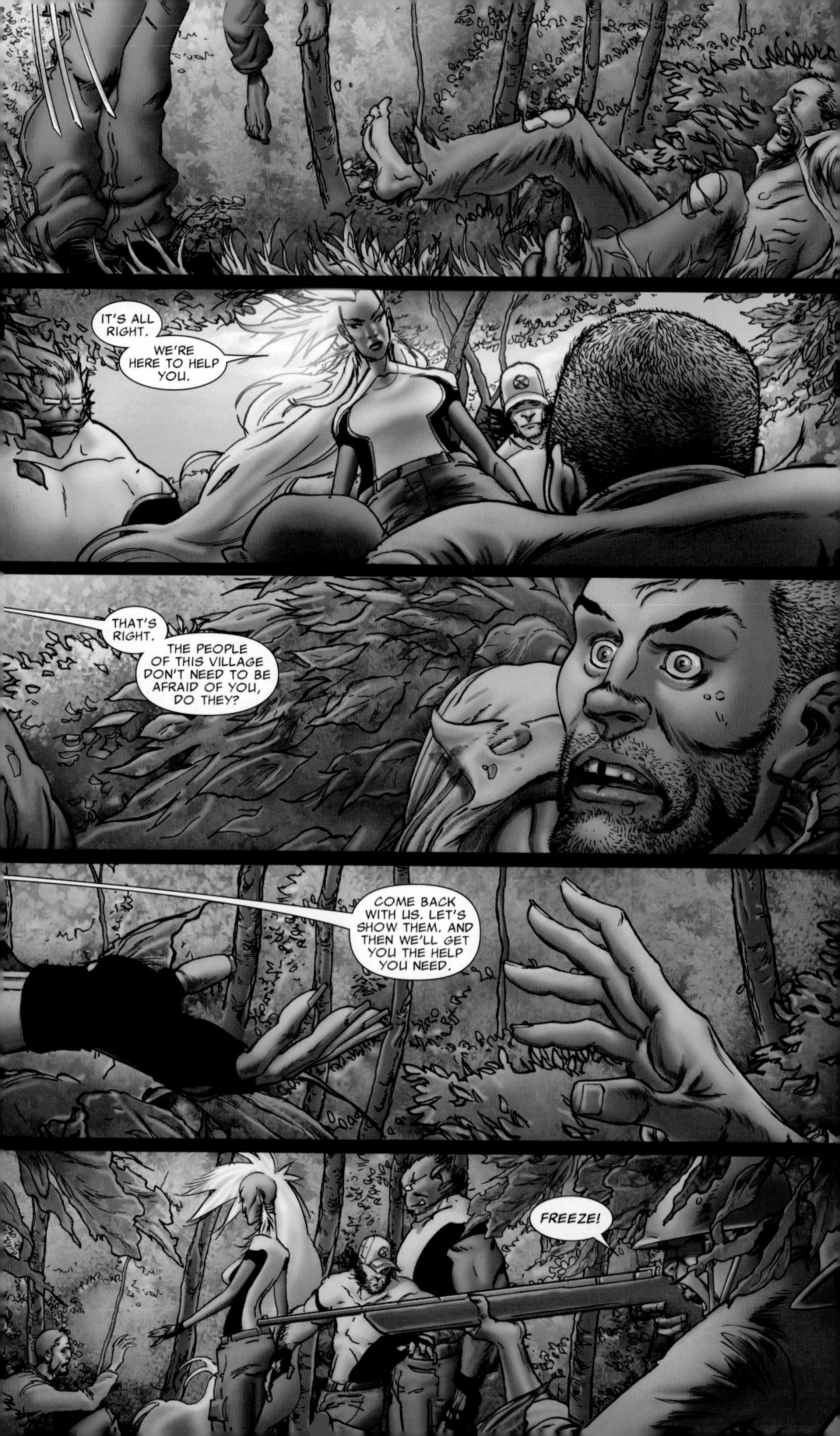

IT'S ALL RIGHT.
WE'RE HERE TO HELP YOU.
THAT'S RIGHT.
THE PEOPLE OF THIS VILLAGE DON'T NEED TO BE AFRAID OF YOU, DO THEY?
COME BACK WITH US. LET'S SHOW THEM, AND THEN WE'LL GET YOU THE HELP YOU NEED.
FREEZE!

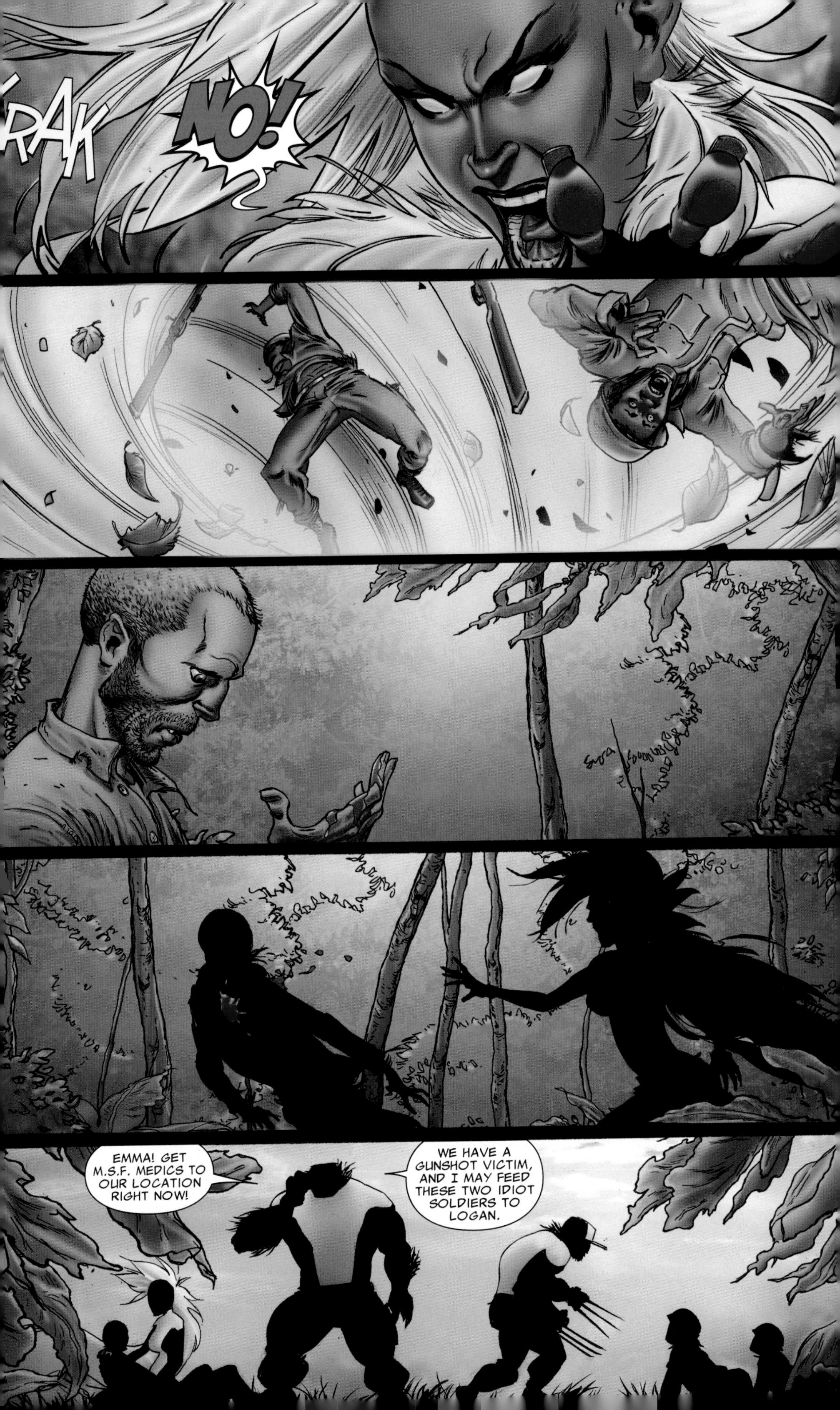
RAK
NO!
EMMA! GET M.S.F. MEDICS TO OUR LOCATION RIGHT NOW!
WE HAVE A GUNSHOT VICTIM, AND I MAY FEED THESE TWO IDIOT SOLDIERS TO LOGAN.

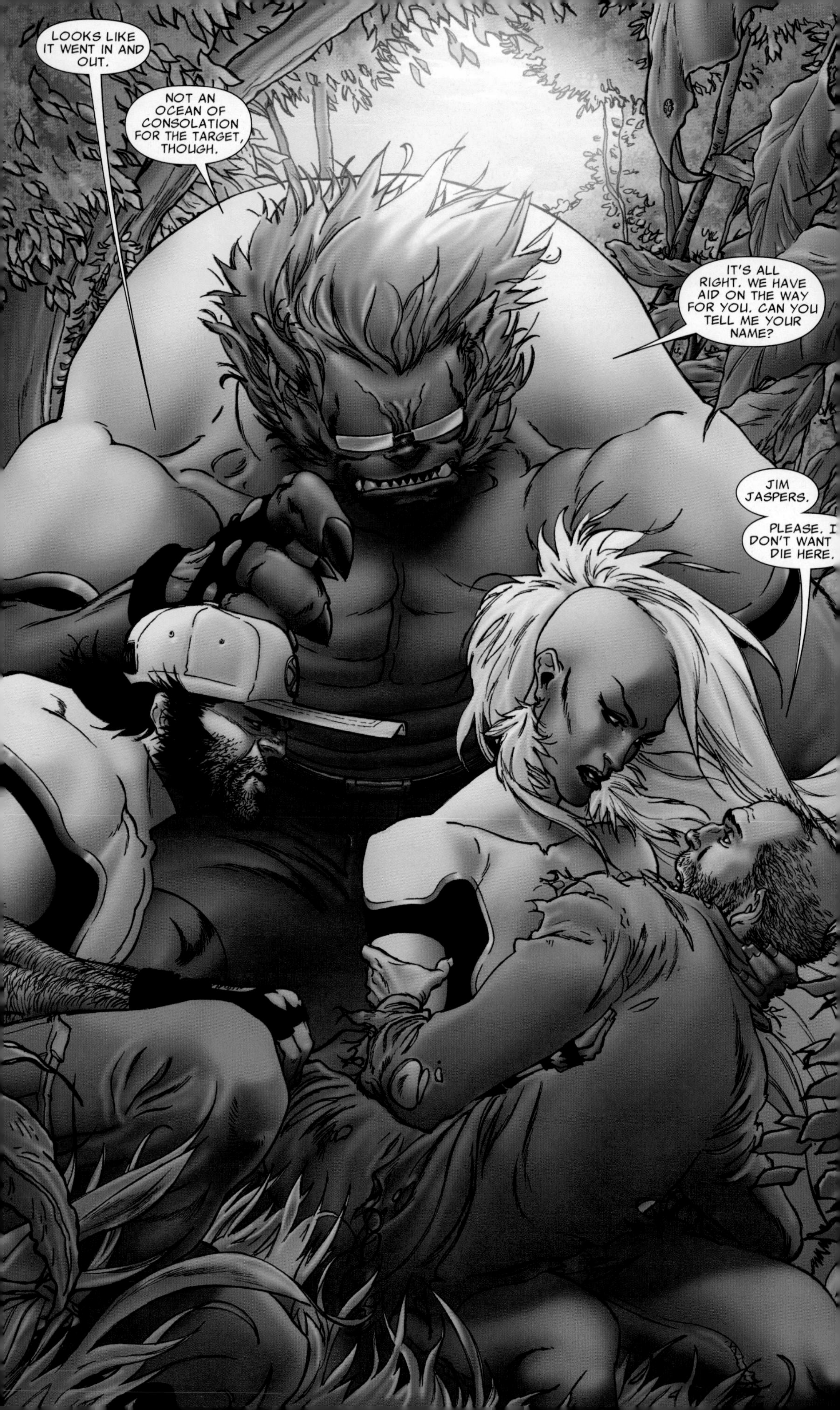
LOOKS LIKE IT WENT IN AND OUT.
NOT AN OCEAN OF CONSOLATION FOR THE TARGET, THOUGH.
IT'S ALL RIGHT. WE HAVE AID ON THE WAY FOR YOU. CAN YOU TELL ME YOUR NAME?
JIM JASPERS.
PLEASE. I DON'T WANT DIE HERE.

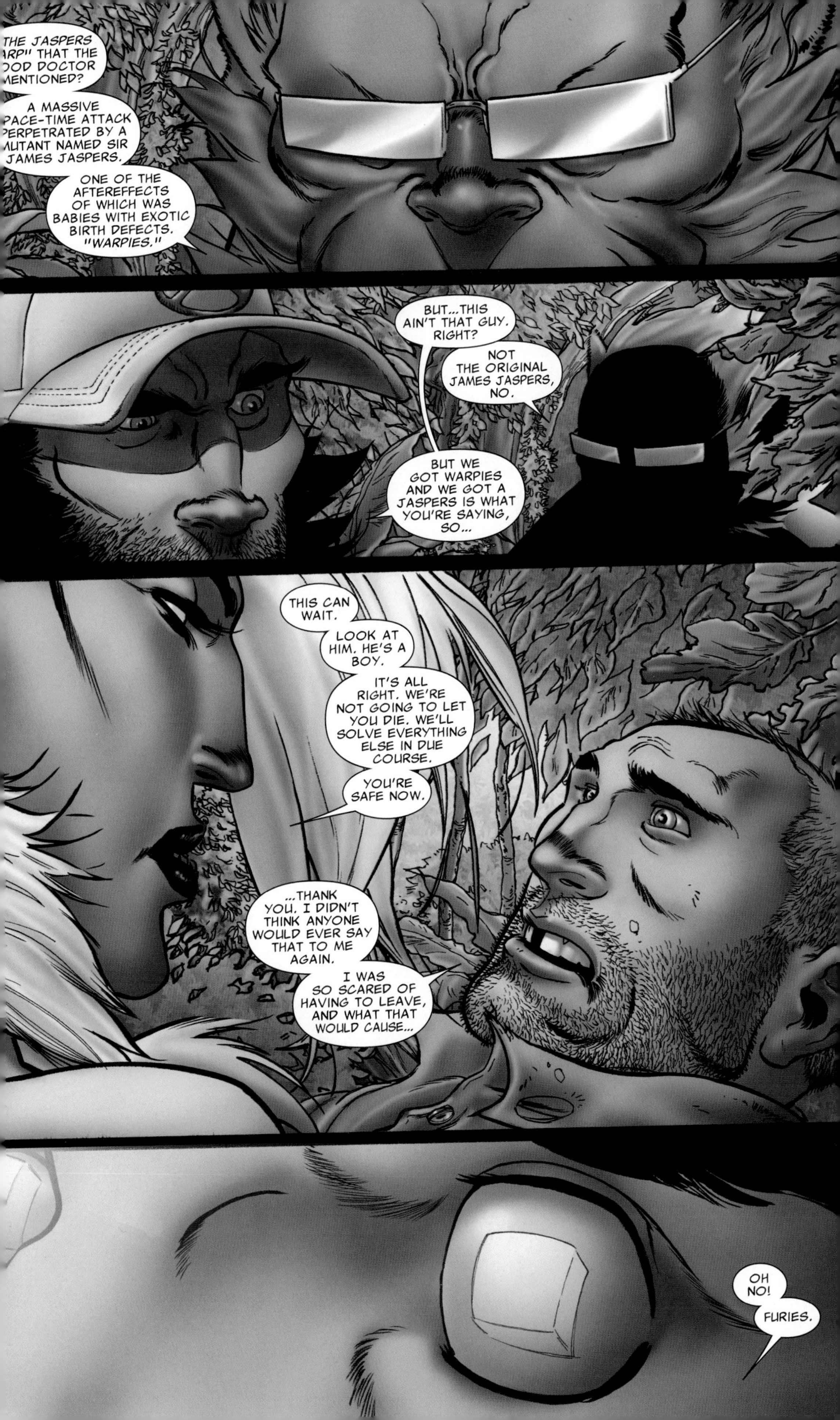
THE JASPERS "WARP" THAT THE GOOD DOCTOR MENTIONED?
A MASSIVE SPACE-TIME ATTACK PERPETRATED BY A MUTANT NAMED SIR JAMES JASPERS.
ONE OF THE AFTEREFFECTS OF WHICH WAS BABIES WITH EXOTIC BIRTH DEFECTS. "WARPIES."
BUT...THIS AIN'T THAT GUY. RIGHT?
NOT THE ORIGINAL JAMES JASPERS, NO.
BUT WE GOT WARPIES AND WE GOT A JASPERS IS WHAT YOU'RE SAYING, SO...
THIS CAN WAIT.
LOOK AT HIM. HE'S A BOY.
IT'S ALL RIGHT. WE'RE NOT GOING TO LET YOU DIE. WE'LL SOLVE EVERYTHING ELSE IN DUE COURSE.
YOU'RE SAFE NOW.
...THANK YOU. I DIDN'T THINK ANYONE WOULD EVER SAY THAT TO ME AGAIN.
I WAS SO SCARED OF HAVING TO LEAVE, AND WHAT THAT WOULD CAUSE...
OH NO!
FURIES.

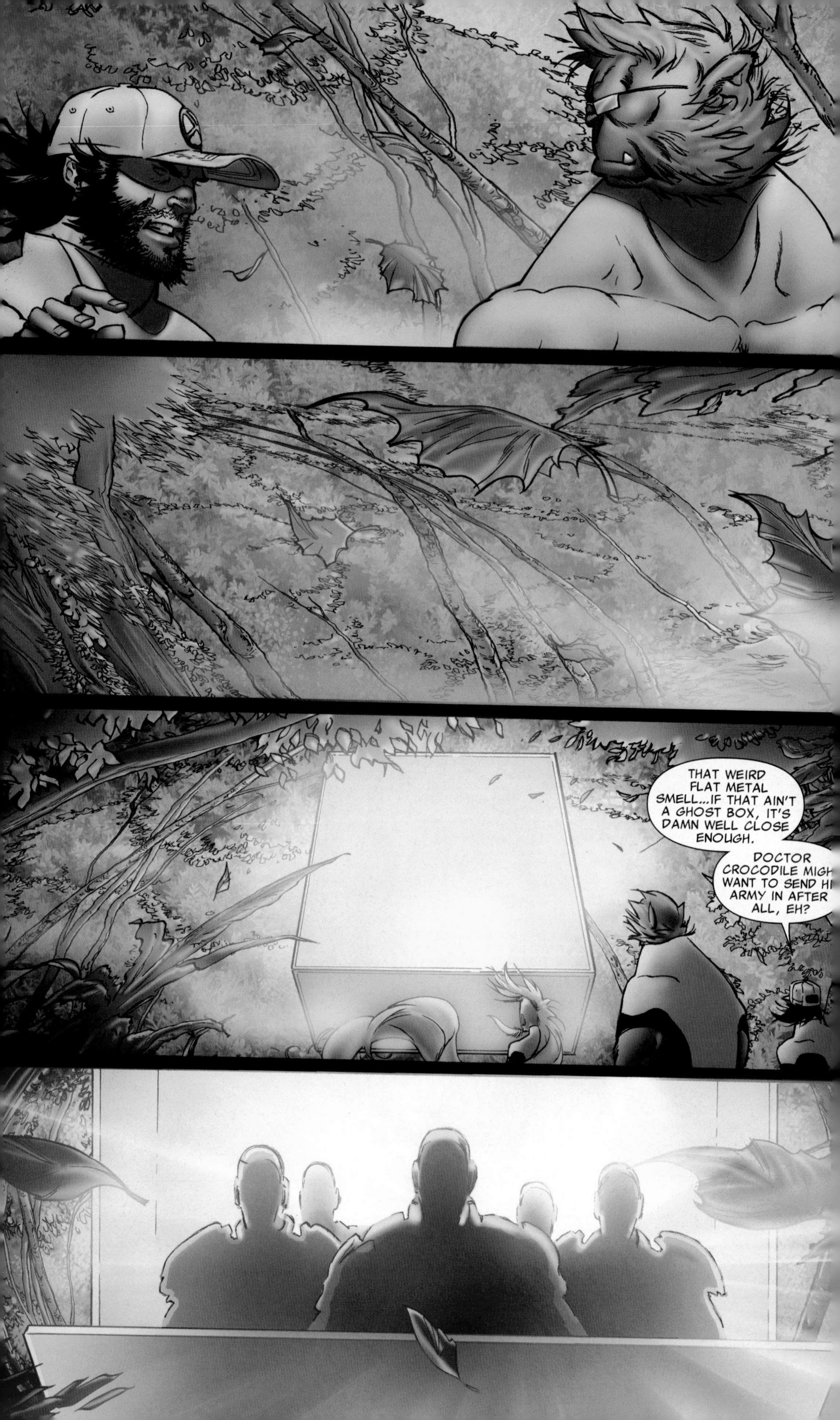
THAT WEIRD FLAT METAL SMELL...IF THAT AIN'T A GHOST BOX, IT'S DAMN WELL CLOSE ENOUGH.
DOCTOR CROCODILE MIGH WANT TO SEND HI ARMY IN AFTER ALL, EH?

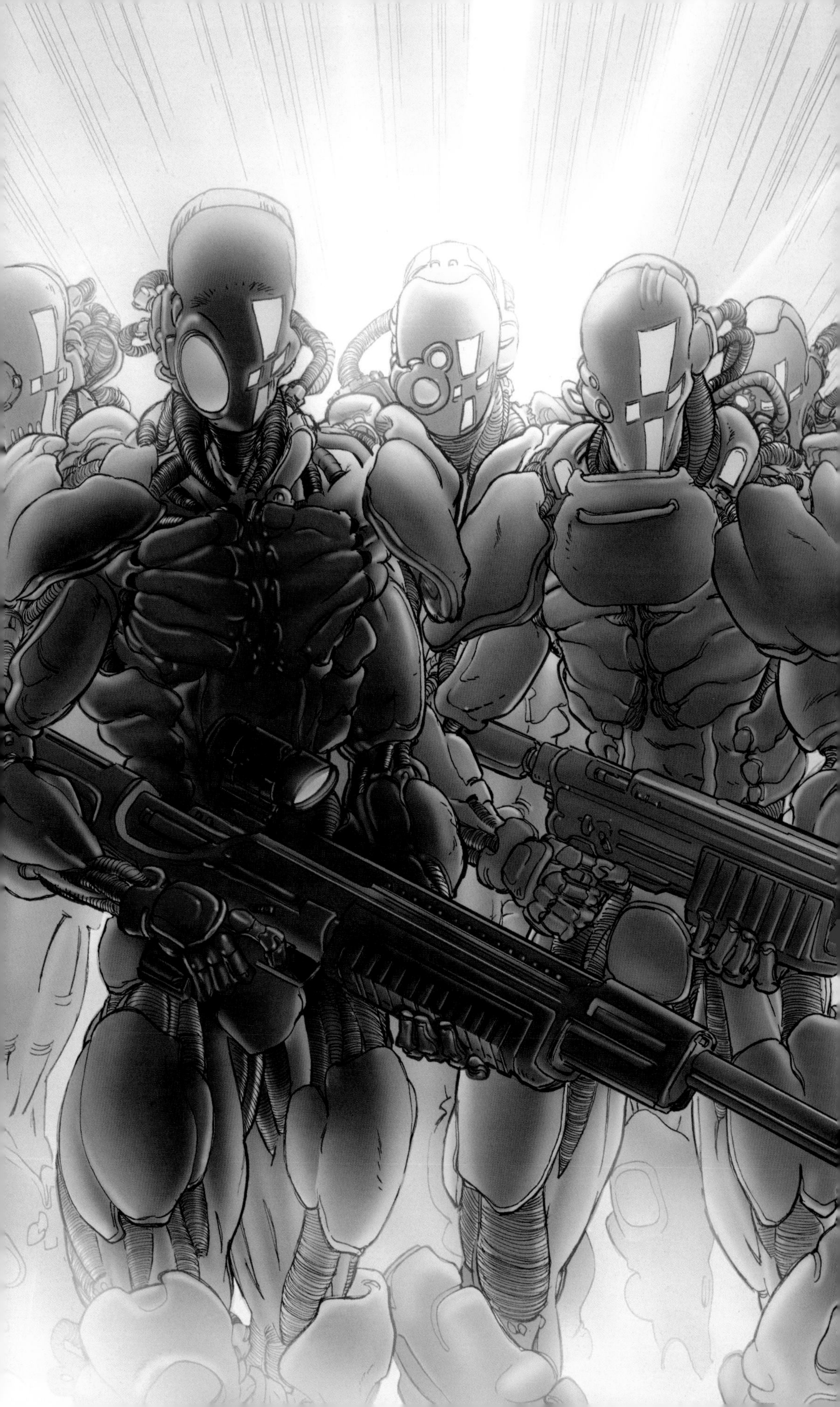

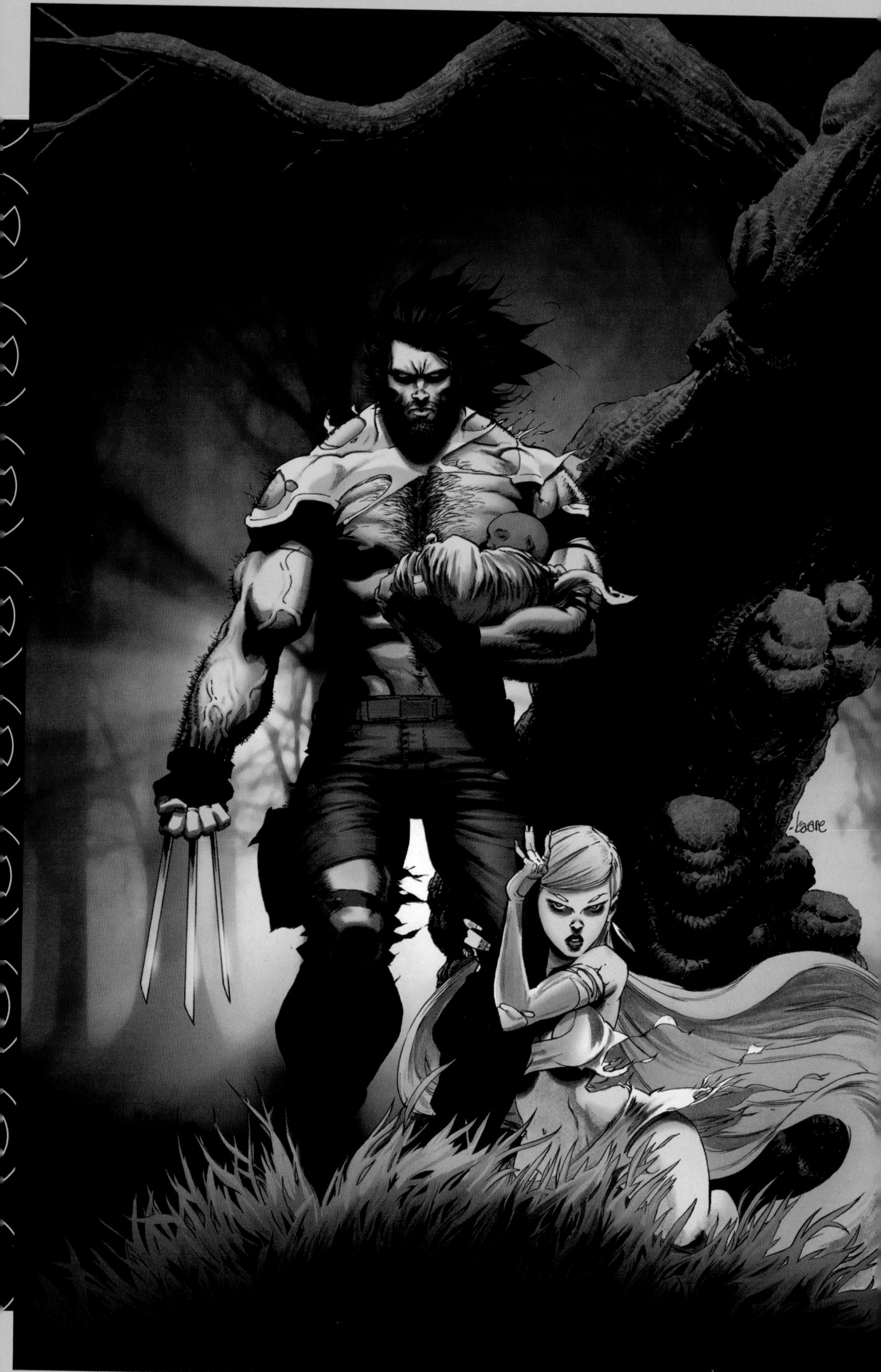

FOUR

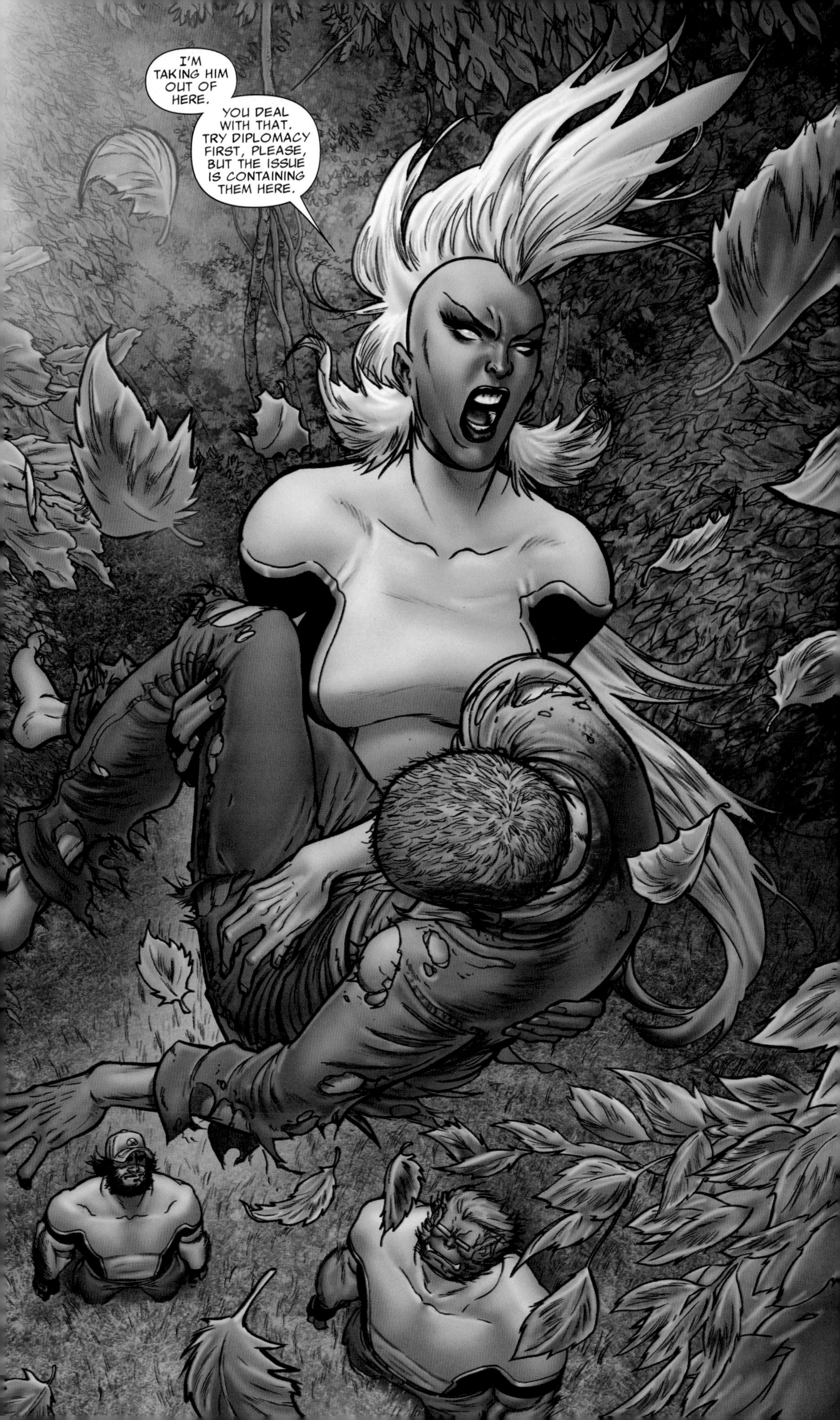
I'M TAKING HIM OUT OF HERE.
YOU DEAL WITH THAT. TRY DIPLOMACY FIRST, PLEASE, BUT THE ISSUE IS CONTAINING THEM HERE.

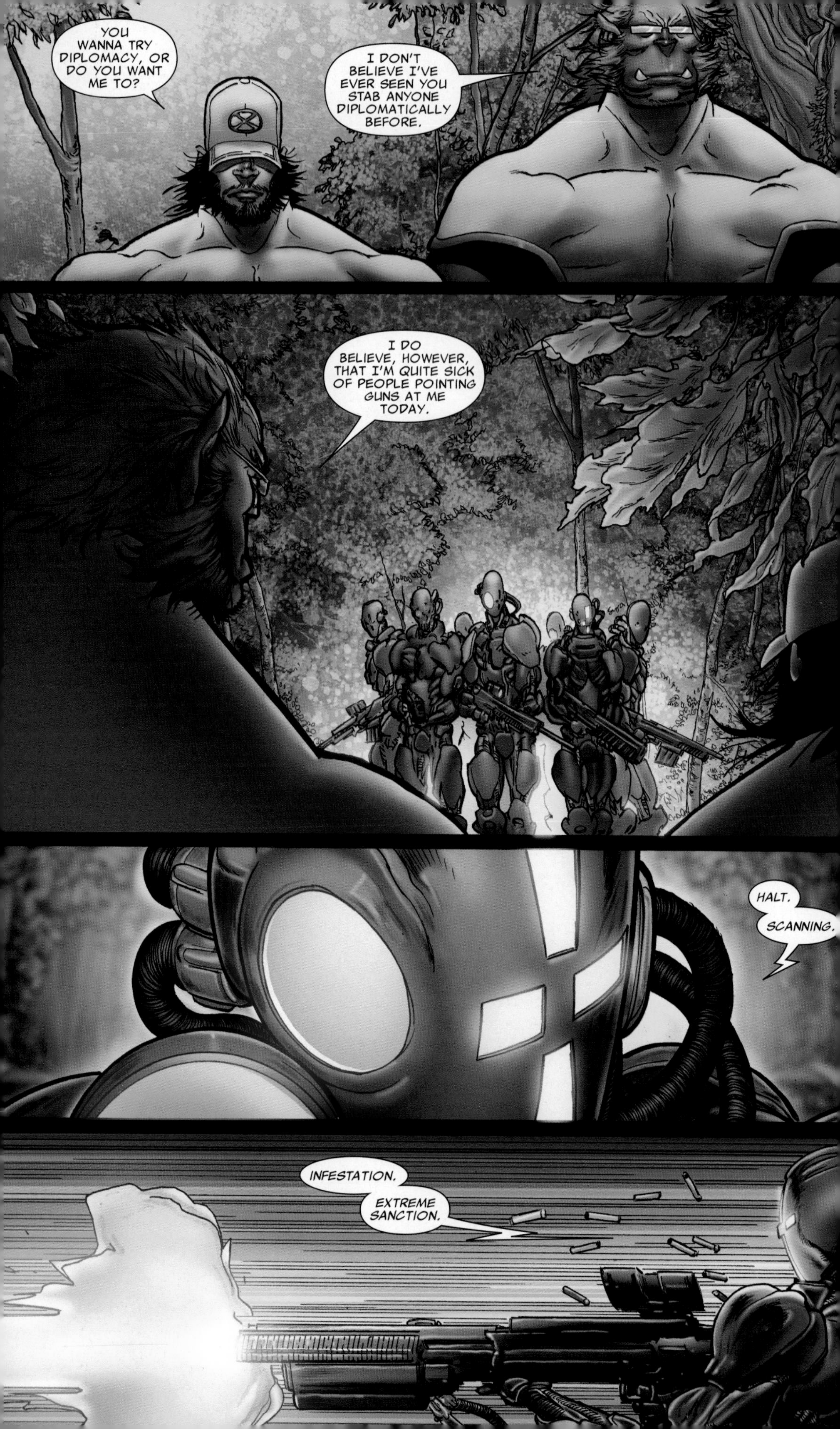

YOU WANNA TRY DIPLOMACY, OR DO YOU WANT ME TO?
I DON'T BELIEVE I'VE EVER SEEN YOU STAB ANYONE DIPLOMATICALLY BEFORE.
I DO BELIEVE, HOWEVER, THAT I'M QUITE SICK OF PEOPLE POINTING GUNS AT ME TODAY.
HALT.
SCANNING.
INFESTATION.
EXTREME SANCTION.

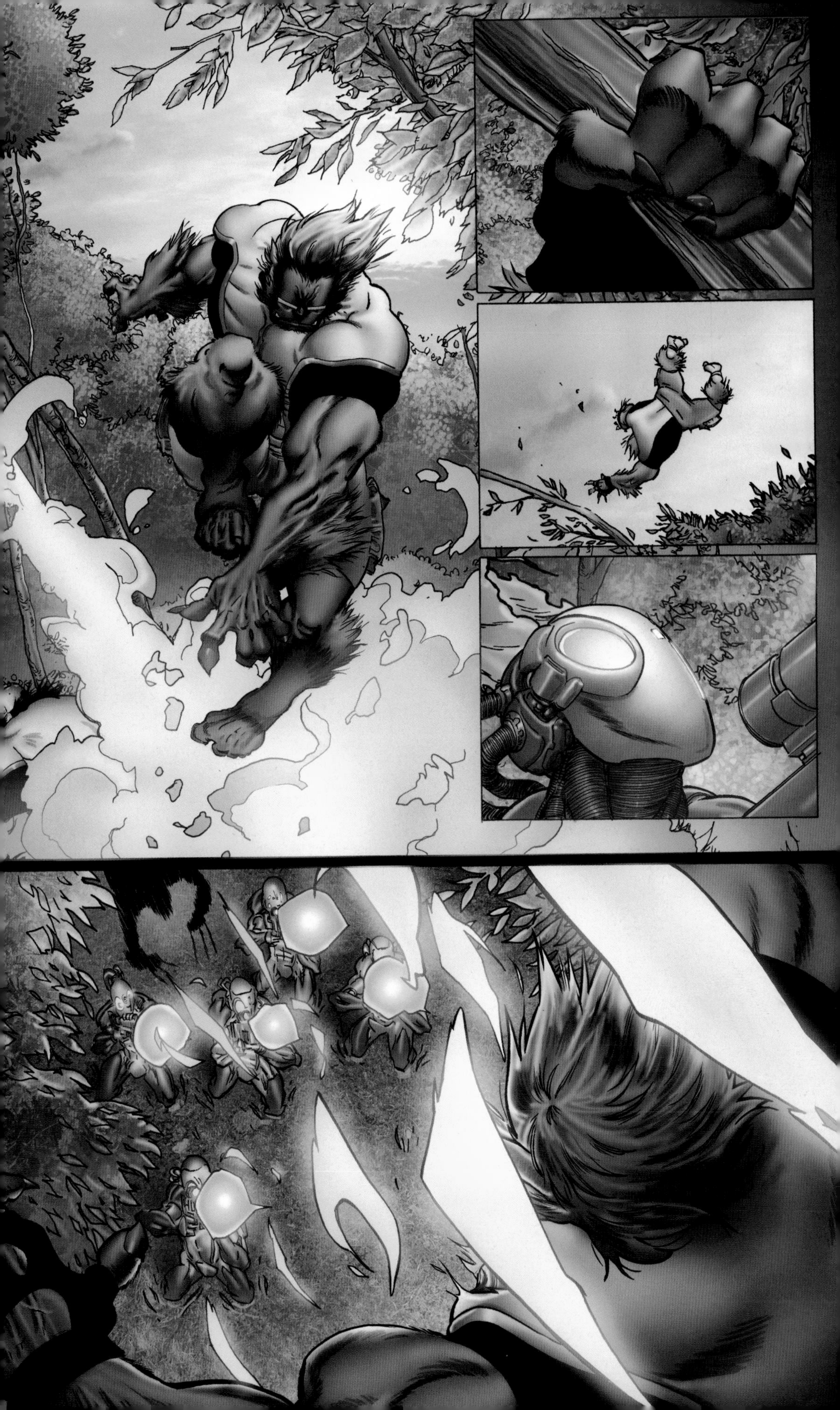

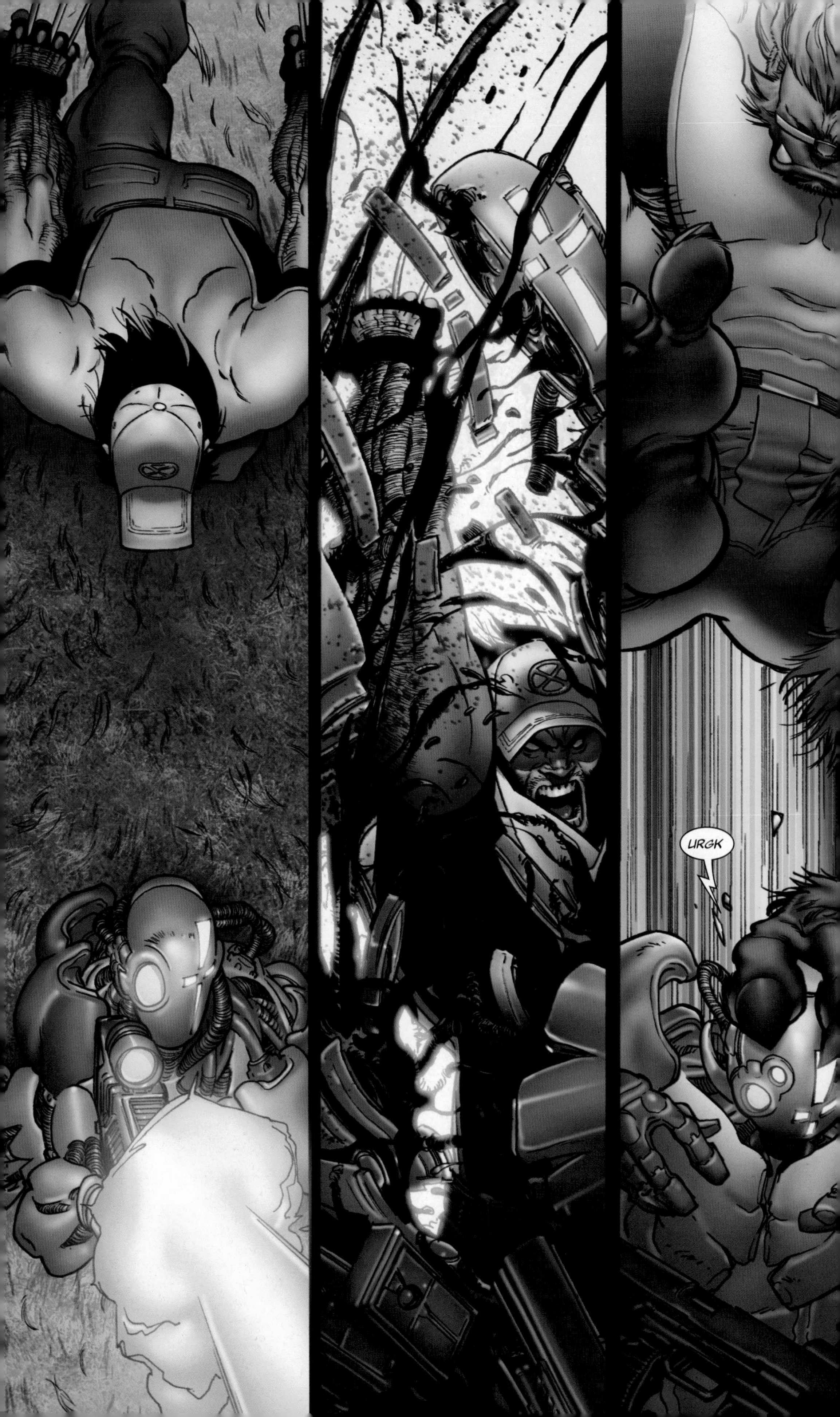
URGK

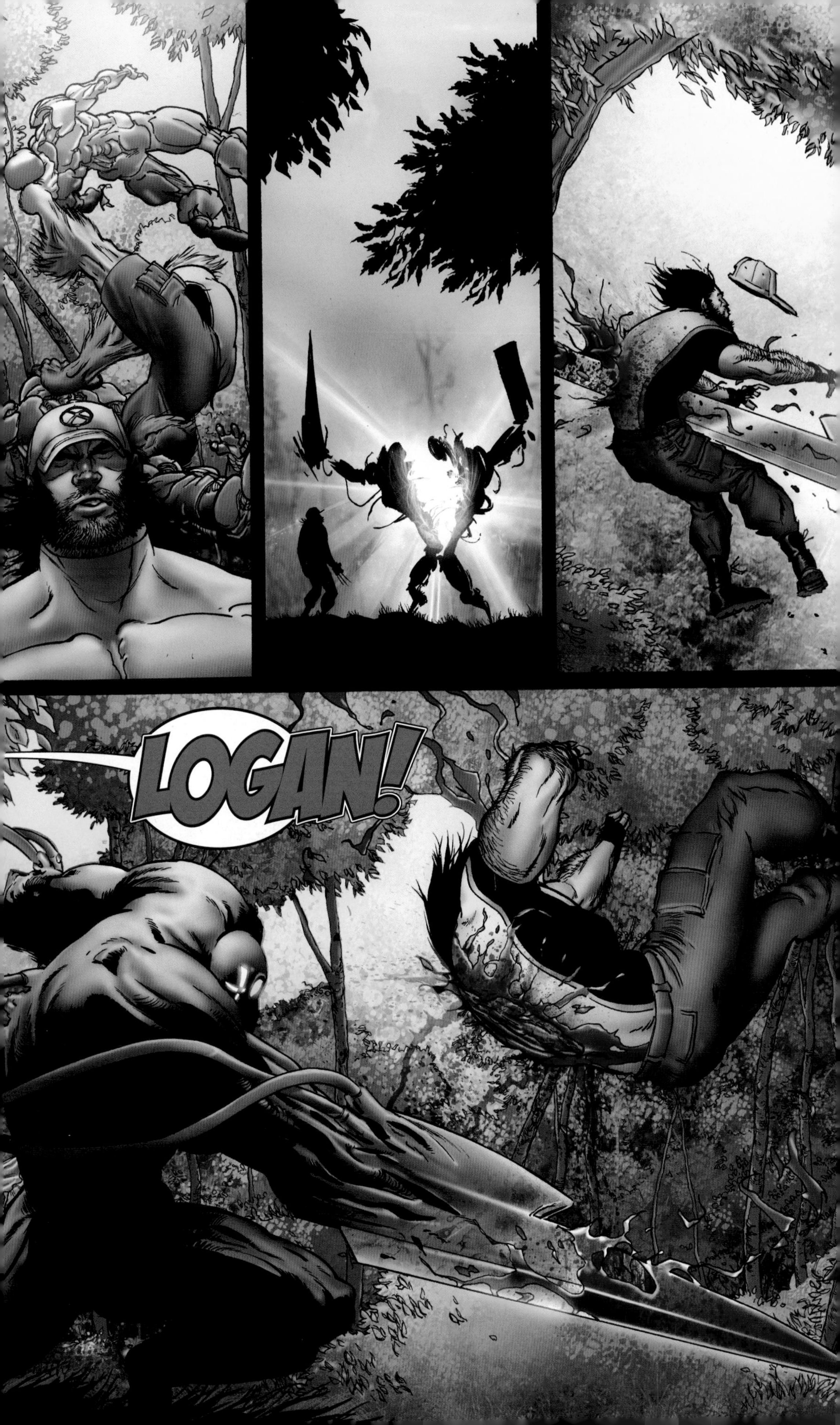
LOGAN!

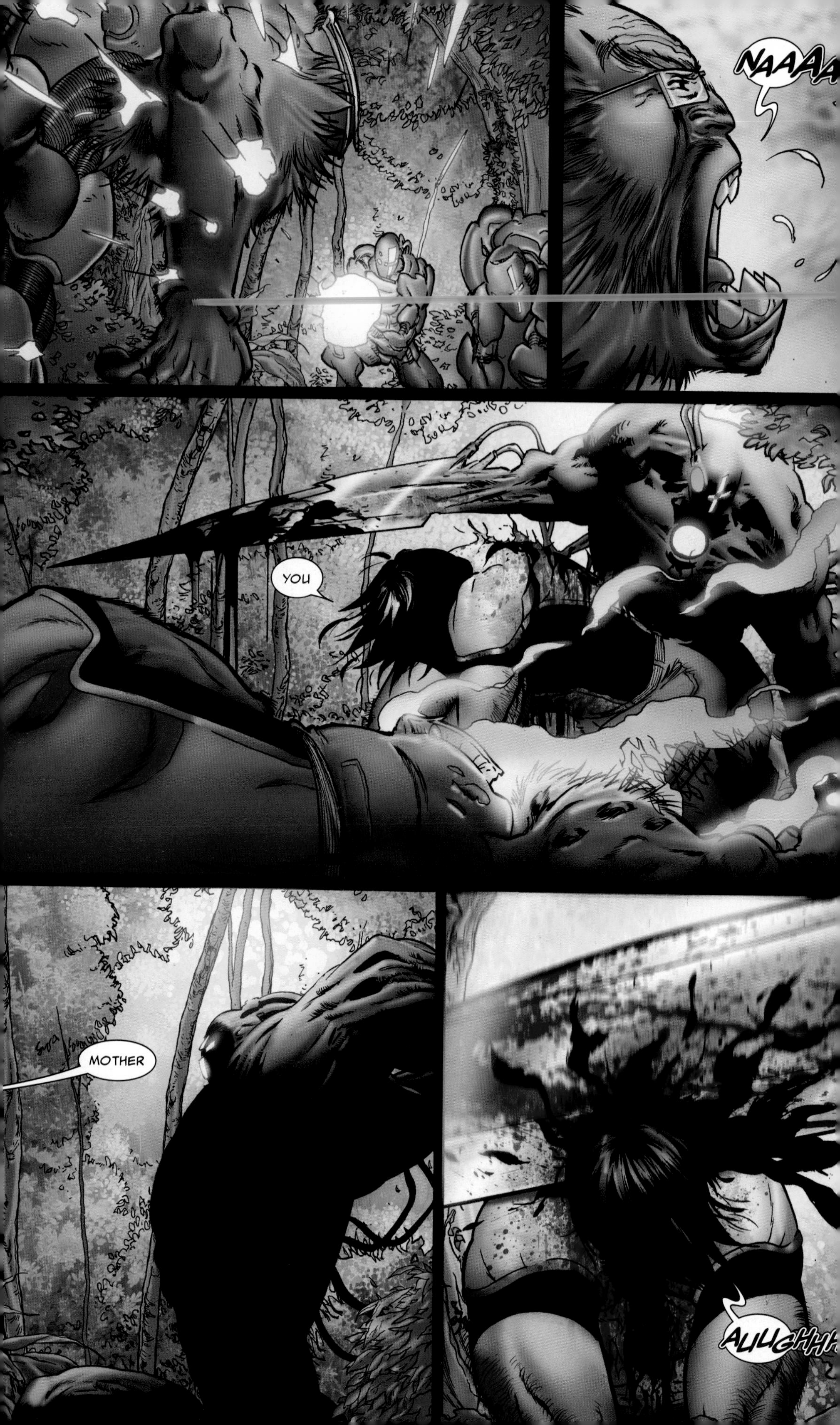
NAAAA
YOU
MOTHER
AUUGHHH

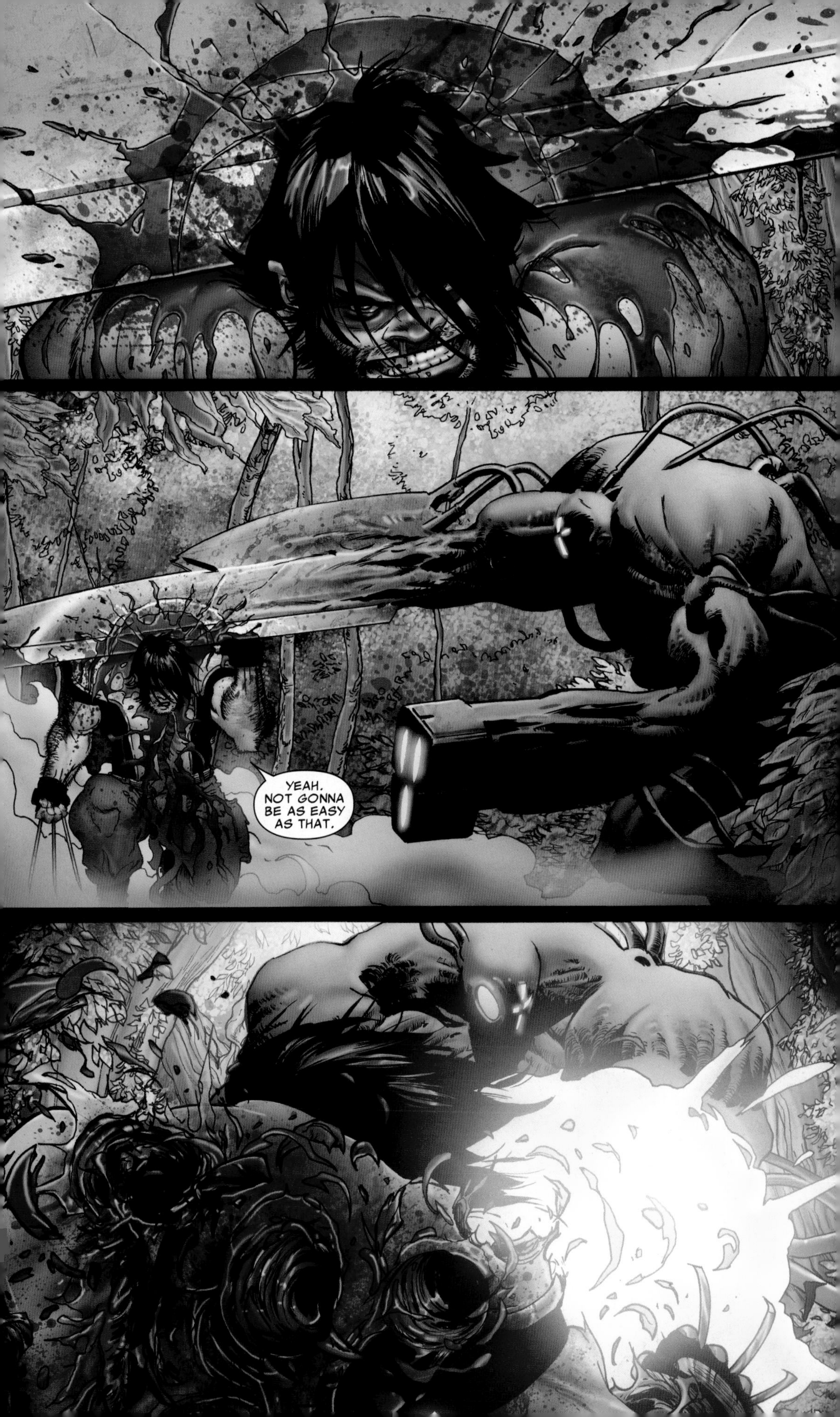
YEAH. NOT GONNA BE AS EASY AS THAT.

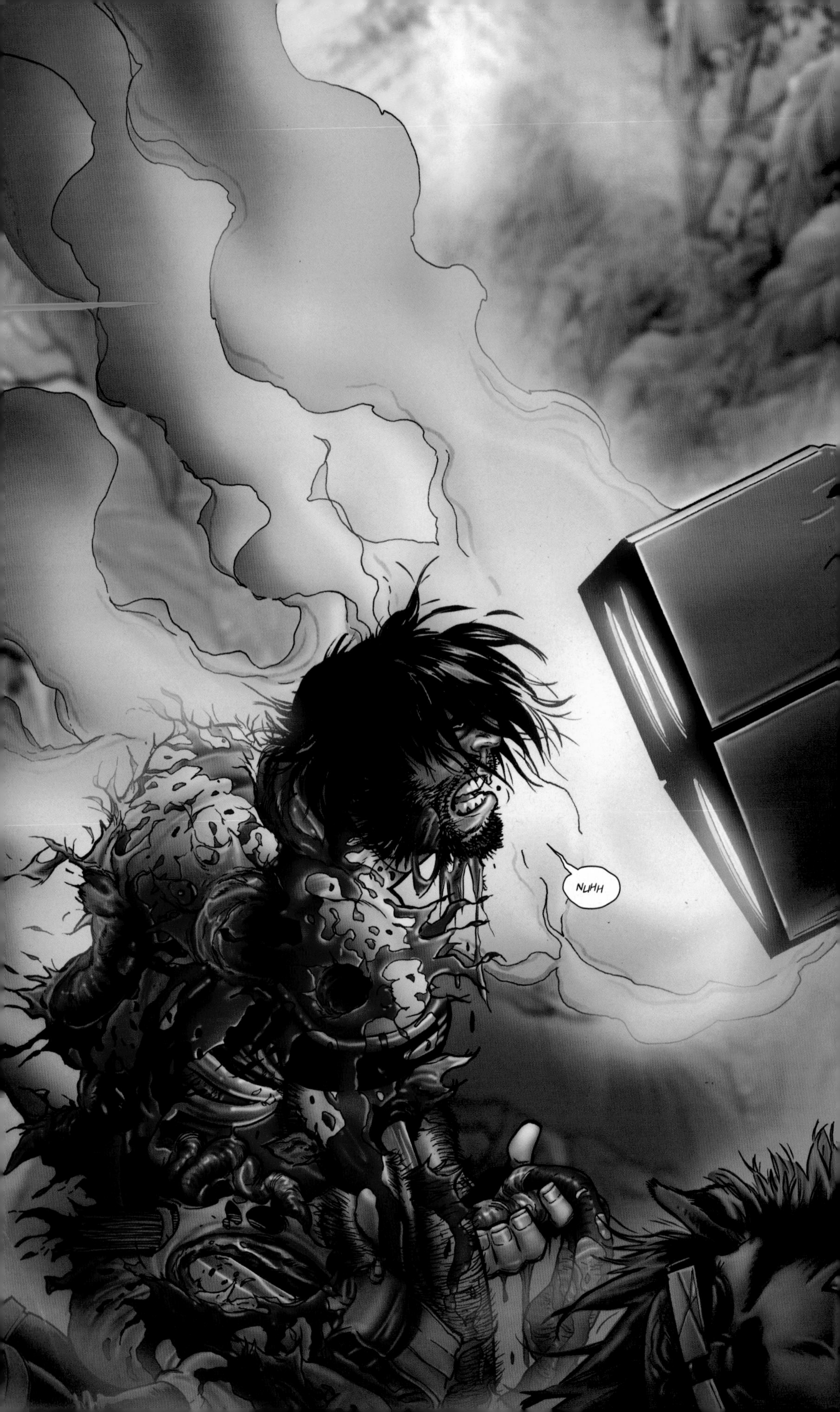
NUHH

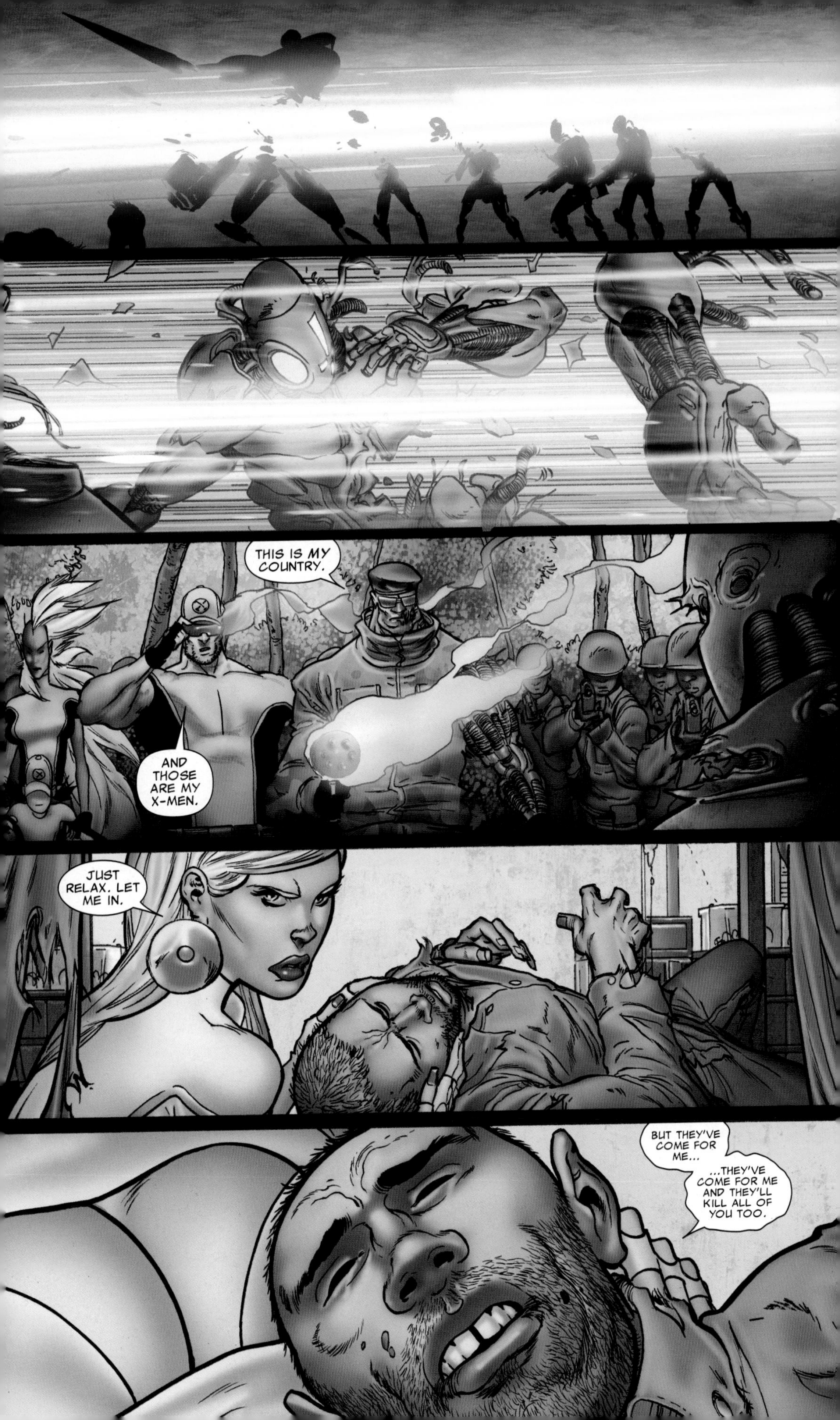
THIS IS MY COUNTRY.
AND THOSE ARE MY X-MEN.
JUST RELAX. LET ME IN.
BUT THEY'VE COME FOR ME...
...THEY'VE COME FOR ME AND THEY'LL KILL ALL OF YOU TOO.

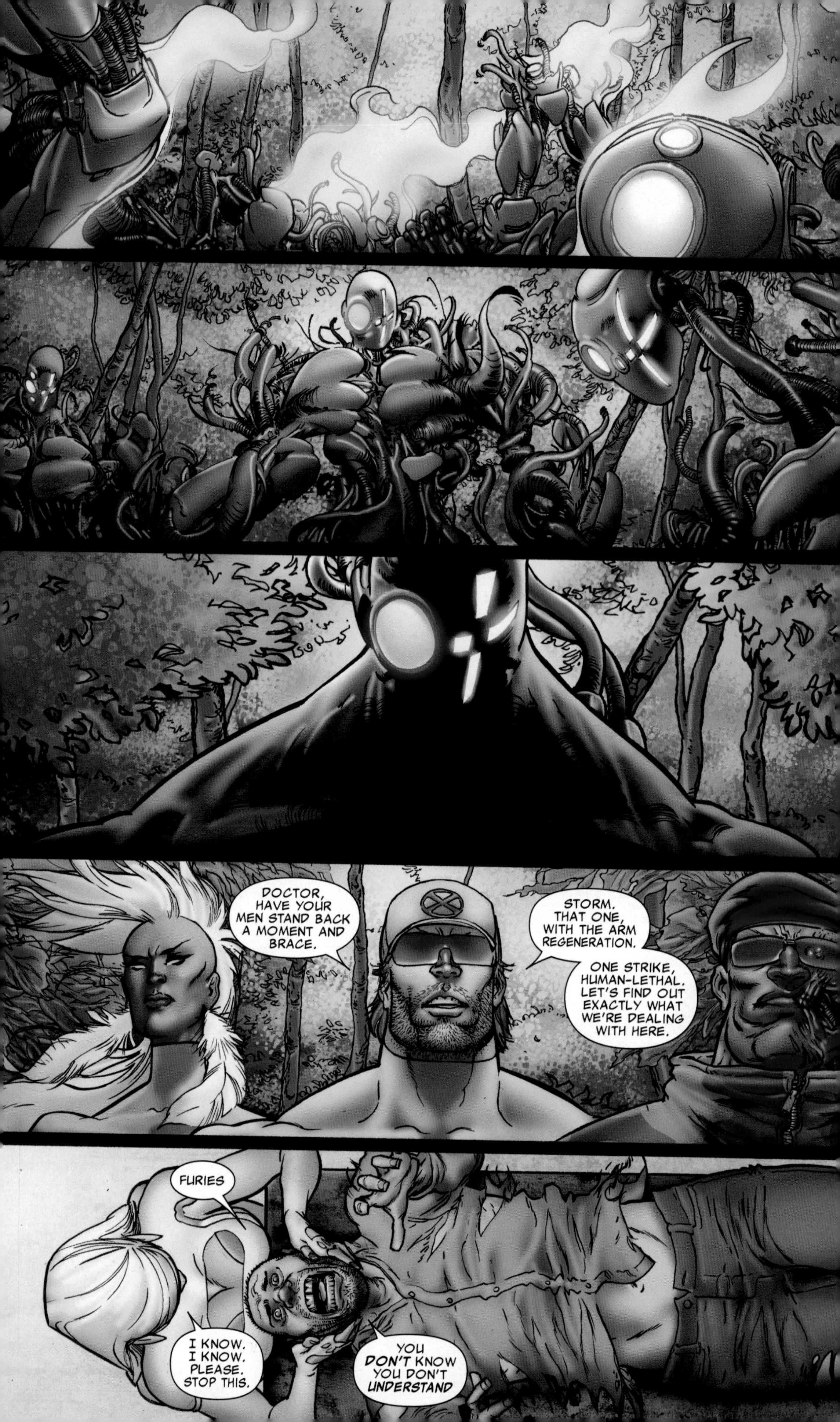
DOCTOR, HAVE YOUR MEN STAND BACK A MOMENT AND BRACE.
STORM. THAT ONE, WITH THE ARM REGENERATION.
ONE STRIKE, HUMAN-LETHAL. LET'S FIND OUT EXACTLY WHAT WE'RE DEALING WITH HERE.
FURIES
I KNOW. I KNOW. PLEASE. STOP THIS.
YOU *DON'T* KNOW YOU DON'T *UNDERSTAND*

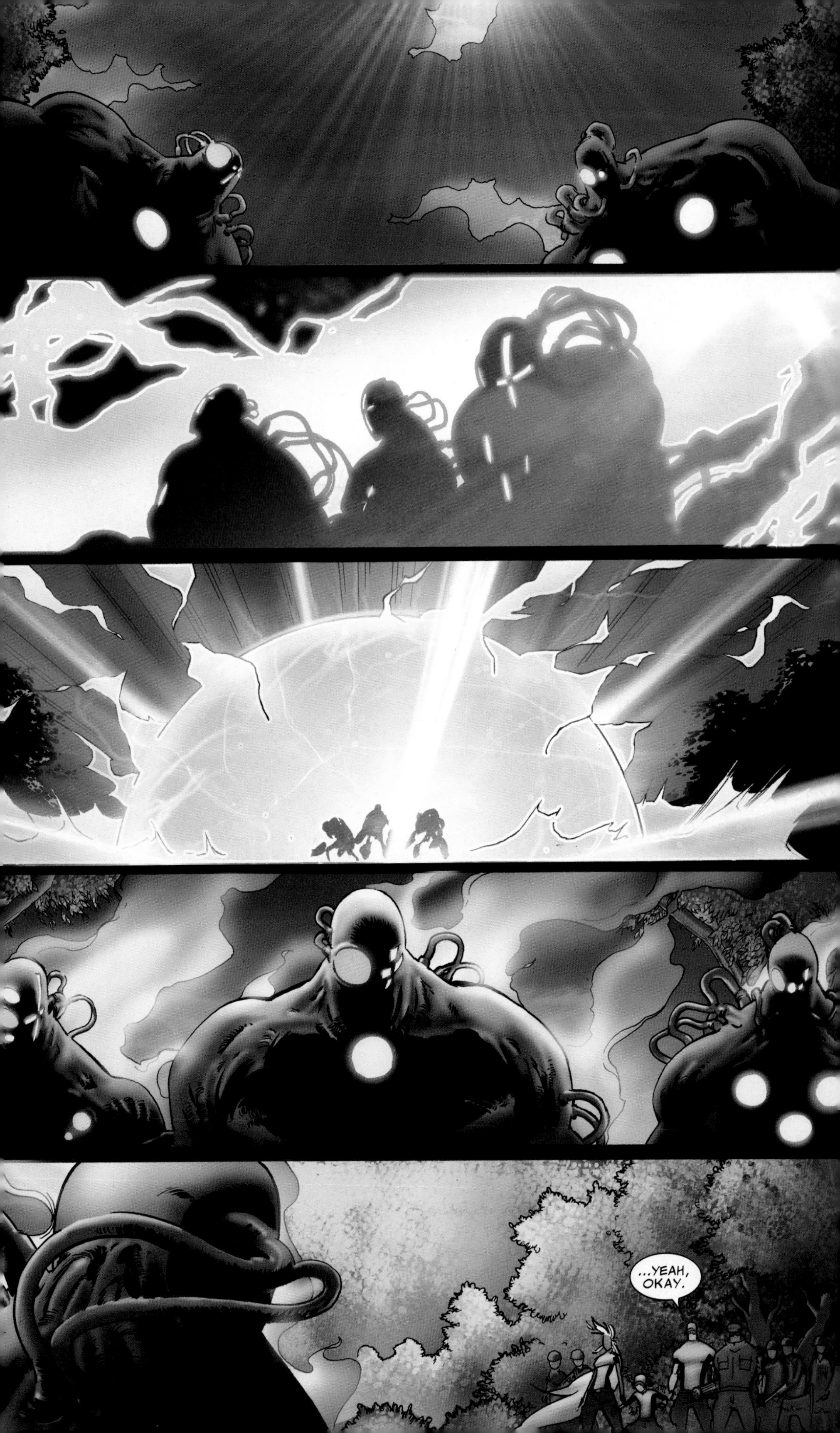
...YEAH, OKAY.

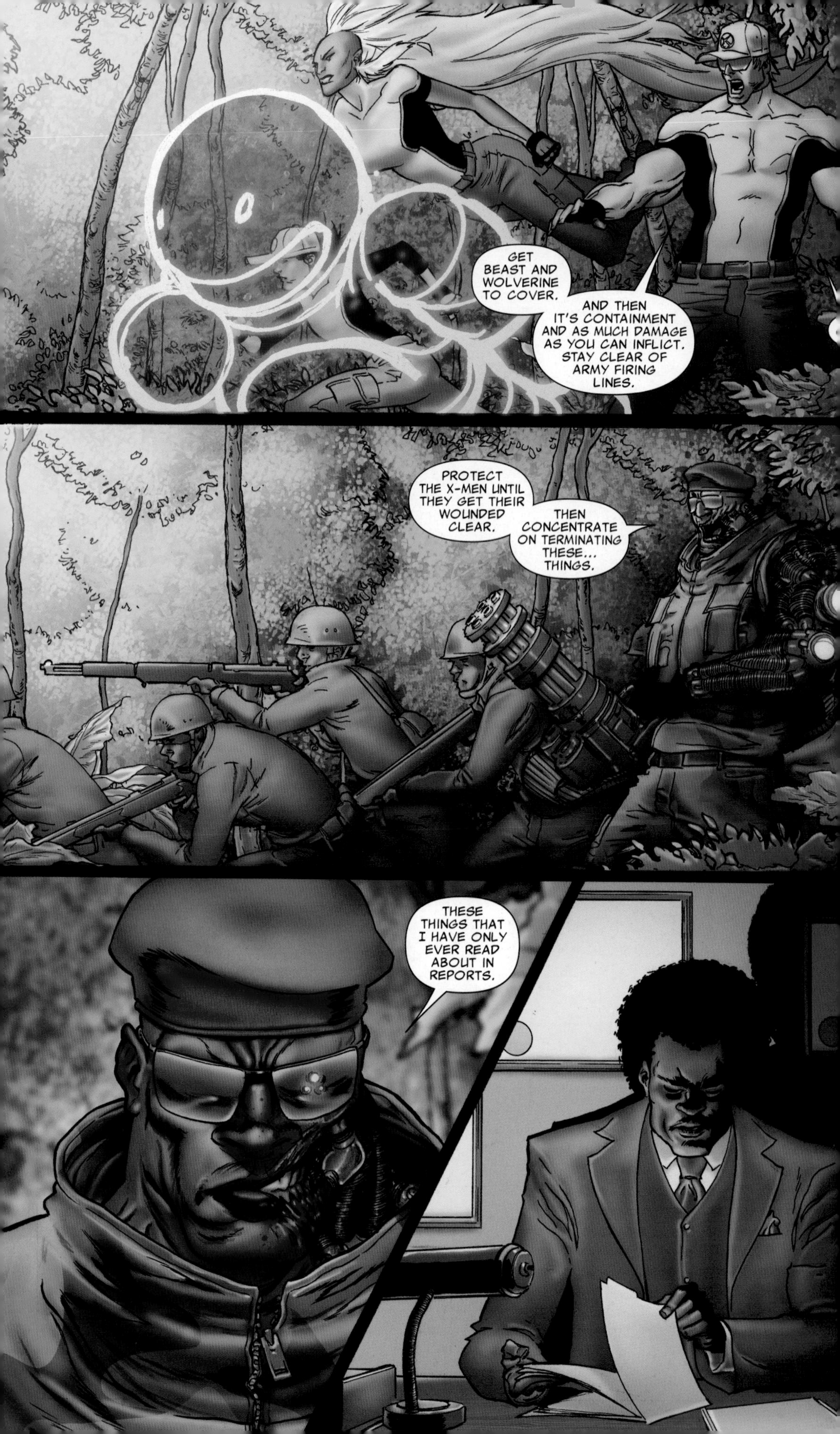
GET BEAST AND WOLVERINE TO COVER.
AND THEN IT'S CONTAINMENT AND AS MUCH DAMAGE AS YOU CAN INFLICT. STAY CLEAR OF ARMY FIRING LINES.
PROTECT THE X-MEN UNTIL THEY GET THEIR WOUNDED CLEAR.
THEN CONCENTRATE ON TERMINATING THESE... THINGS.
THESE THINGS THAT I HAVE ONLY EVER READ ABOUT IN REPORTS.

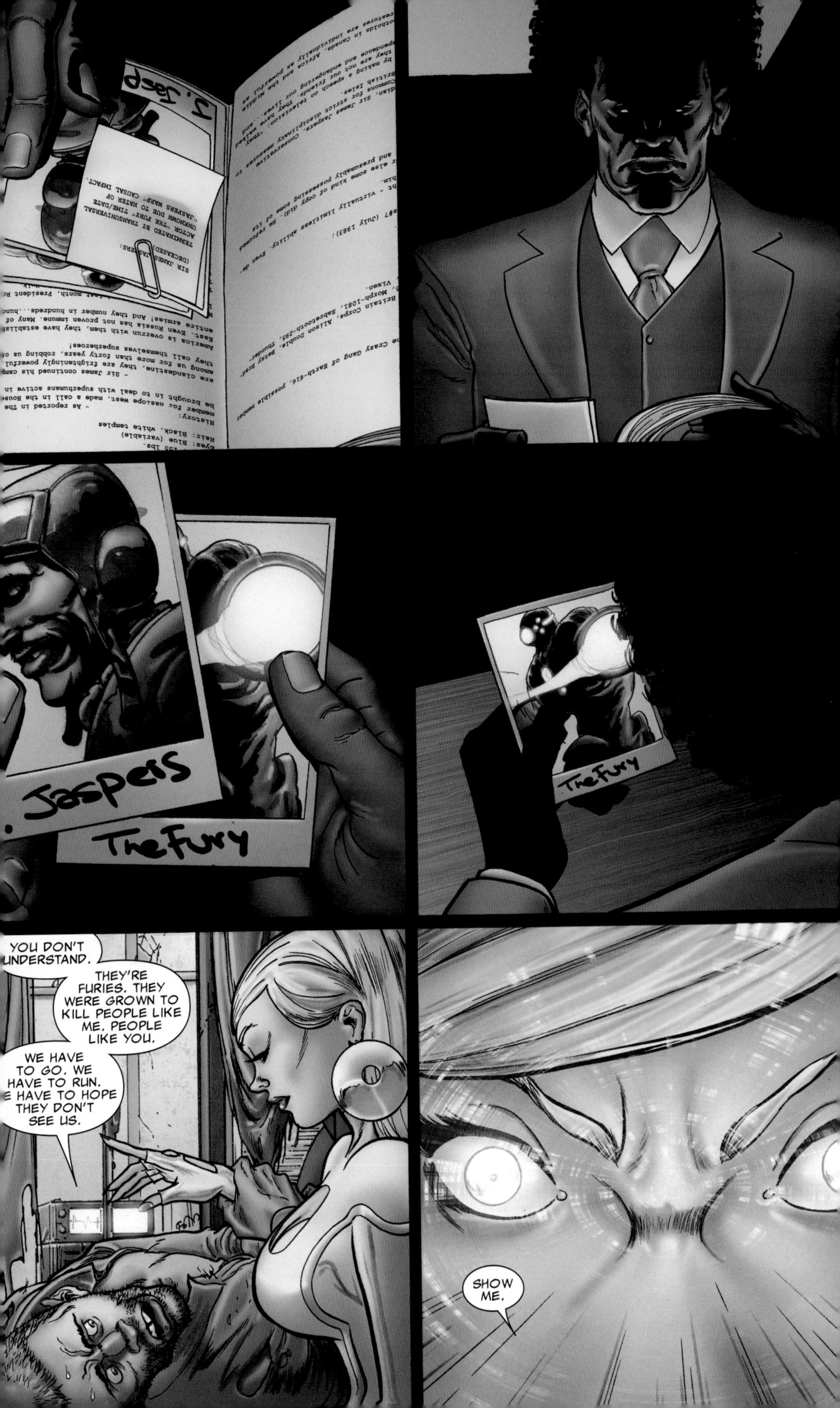
Jaspers
The Fury
The Fury
YOU DON'T UNDERSTAND.
THEY'RE FURIES. THEY WERE GROWN TO KILL PEOPLE LIKE ME. PEOPLE LIKE YOU.
WE HAVE TO GO. WE HAVE TO RUN. E HAVE TO HOPE THEY DON'T SEE US.
SHOW ME.

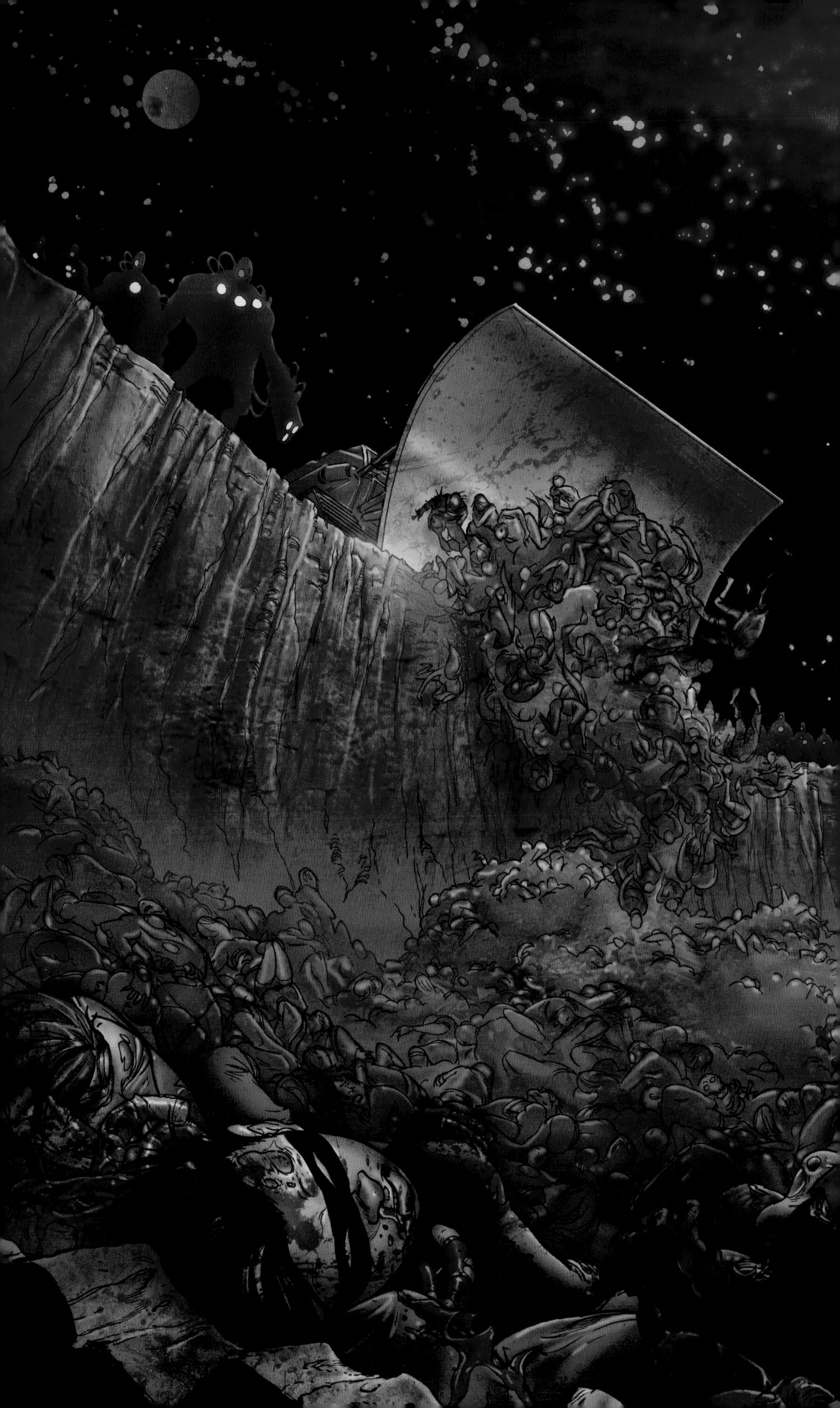

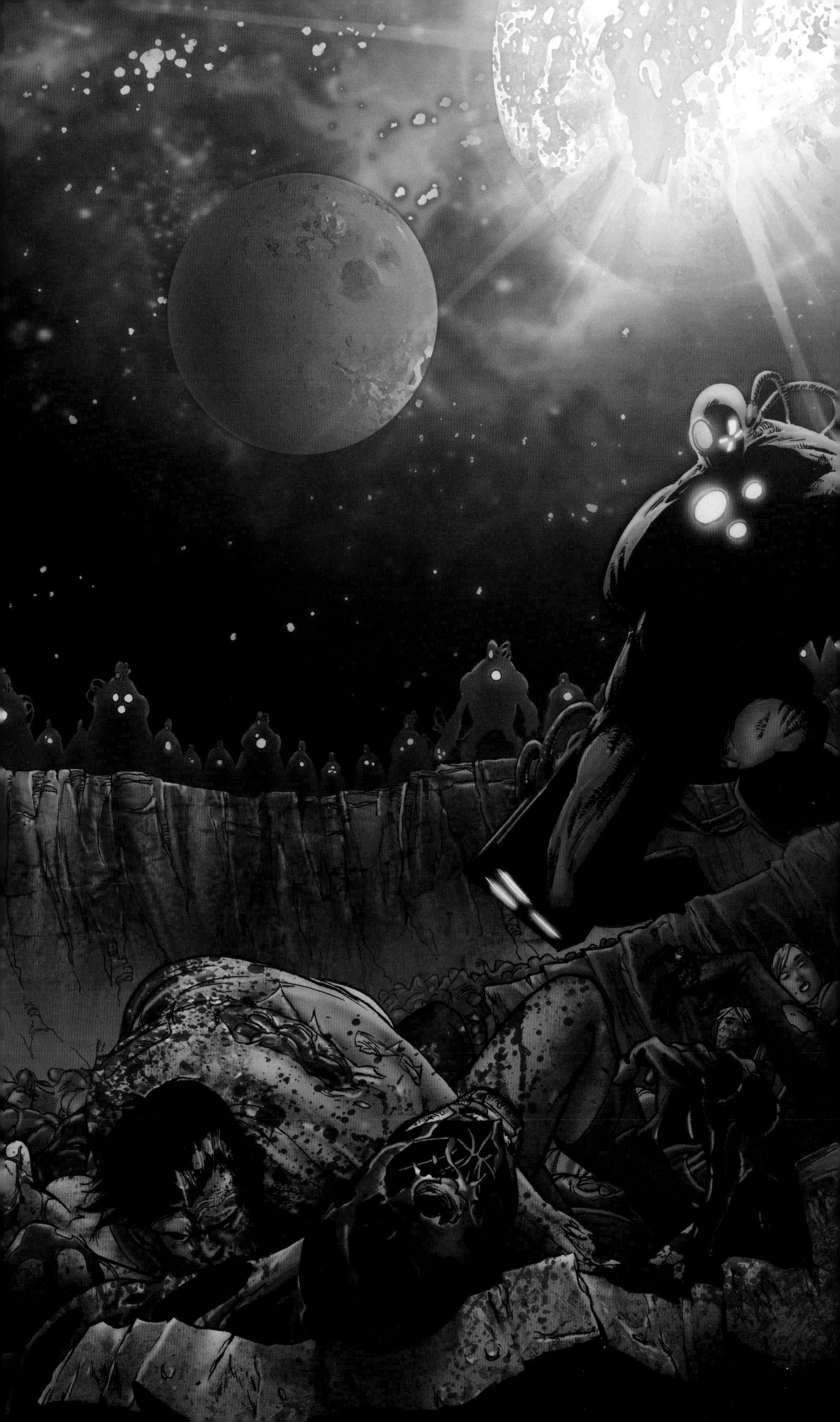

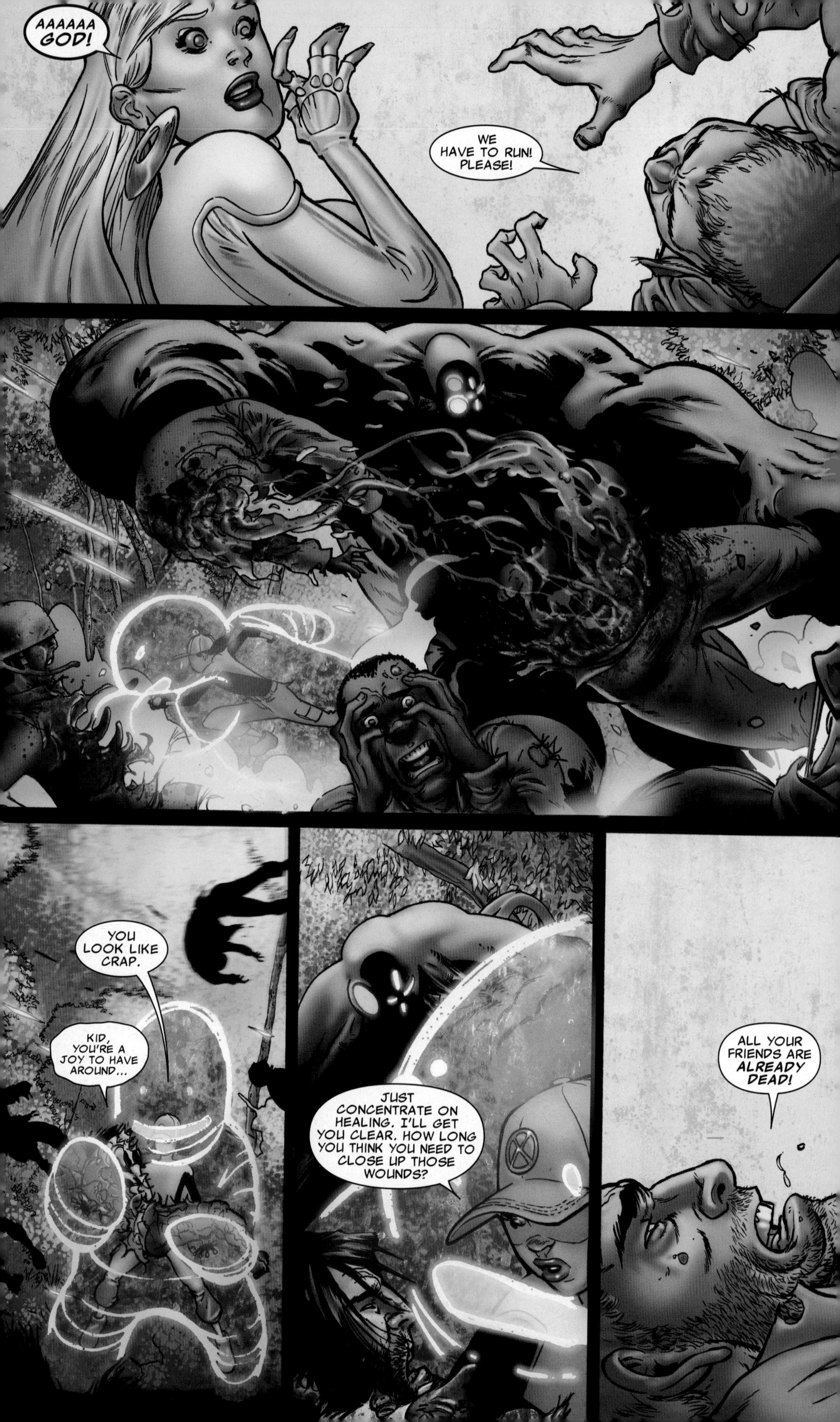
AAAAAA GOD!
WE HAVE TO RUN! PLEASE!
YOU LOOK LIKE CRAP.
KID, YOU'RE A JOY TO HAVE AROUND...
JUST CONCENTRATE ON HEALING. I'LL GET YOU CLEAR. HOW LONG YOU THINK YOU NEED TO CLOSE UP THOSE WOUNDS?
ALL YOUR FRIENDS ARE *ALREADY DEAD!*

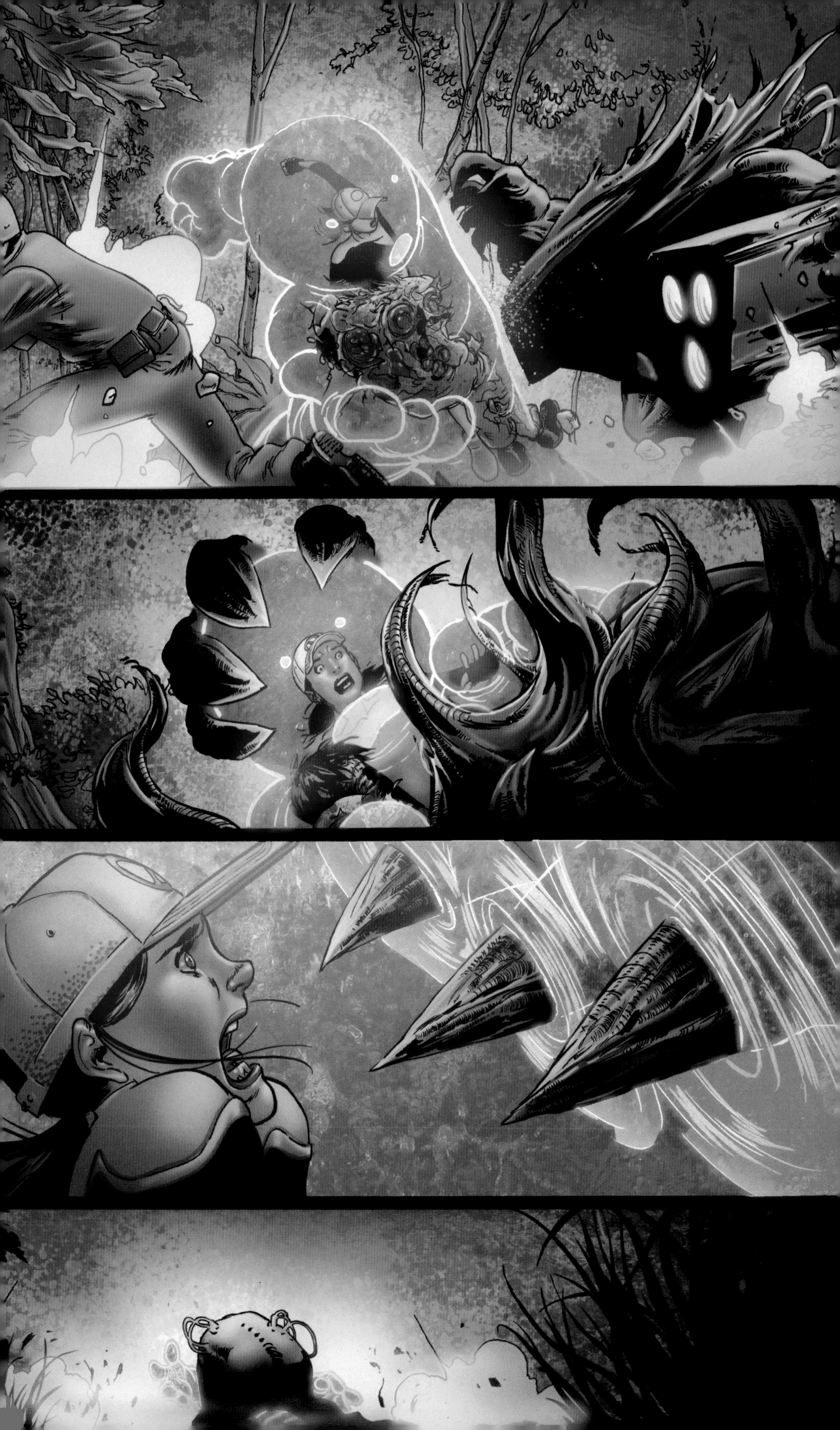

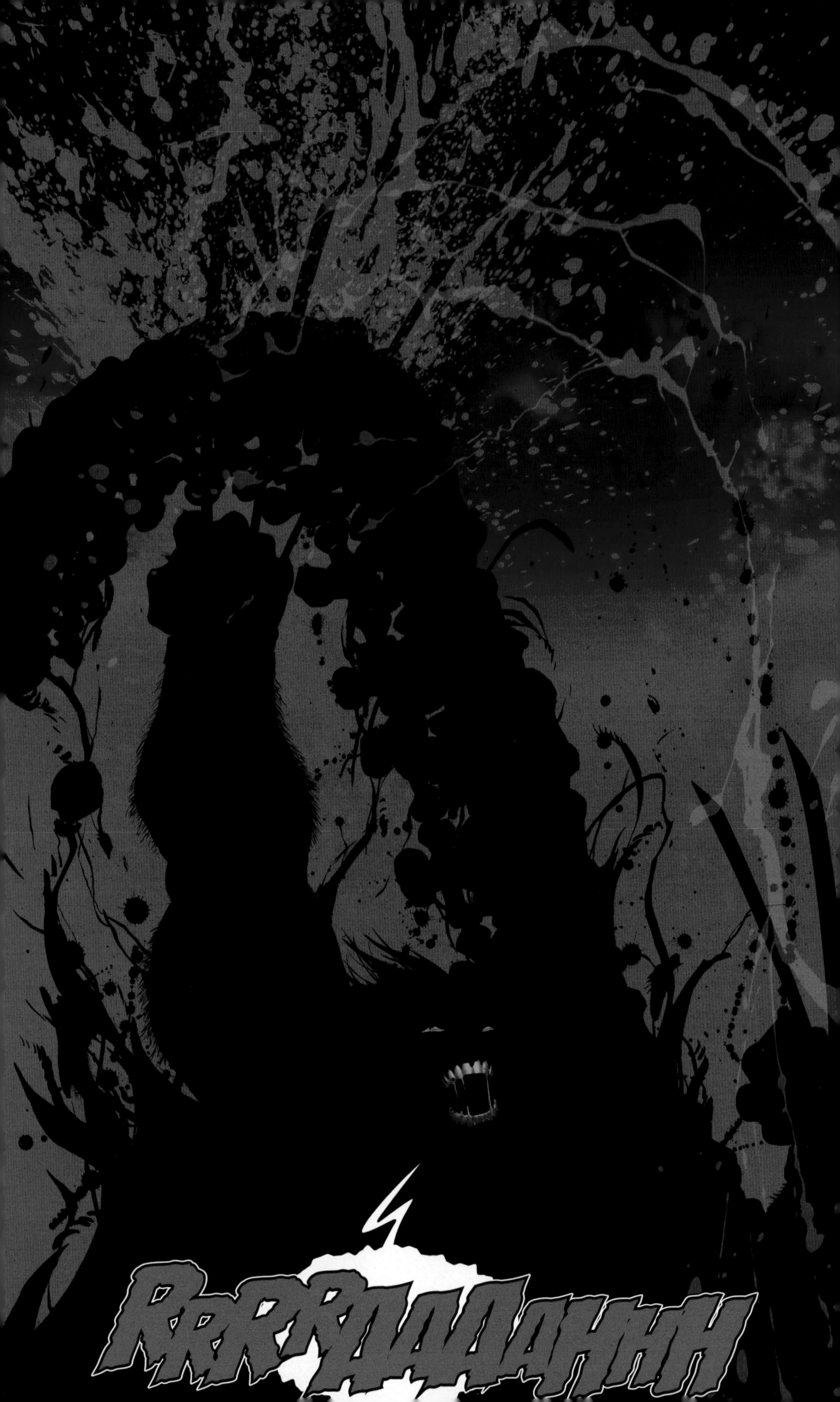
RRRRAAAAHHH

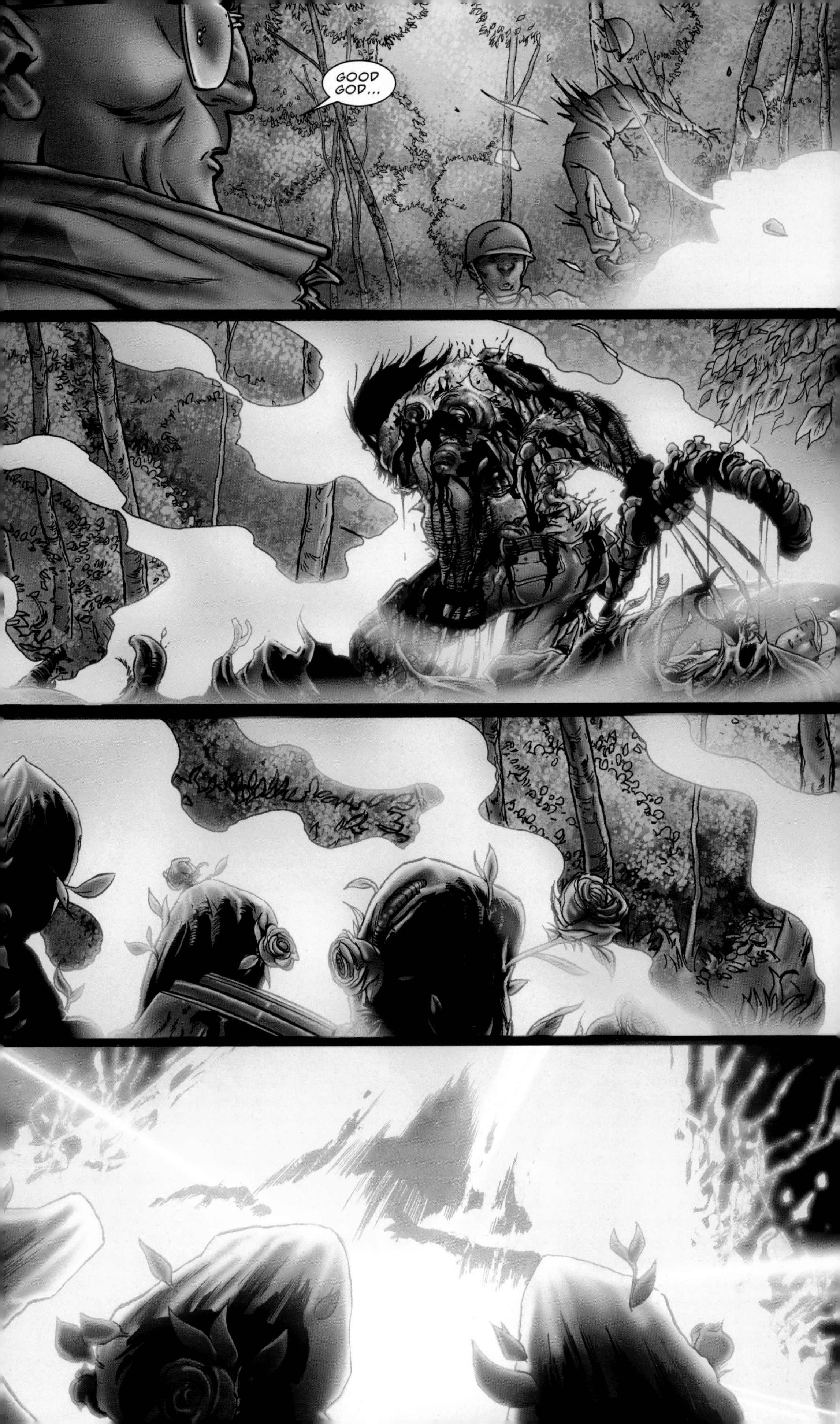
GOOD GOD...

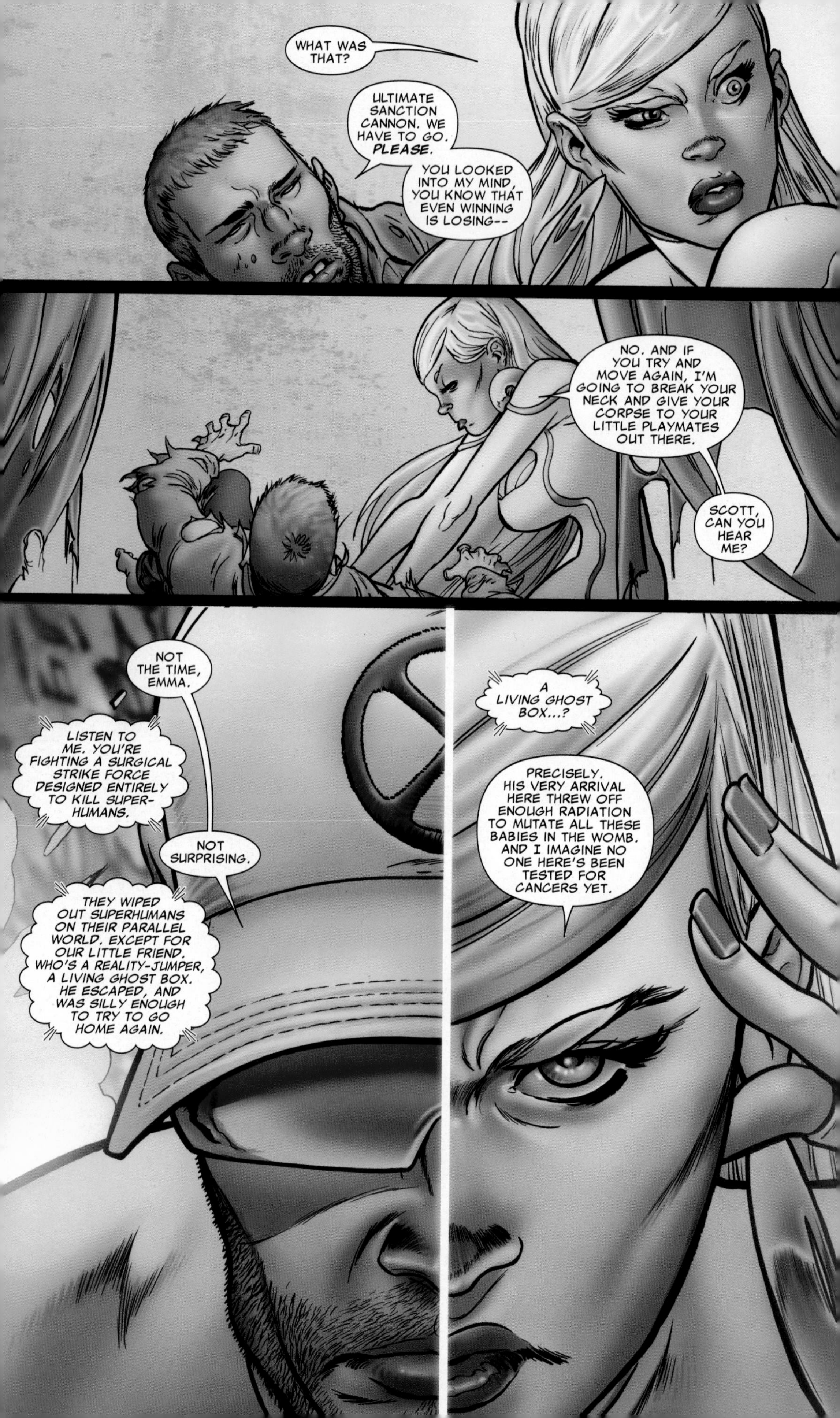
WHAT WAS THAT?
ULTIMATE SANCTION CANNON. WE HAVE TO GO. PLEASE.
YOU LOOKED INTO MY MIND, YOU KNOW THAT EVEN WINNING IS LOSING--
NO. AND IF YOU TRY AND MOVE AGAIN, I'M GOING TO BREAK YOUR NECK AND GIVE YOUR CORPSE TO YOUR LITTLE PLAYMATES OUT THERE.
SCOTT, CAN YOU HEAR ME?
NOT THE TIME, EMMA.
LISTEN TO ME. YOU'RE FIGHTING A SURGICAL STRIKE FORCE DESIGNED ENTIRELY TO KILL SUPER-HUMANS.
NOT SURPRISING.
THEY WIPED OUT SUPERHUMANS ON THEIR PARALLEL WORLD. EXCEPT FOR OUR LITTLE FRIEND. WHO'S A REALITY-JUMPER, A LIVING GHOST BOX. HE ESCAPED, AND WAS SILLY ENOUGH TO TRY TO GO HOME AGAIN.
A LIVING GHOST BOX...?
PRECISELY. HIS VERY ARRIVAL HERE THREW OFF ENOUGH RADIATION TO MUTATE ALL THESE BABIES IN THE WOMB. AND I IMAGINE NO ONE HERE'S BEEN TESTED FOR CANCERS YET.

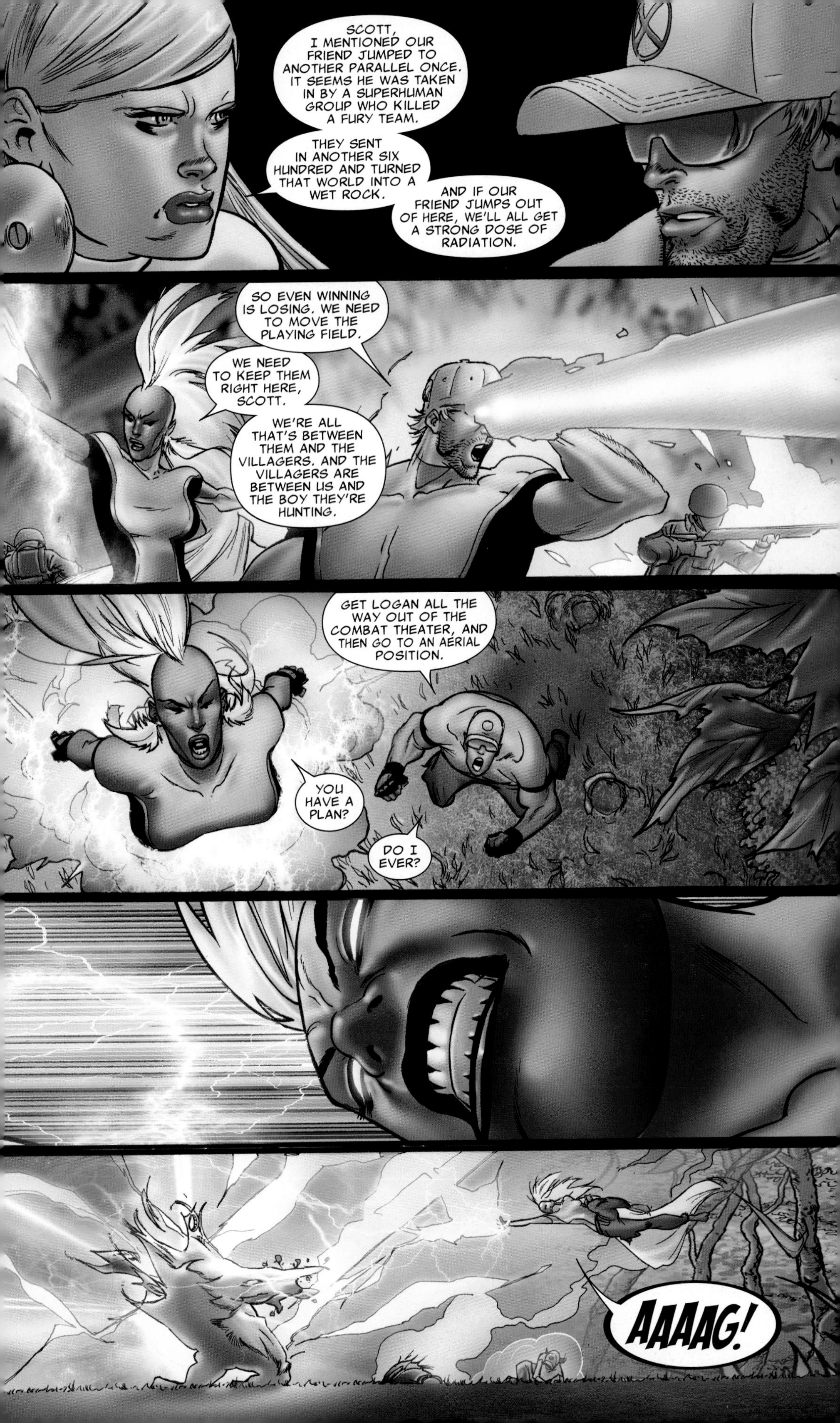
SCOTT, I MENTIONED OUR FRIEND JUMPED TO ANOTHER PARALLEL ONCE. IT SEEMS HE WAS TAKEN IN BY A SUPERHUMAN GROUP WHO KILLED A FURY TEAM.
THEY SENT IN ANOTHER SIX HUNDRED AND TURNED THAT WORLD INTO A WET ROCK.
AND IF OUR FRIEND JUMPS OUT OF HERE, WE'LL ALL GET A STRONG DOSE OF RADIATION.
SO EVEN WINNING IS LOSING. WE NEED TO MOVE THE PLAYING FIELD.
WE NEED TO KEEP THEM RIGHT HERE, SCOTT.
WE'RE ALL THAT'S BETWEEN THEM AND THE VILLAGERS. AND THE VILLAGERS ARE BETWEEN US AND THE BOY THEY'RE HUNTING.
GET LOGAN ALL THE WAY OUT OF THE COMBAT THEATER, AND THEN GO TO AN AERIAL POSITION.
YOU HAVE A PLAN?
DO I EVER?
AAAAG!

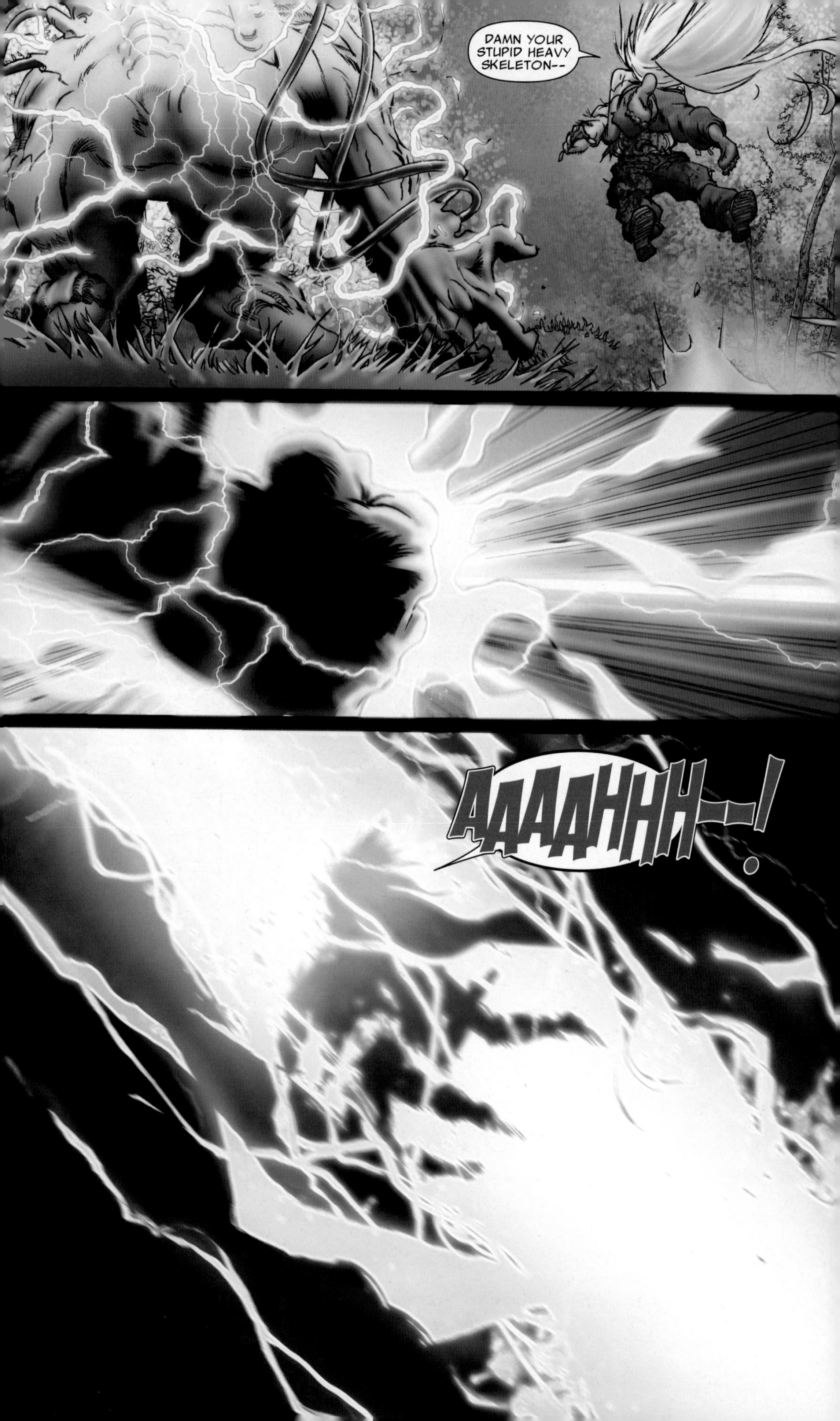
DAMN YOUR STUPID HEAVY SKELETON--
AAAAHHH--!

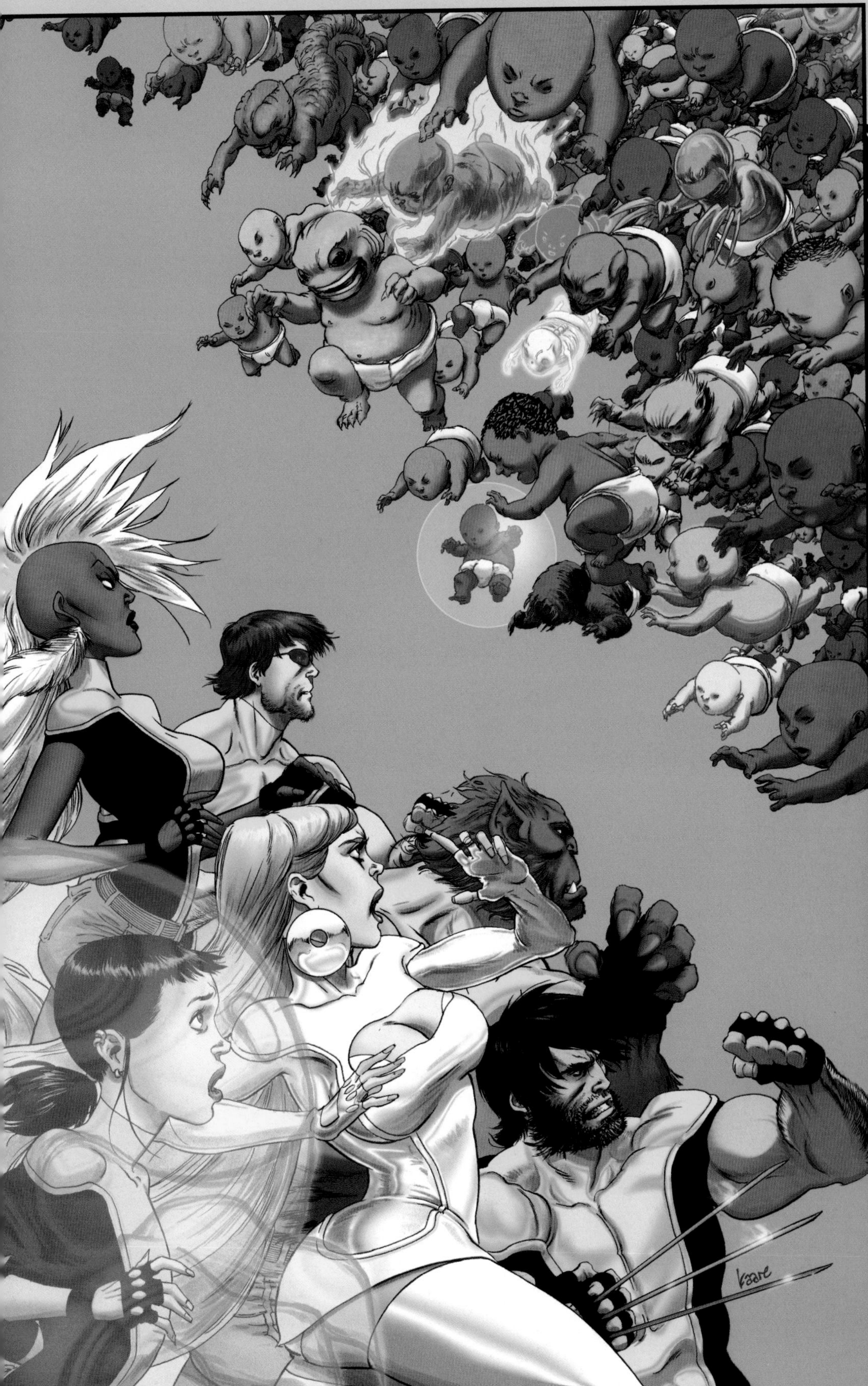

FIVE

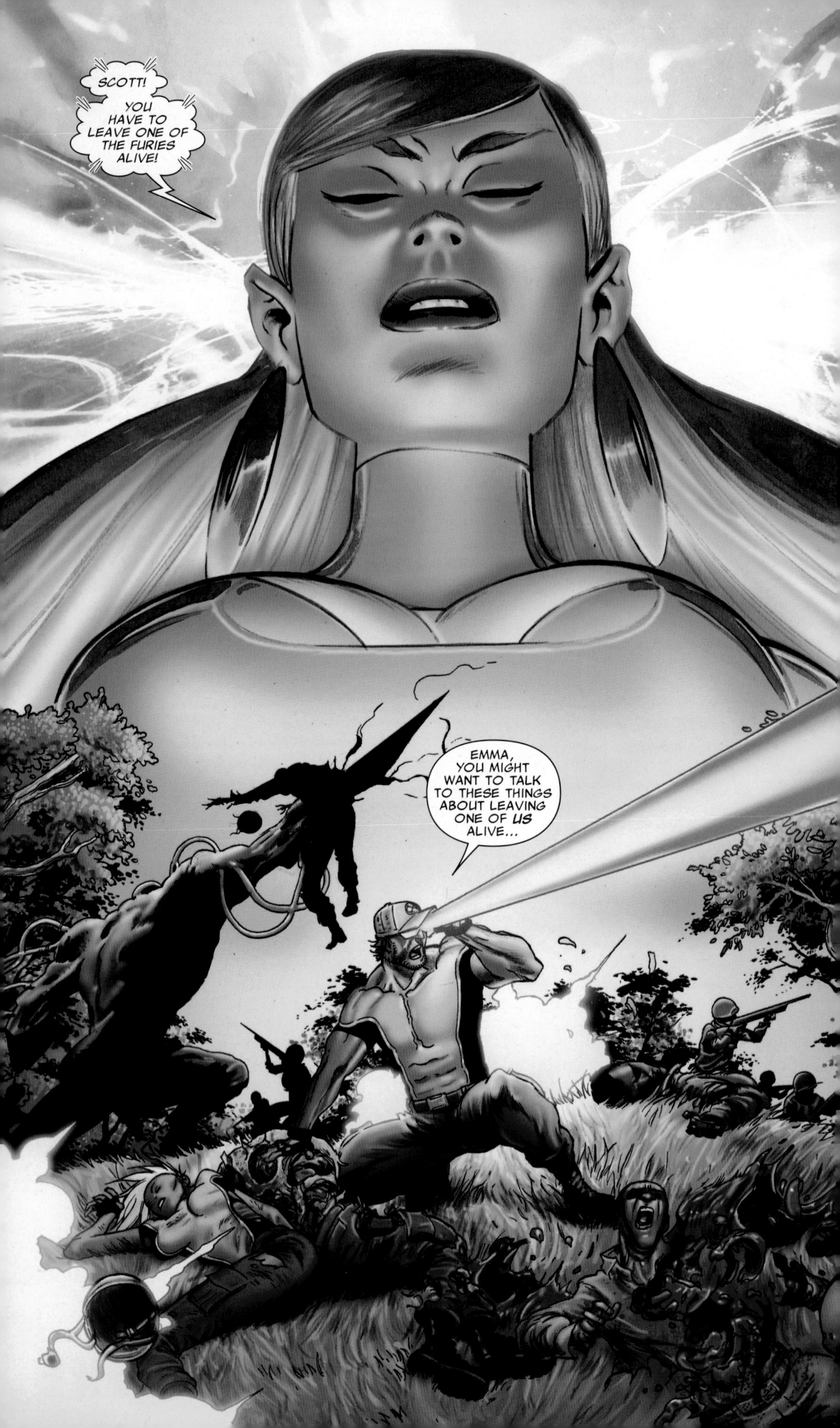
SCOTT!
YOU HAVE TO LEAVE ONE OF THE FURIES ALIVE!
EMMA, YOU MIGHT WANT TO TALK TO THESE THINGS ABOUT LEAVING ONE OF US ALIVE...

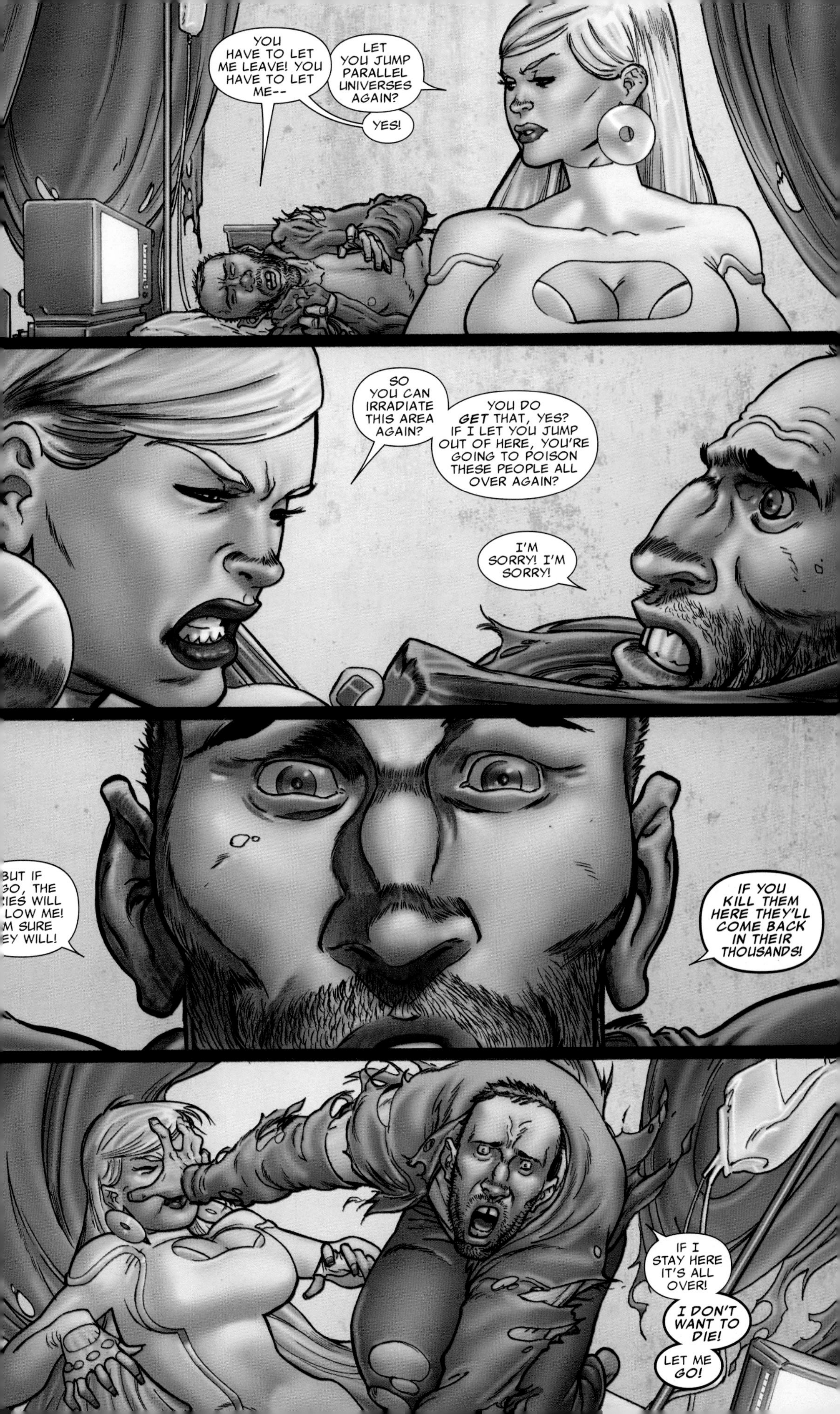
YOU HAVE TO LET ME LEAVE! YOU HAVE TO LET ME--
LET YOU JUMP PARALLEL UNIVERSES AGAIN?
YES!
SO YOU CAN IRRADIATE THIS AREA AGAIN?
YOU DO GET THAT, YES? IF I LET YOU JUMP OUT OF HERE, YOU'RE GOING TO POISON THESE PEOPLE ALL OVER AGAIN?
I'M SORRY! I'M SORRY!
BUT IF GO, THE IES WILL LOW ME! M SURE EY WILL!
IF YOU KILL THEM HERE THEY'LL COME BACK IN THEIR THOUSANDS!
IF I STAY HERE IT'S ALL OVER!
I DON'T WANT TO DIE!
LET ME GO!

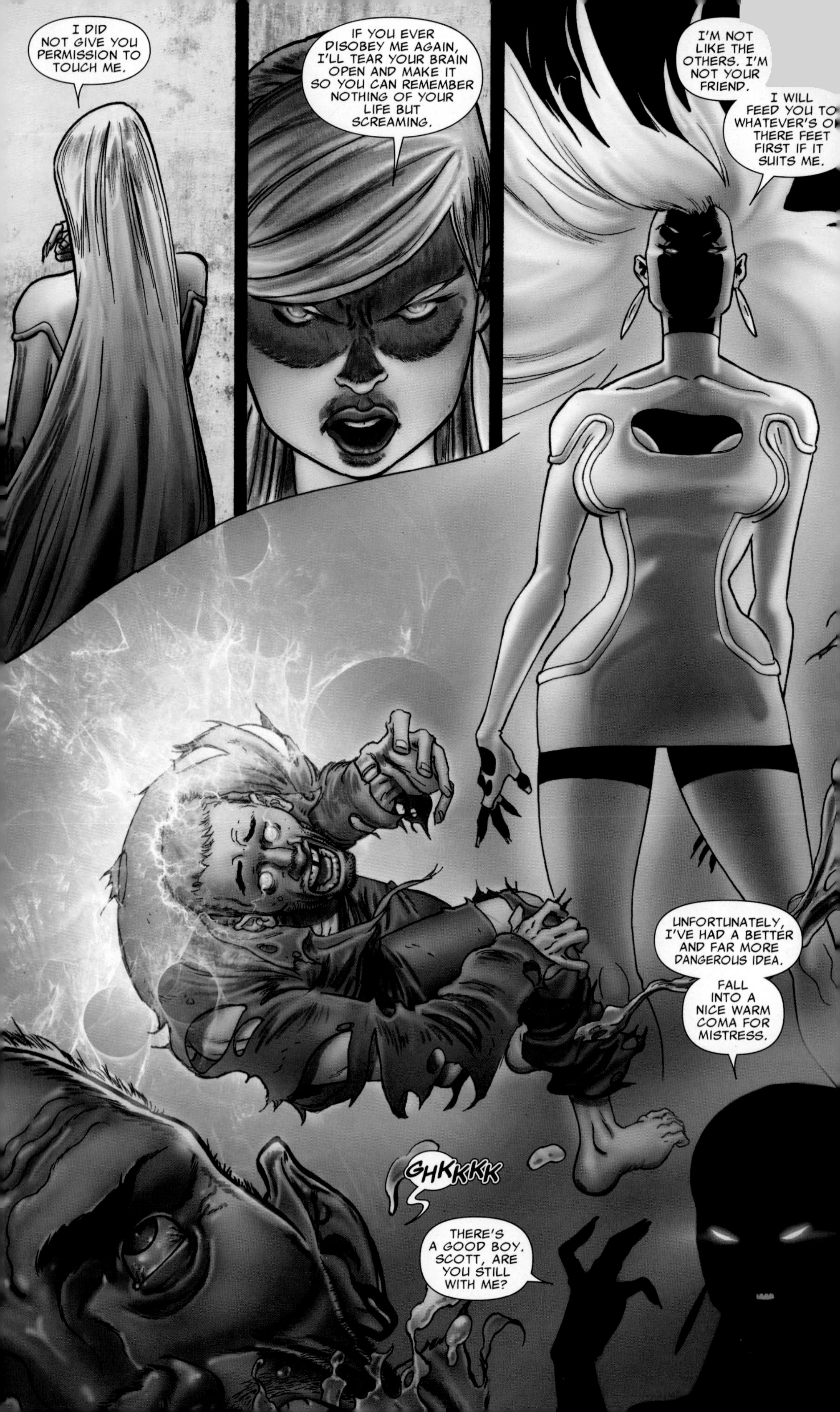

I DID NOT GIVE YOU PERMISSION TO TOUCH ME.
IF YOU EVER DISOBEY ME AGAIN, I'LL TEAR YOUR BRAIN OPEN AND MAKE IT SO YOU CAN REMEMBER NOTHING OF YOUR LIFE BUT SCREAMING.
I'M NOT LIKE THE OTHERS. I'M NOT YOUR FRIEND.
I WILL FEED YOU TO WHATEVER'S O THERE FEET FIRST IF IT SUITS ME.
UNFORTUNATELY, I'VE HAD A BETTER AND FAR MORE DANGEROUS IDEA.
FALL INTO A NICE WARM COMA FOR MISTRESS.
GHKKKK
THERE'S A GOOD BOY. SCOTT, ARE YOU STILL WITH ME?

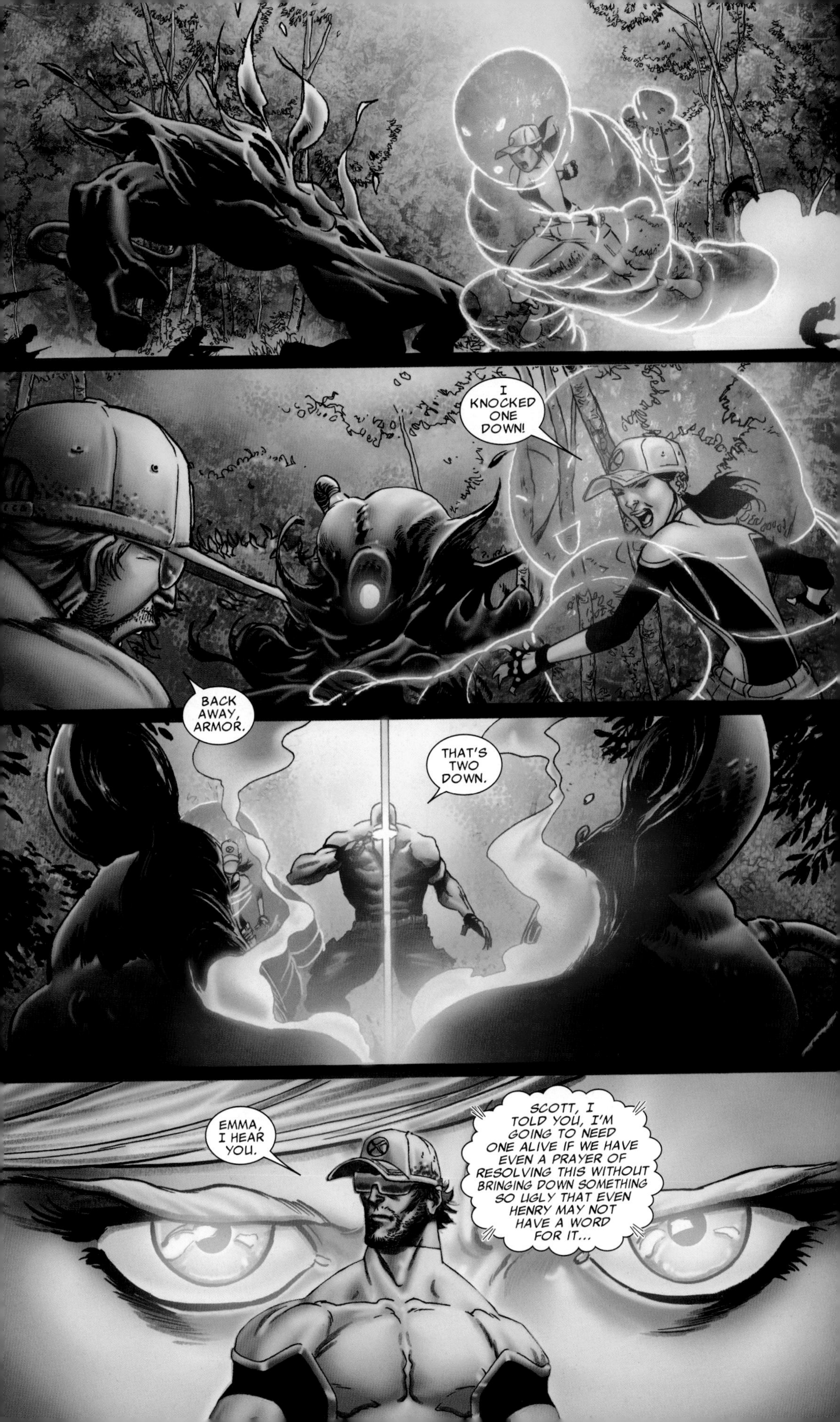
I KNOCKED ONE DOWN!
BACK AWAY, ARMOR.
THAT'S TWO DOWN.
EMMA, I HEAR YOU.
SCOTT, I TOLD YOU, I'M GOING TO NEED ONE ALIVE IF WE HAVE EVEN A PRAYER OF RESOLVING THIS WITHOUT BRINGING DOWN SOMETHING SO UGLY THAT EVEN HENRY MAY NOT HAVE A WORD FOR IT...

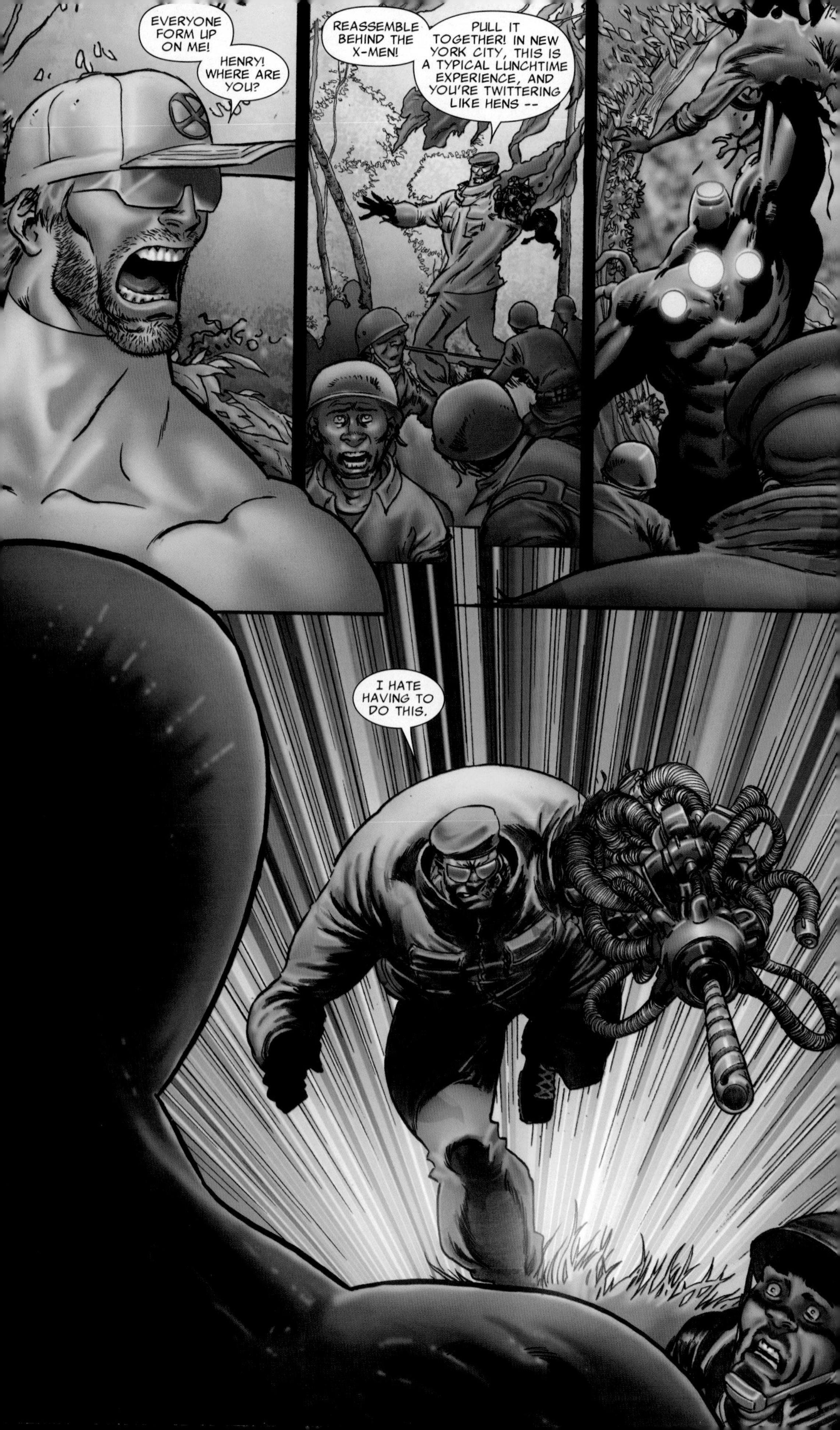
EVERYONE FORM UP ON ME!
HENRY! WHERE ARE YOU?
REASSEMBLE BEHIND THE X-MEN!
PULL IT TOGETHER! IN NEW YORK CITY, THIS IS A TYPICAL LUNCHTIME EXPERIENCE, AND YOU'RE TWITTERING LIKE HENS --
I HATE HAVING TO DO THIS.

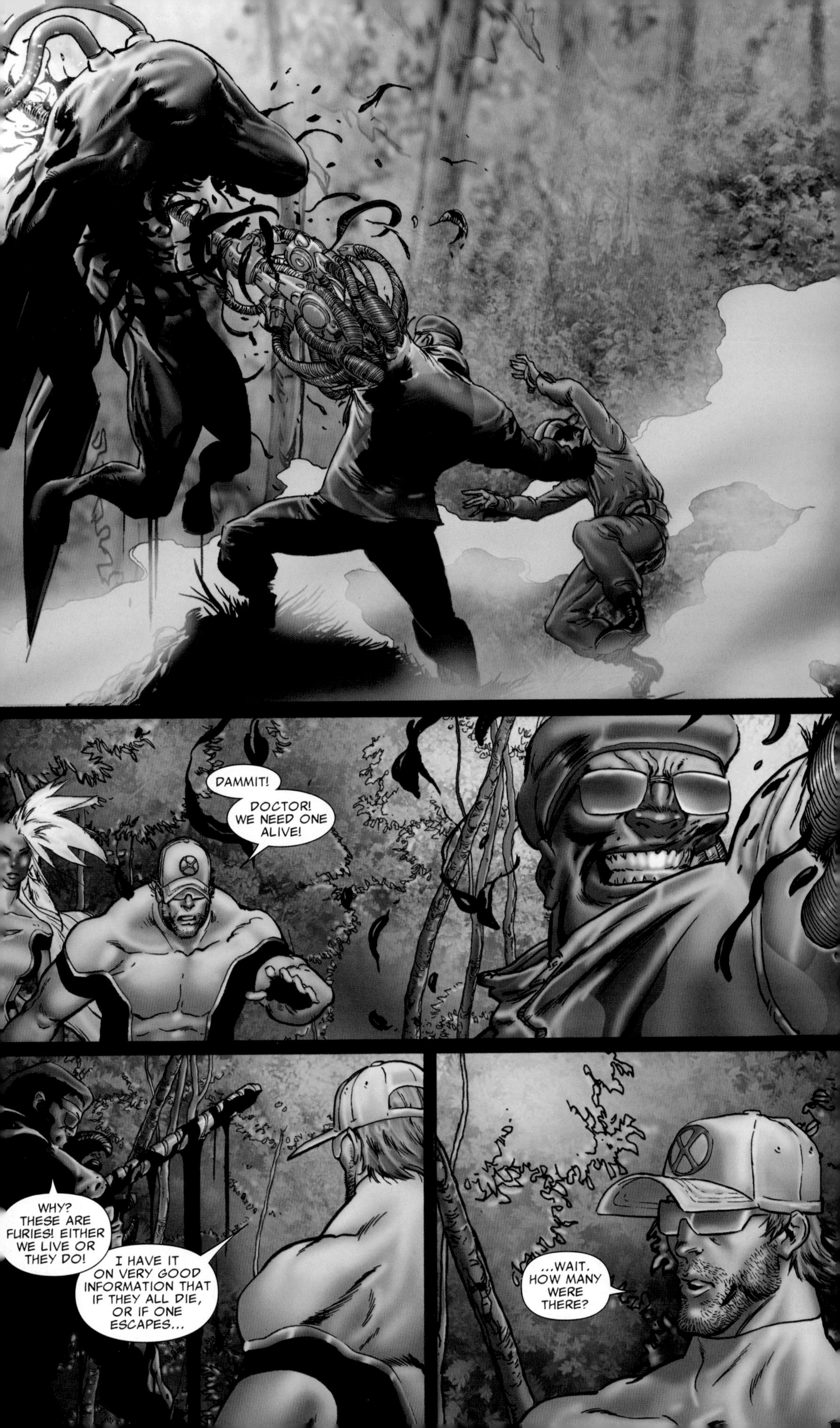
DAMMIT!
DOCTOR! WE NEED ONE ALIVE!
WHY? THESE ARE FURIES! EITHER WE LIVE OR THEY DO!
I HAVE IT ON VERY GOOD INFORMATION THAT IF THEY ALL DIE, OR IF ONE ESCAPES...
...WAIT. HOW MANY WERE THERE?

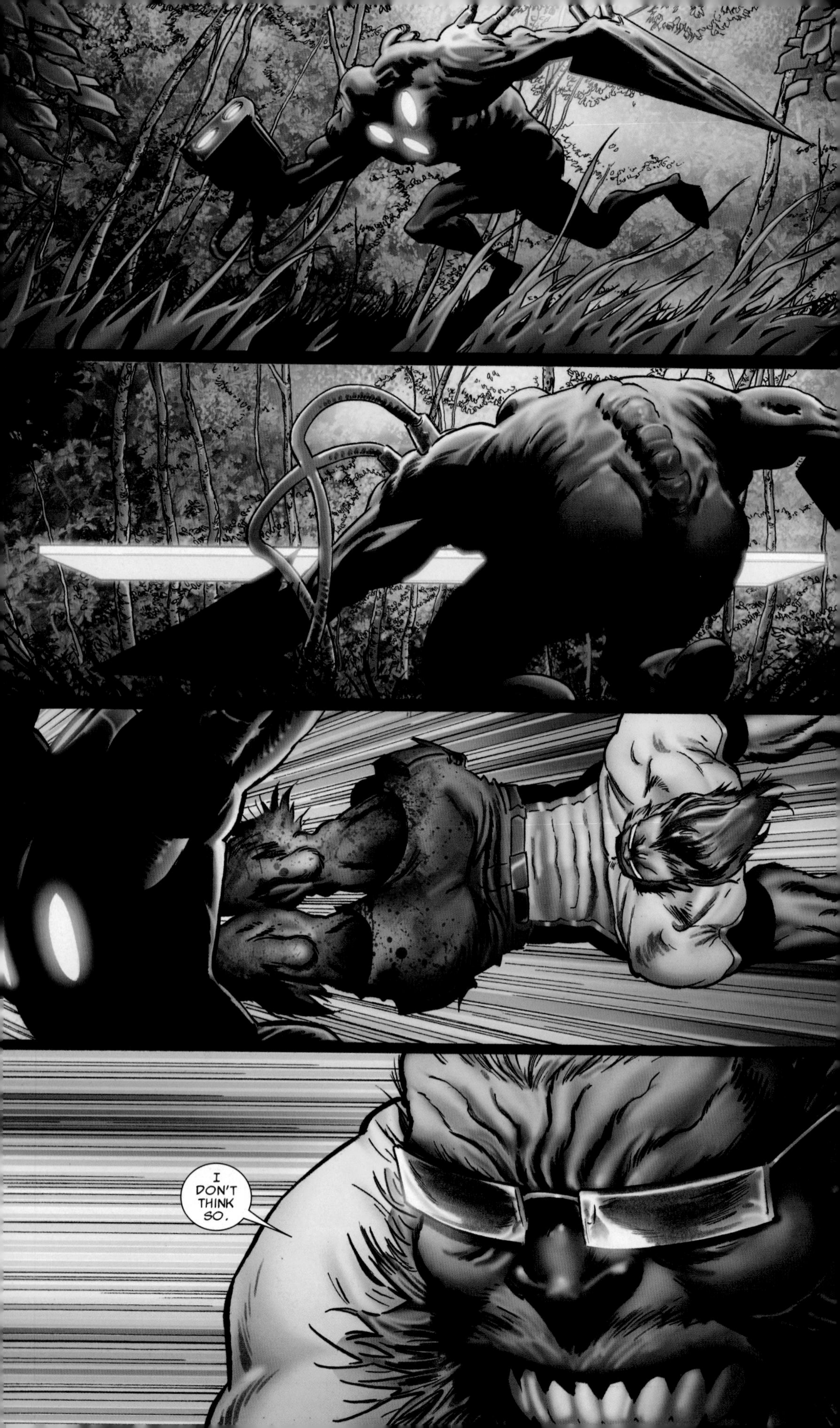
I DON'T THINK SO.

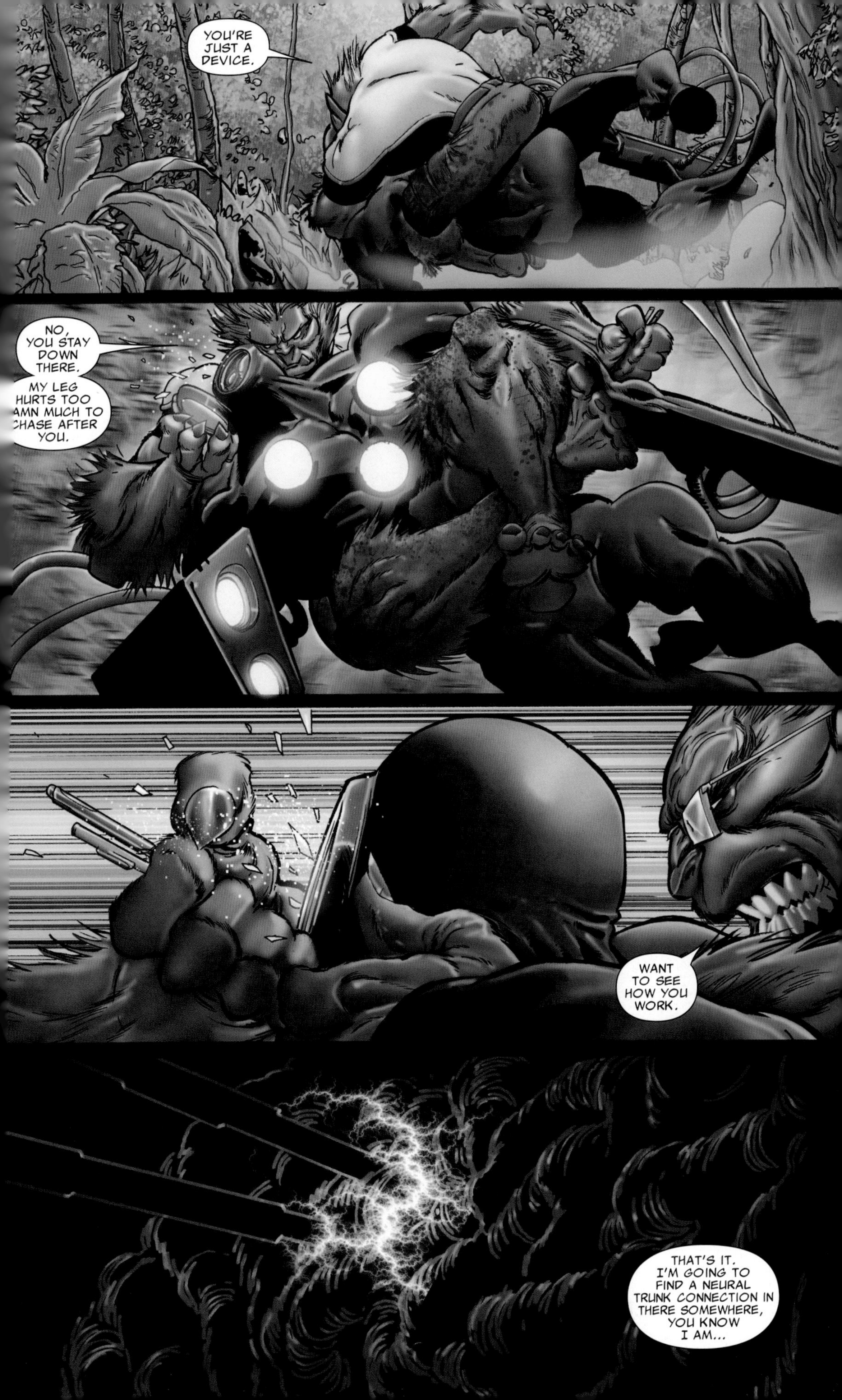
YOU'RE JUST A DEVICE.
NO, YOU STAY DOWN THERE.
MY LEG HURTS TOO AMN MUCH TO CHASE AFTER YOU.
WANT TO SEE HOW YOU WORK.
THAT'S IT. I'M GOING TO FIND A NEURAL TRUNK CONNECTION IN THERE SOMEWHERE, YOU KNOW I AM...

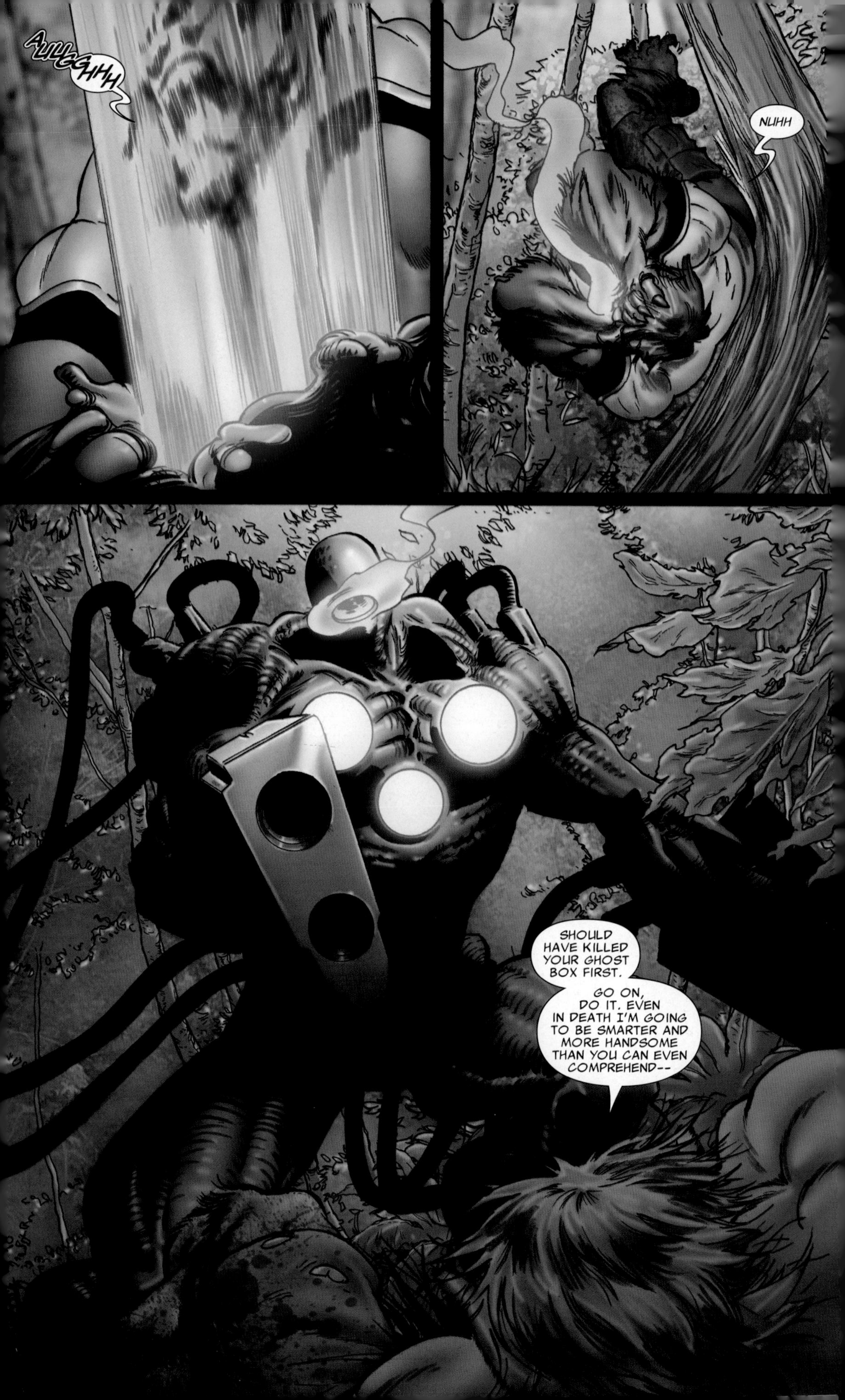
AUUGGHHH
NUHH
SHOULD HAVE KILLED YOUR GHOST BOX FIRST.
GO ON, DO IT. EVEN IN DEATH I'M GOING TO BE SMARTER AND MORE HANDSOME THAN YOU CAN EVEN COMPREHEND--

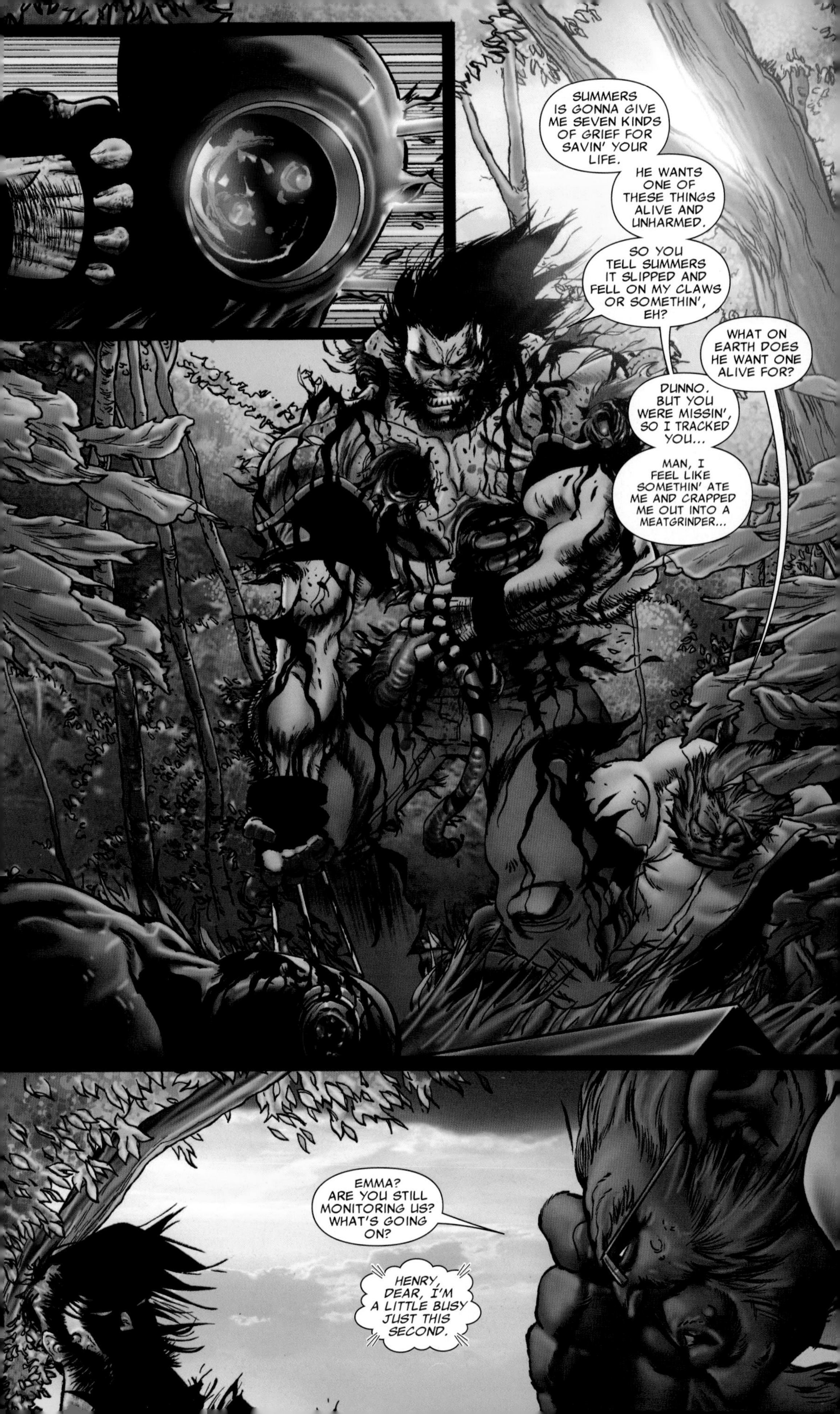
SUMMERS IS GONNA GIVE ME SEVEN KINDS OF GRIEF FOR SAVIN' YOUR LIFE.
HE WANTS ONE OF THESE THINGS ALIVE AND UNHARMED.
SO YOU TELL SUMMERS IT SLIPPED AND FELL ON MY CLAWS OR SOMETHIN', EH?
WHAT ON EARTH DOES HE WANT ONE ALIVE FOR?
DUNNO. BUT YOU WERE MISSIN', SO I TRACKED YOU...
MAN, I FEEL LIKE SOMETHIN' ATE ME AND CRAPPED ME OUT INTO A MEATGRINDER...
EMMA? ARE YOU STILL MONITORING US? WHAT'S GOING ON?
HENRY, DEAR, I'M A LITTLE BUSY JUST THIS SECOND.

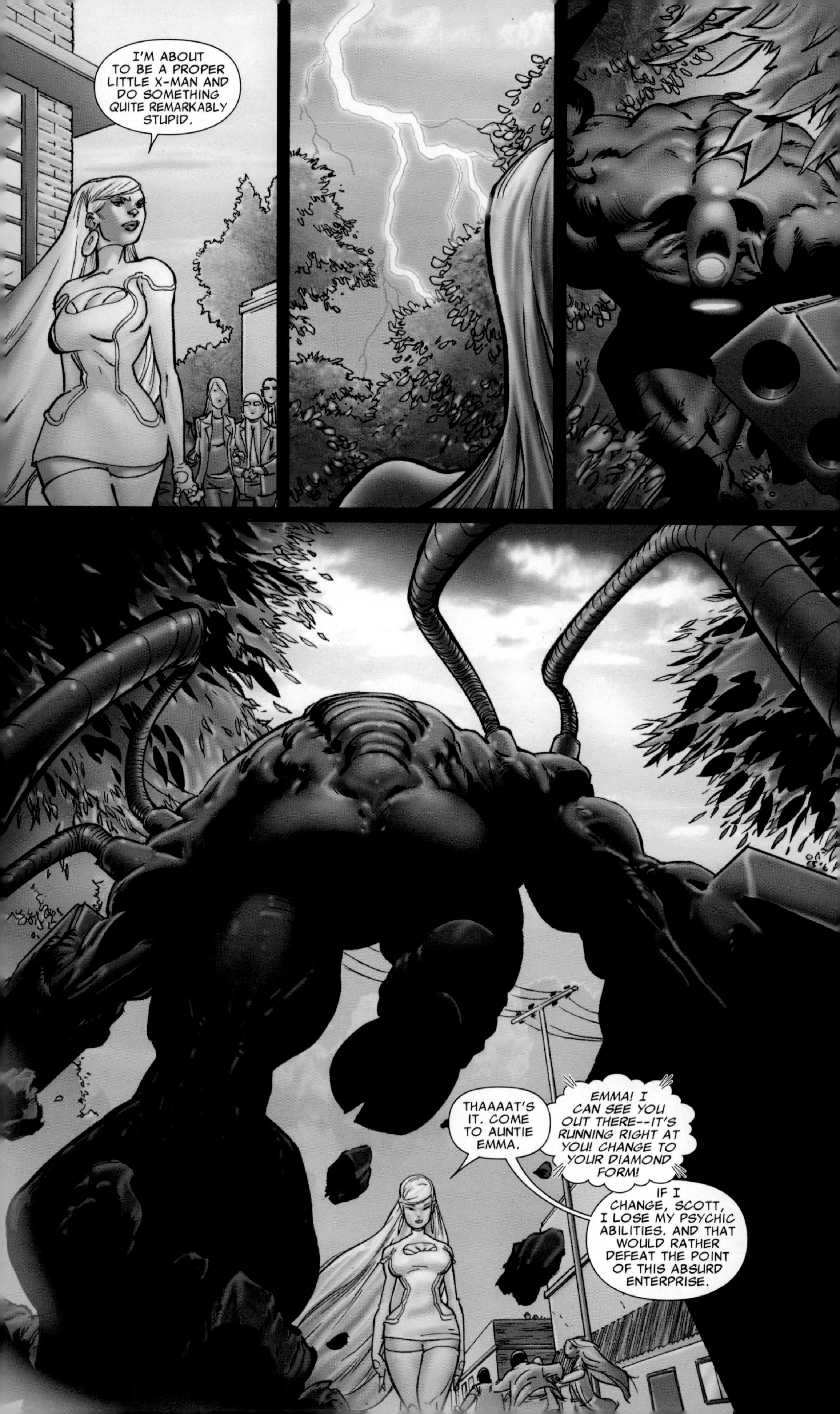
I'M ABOUT TO BE A PROPER LITTLE X-MAN AND DO SOMETHING QUITE REMARKABLY STUPID.
THAAAAT'S IT. COME TO AUNTIE EMMA.
EMMA! I CAN SEE YOU OUT THERE--IT'S RUNNING RIGHT AT YOU! CHANGE TO YOUR DIAMOND FORM!
IF I CHANGE, SCOTT, I LOSE MY PSYCHIC ABILITIES. AND THAT WOULD RATHER DEFEAT THE POINT OF THIS ABSURD ENTERPRISE.

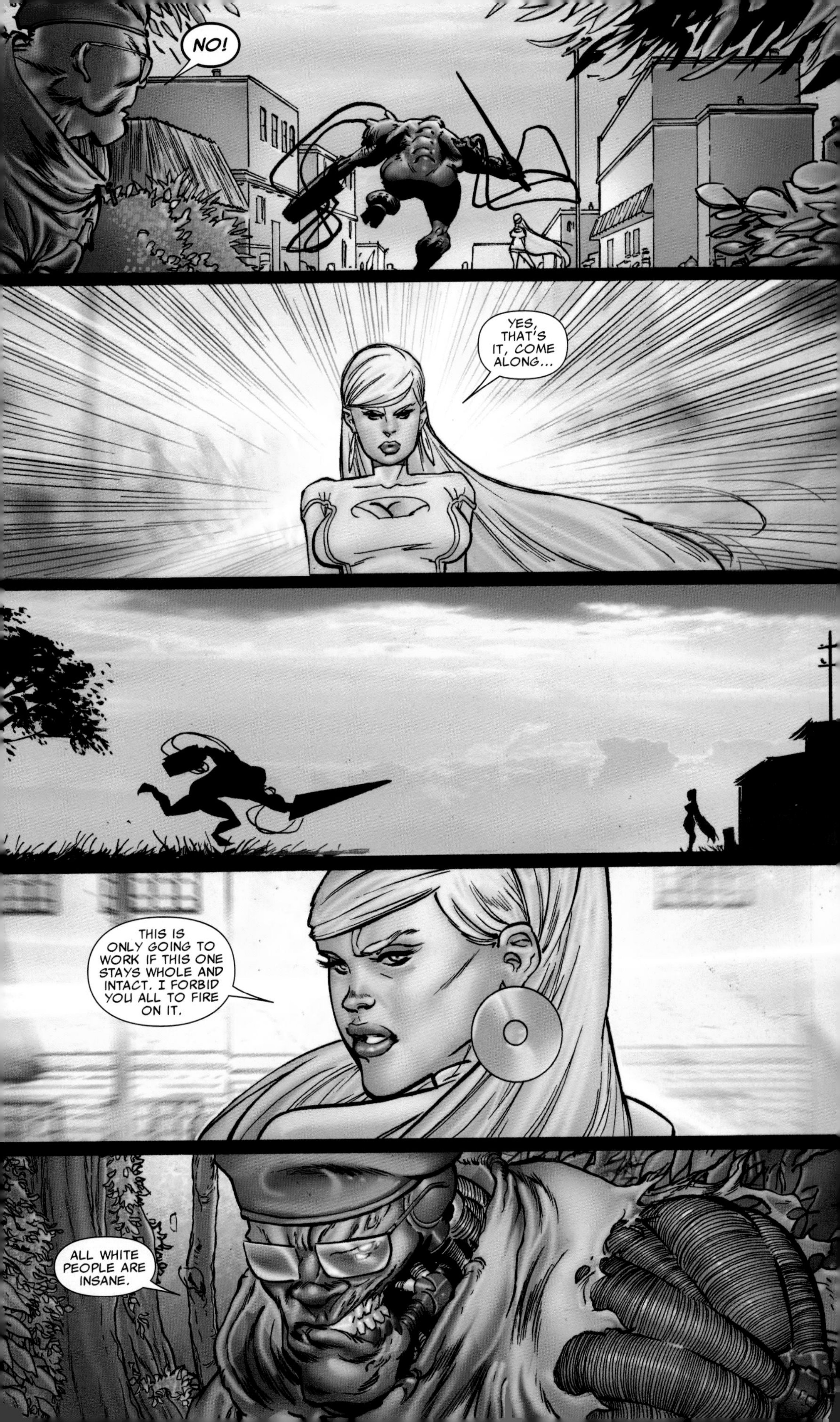
NO!
YES, THAT'S IT, COME ALONG...
THIS IS ONLY GOING TO WORK IF THIS ONE STAYS WHOLE AND INTACT. I FORBID YOU ALL TO FIRE ON IT.
ALL WHITE PEOPLE ARE INSANE.

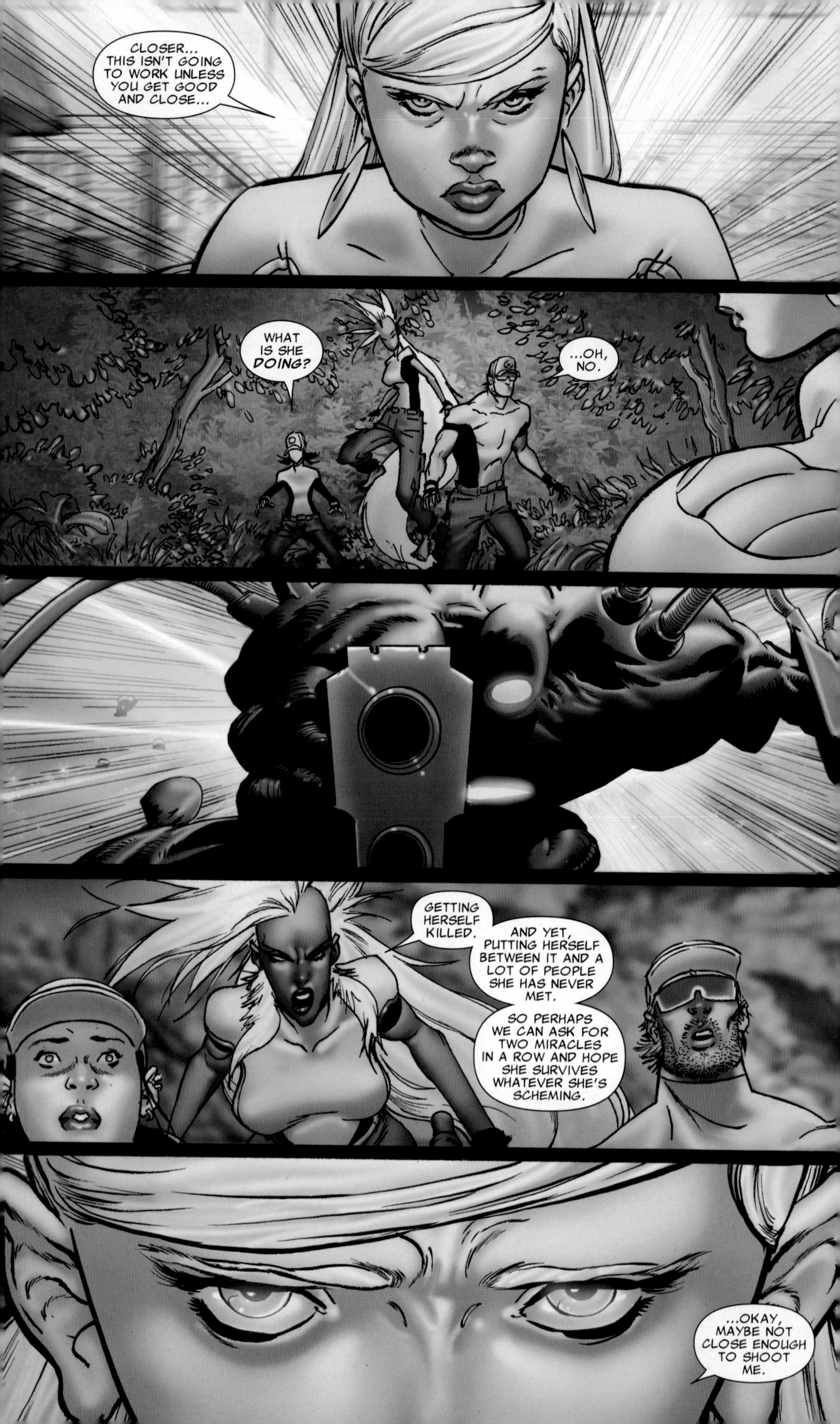
CLOSER... THIS ISN'T GOING TO WORK UNLESS YOU GET GOOD AND CLOSE...
WHAT IS SHE DOING?
...OH, NO.
GETTING HERSELF KILLED.
AND YET, PUTTING HERSELF BETWEEN IT AND A LOT OF PEOPLE SHE HAS NEVER MET.
SO PERHAPS WE CAN ASK FOR TWO MIRACLES IN A ROW AND HOPE SHE SURVIVES WHATEVER SHE'S SCHEMING.
...OKAY, MAYBE NOT CLOSE ENOUGH TO SHOOT ME.

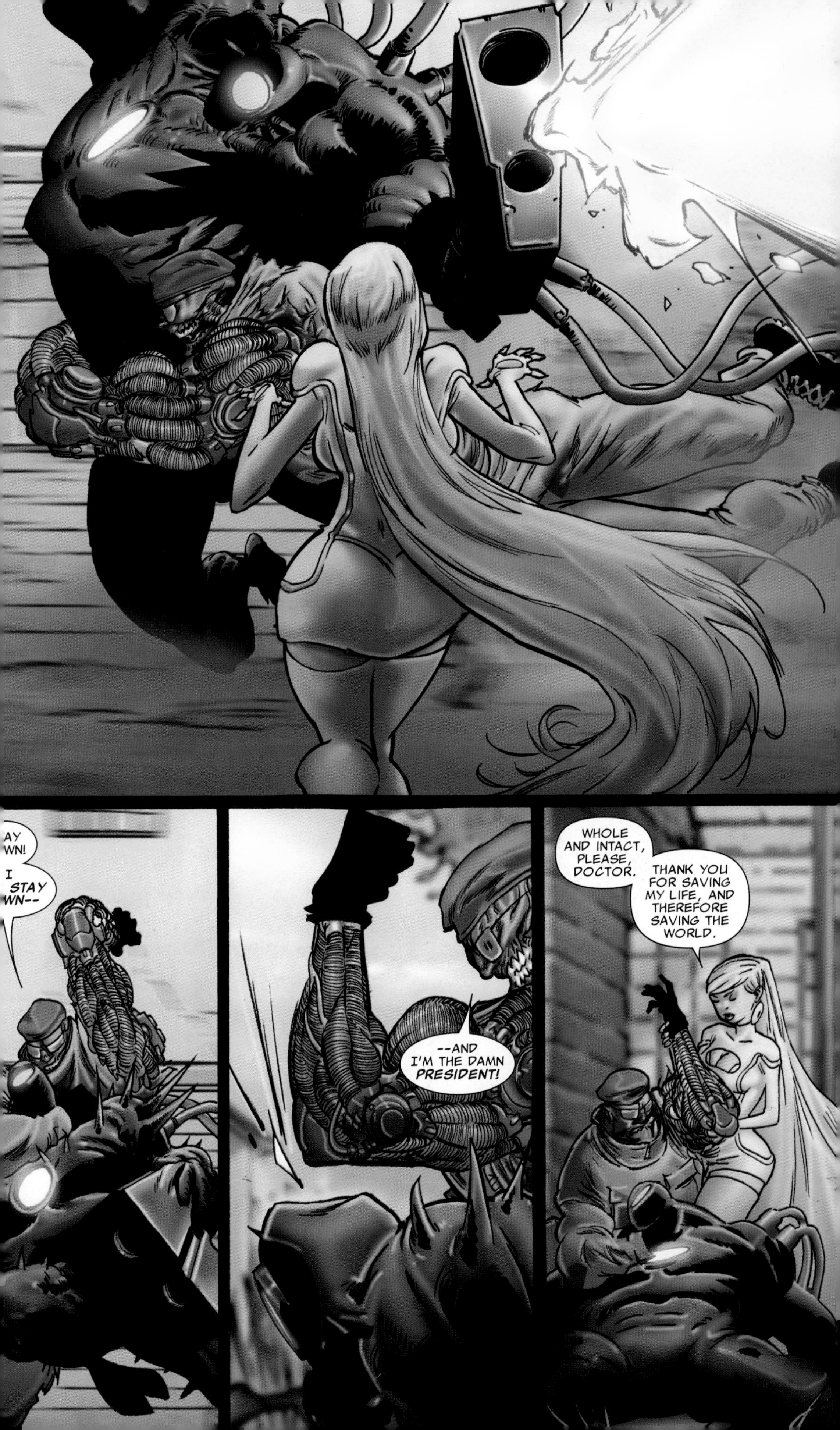

AY
WN!
I STAY
WN--
--AND I'M THE DAMN PRESIDENT!
WHOLE AND INTACT, PLEASE, DOCTOR.
THANK YOU FOR SAVING MY LIFE, AND THEREFORE SAVING THE WORLD.

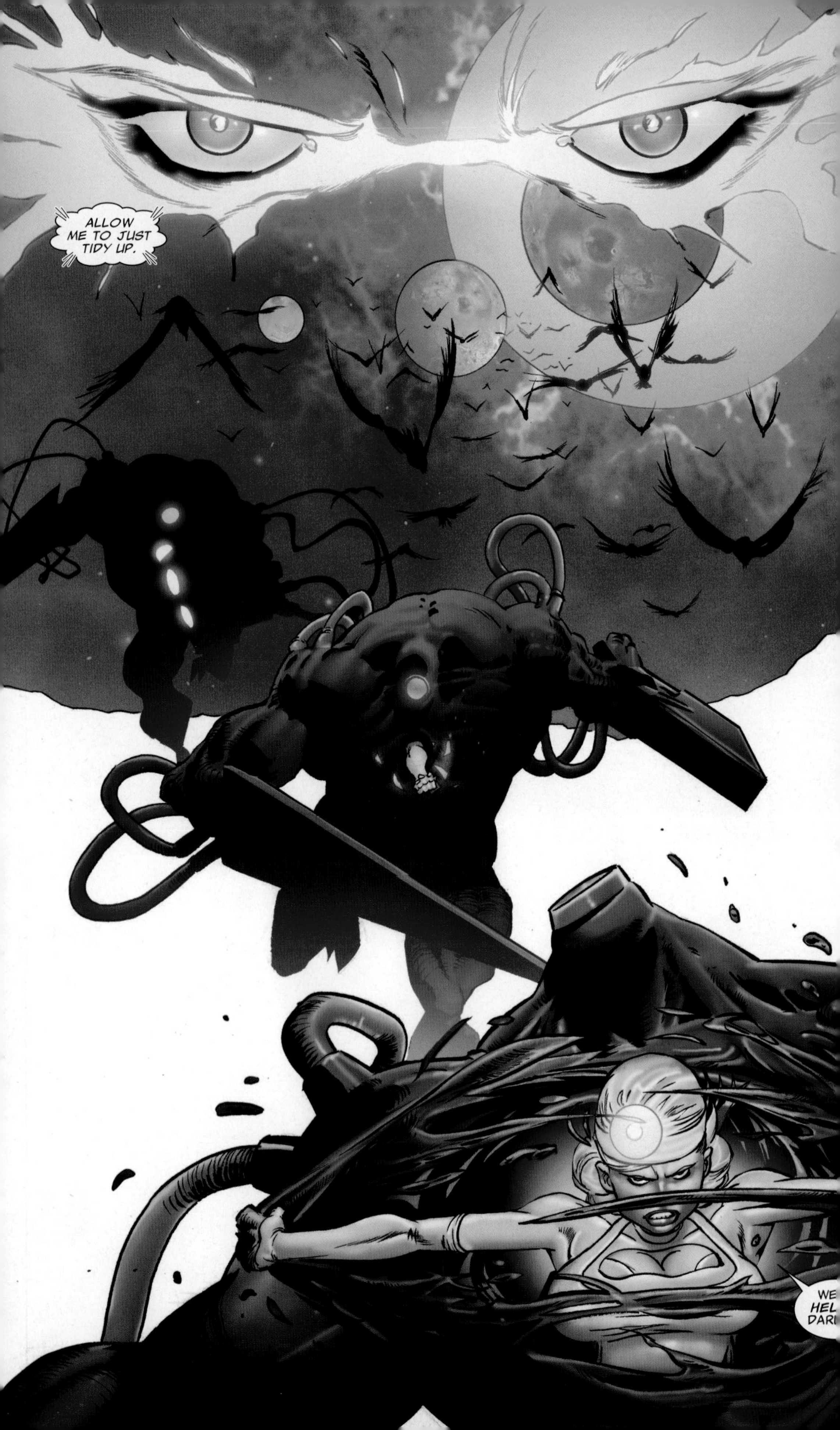
ALLOW ME TO JUST TIDY UP.

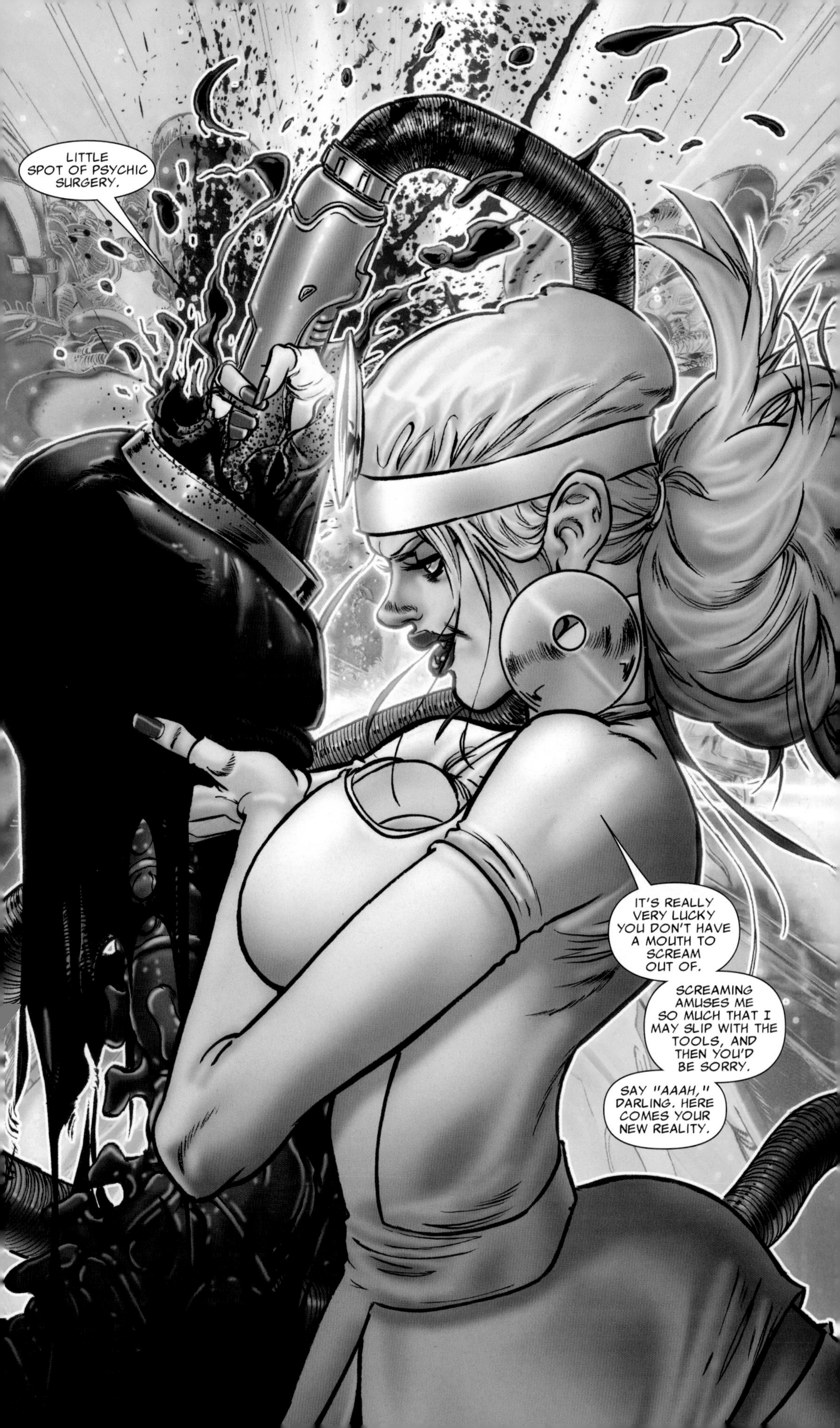
LITTLE SPOT OF PSYCHIC SURGERY.
IT'S REALLY VERY LUCKY YOU DON'T HAVE A MOUTH TO SCREAM OUT OF.
SCREAMING AMUSES ME SO MUCH THAT I MAY SLIP WITH THE TOOLS, AND THEN YOU'D BE SORRY.
SAY "AAAH," DARLING. HERE COMES YOUR NEW REALITY.

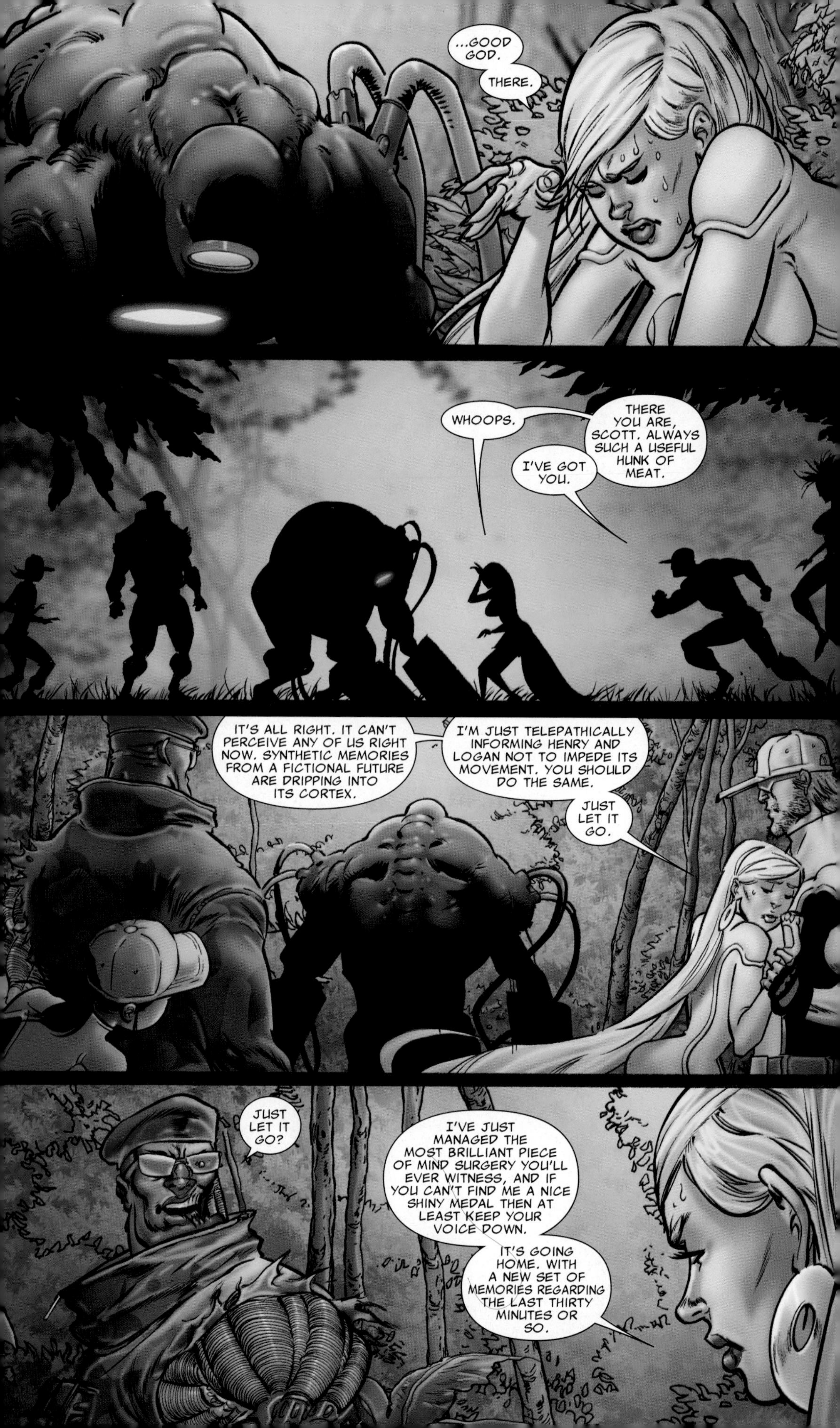
...GOOD GOD.
THERE.
WHOOPS.
THERE YOU ARE, SCOTT. ALWAYS SUCH A USEFUL HUNK OF MEAT.
I'VE GOT YOU.
IT'S ALL RIGHT. IT CAN'T PERCEIVE ANY OF US RIGHT NOW. SYNTHETIC MEMORIES FROM A FICTIONAL FUTURE ARE DRIPPING INTO ITS CORTEX.
I'M JUST TELEPATHICALLY INFORMING HENRY AND LOGAN NOT TO IMPEDE ITS MOVEMENT. YOU SHOULD DO THE SAME.
JUST LET IT GO.
JUST LET IT GO?
I'VE JUST MANAGED THE MOST BRILLIANT PIECE OF MIND SURGERY YOU'LL EVER WITNESS, AND IF YOU CAN'T FIND ME A NICE SHINY MEDAL THEN AT LEAST KEEP YOUR VOICE DOWN.
IT'S GOING HOME. WITH A NEW SET OF MEMORIES REGARDING THE LAST THIRTY MINUTES OR SO.

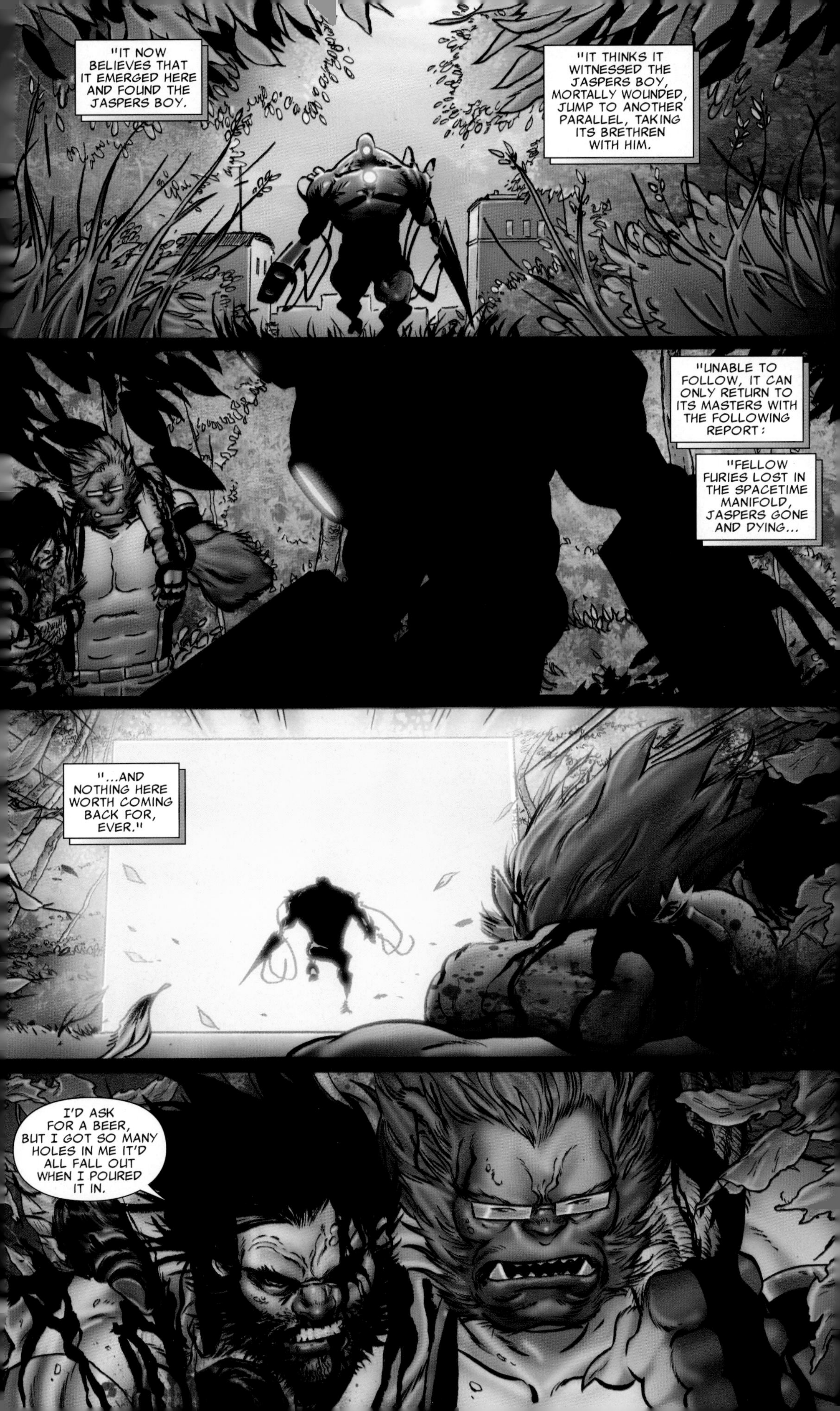
"IT NOW BELIEVES THAT IT EMERGED HERE AND FOUND THE JASPERS BOY.
"IT THINKS IT WITNESSED THE JASPERS BOY, MORTALLY WOUNDED, JUMP TO ANOTHER PARALLEL, TAKING ITS BRETHREN WITH HIM.
"UNABLE TO FOLLOW, IT CAN ONLY RETURN TO ITS MASTERS WITH THE FOLLOWING REPORT:
"FELLOW FURIES LOST IN THE SPACETIME MANIFOLD, JASPERS GONE AND DYING...
"...AND NOTHING HERE WORTH COMING BACK FOR, EVER."
I'D ASK FOR A BEER, BUT I GOT SO MANY HOLES IN ME IT'D ALL FALL OUT WHEN I POURED IT IN.

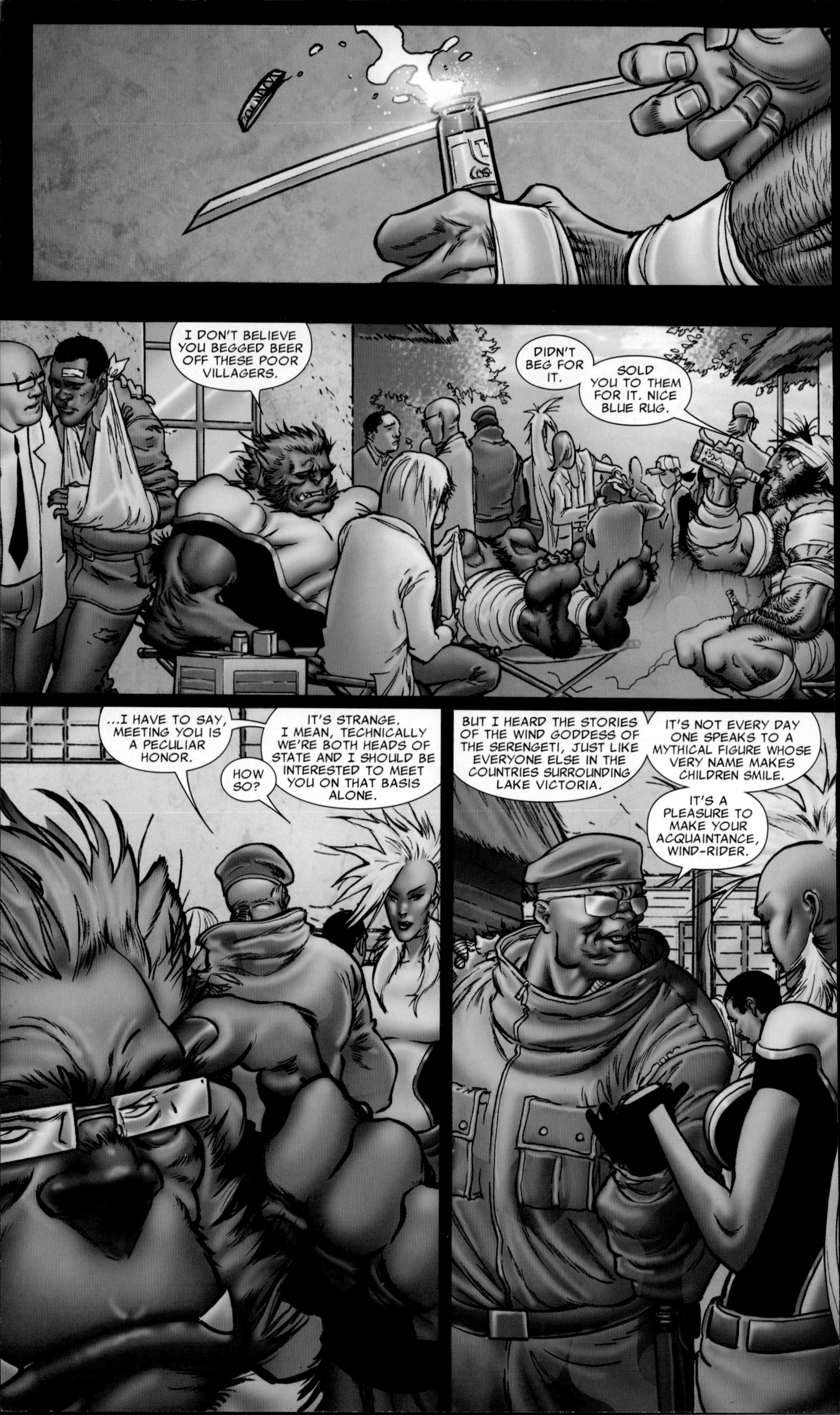
I DON'T BELIEVE YOU BEGGED BEER OFF THESE POOR VILLAGERS.
DIDN'T BEG FOR IT.
SOLD YOU TO THEM FOR IT. NICE BLUE RUG.
...I HAVE TO SAY, MEETING YOU IS A PECULIAR HONOR.
HOW SO?
IT'S STRANGE. I MEAN, TECHNICALLY WE'RE BOTH HEADS OF STATE AND I SHOULD BE INTERESTED TO MEET YOU ON THAT BASIS ALONE.
BUT I HEARD THE STORIES OF THE WIND GODDESS OF THE SERENGETI, JUST LIKE EVERYONE ELSE IN THE COUNTRIES SURROUNDING LAKE VICTORIA.
IT'S NOT EVERY DAY ONE SPEAKS TO A MYTHICAL FIGURE WHOSE VERY NAME MAKES CHILDREN SMILE.
IT'S A PLEASURE TO MAKE YOUR ACQUAINTANCE, WIND-RIDER.

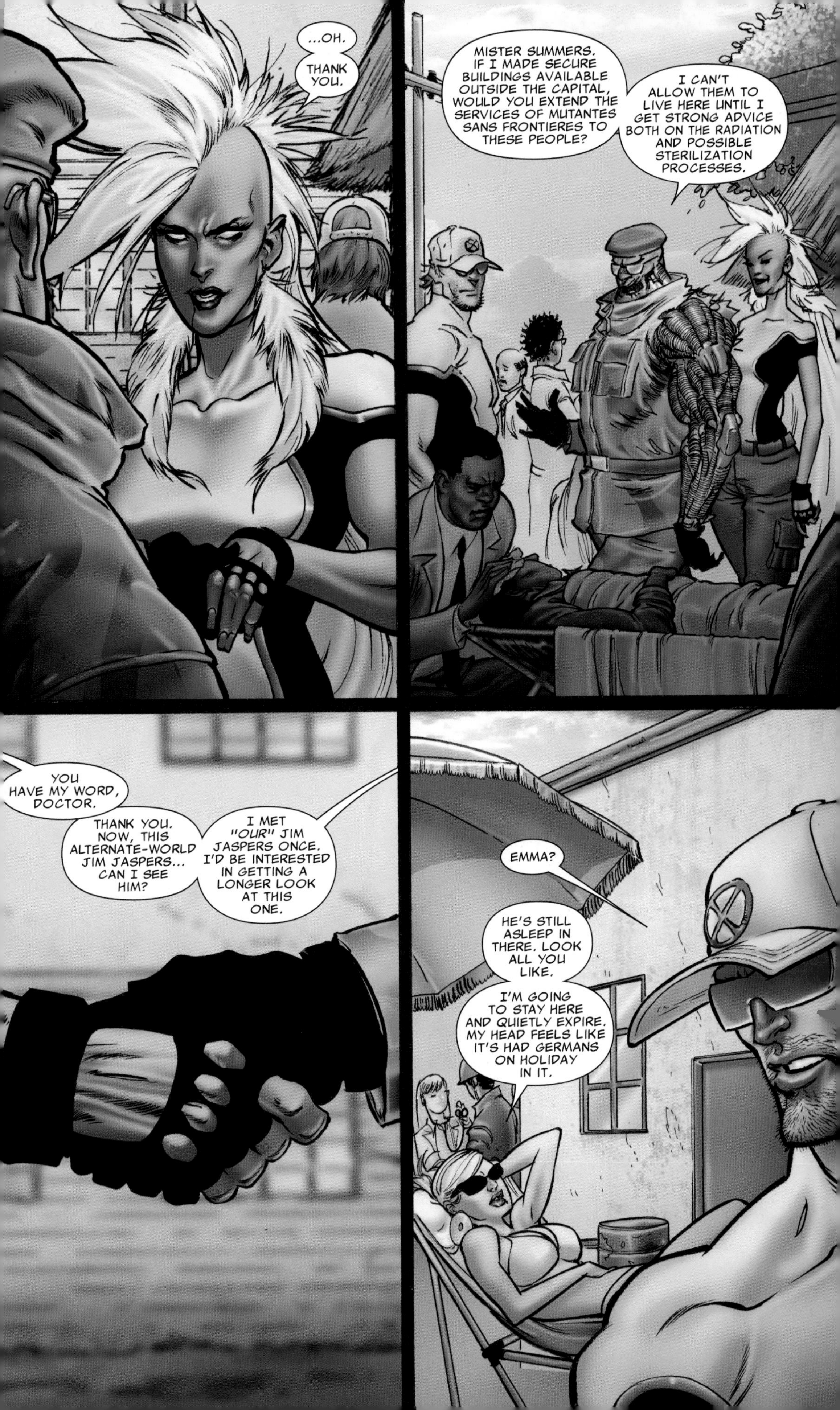

...OH.
THANK YOU.
MISTER SUMMERS. IF I MADE SECURE BUILDINGS AVAILABLE OUTSIDE THE CAPITAL, WOULD YOU EXTEND THE SERVICES OF MUTANTES SANS FRONTIERES TO THESE PEOPLE?
I CAN'T ALLOW THEM TO LIVE HERE UNTIL I GET STRONG ADVICE BOTH ON THE RADIATION AND POSSIBLE STERILIZATION PROCESSES.
YOU HAVE MY WORD, DOCTOR.
THANK YOU. NOW, THIS ALTERNATE-WORLD JIM JASPERS... CAN I SEE HIM?
I MET "OUR" JIM JASPERS ONCE. I'D BE INTERESTED IN GETTING A LONGER LOOK AT THIS ONE.
EMMA?
HE'S STILL ASLEEP IN THERE. LOOK ALL YOU LIKE.
I'M GOING TO STAY HERE AND QUIETLY EXPIRE. MY HEAD FEELS LIKE IT'S HAD GERMANS ON HOLIDAY IN IT.

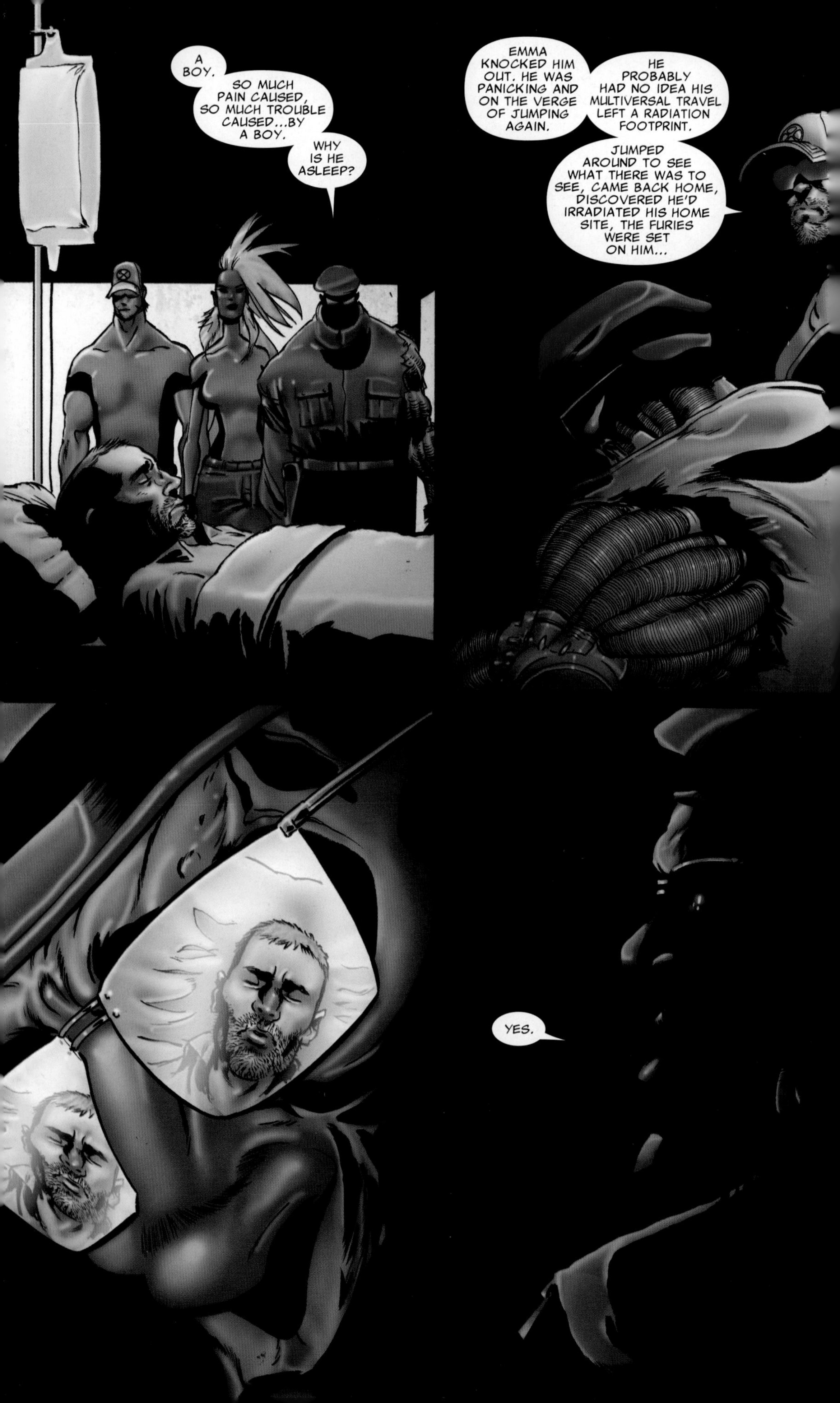
A BOY.
SO MUCH PAIN CAUSED, SO MUCH TROUBLE CAUSED...BY A BOY.
WHY IS HE ASLEEP?
EMMA KNOCKED HIM OUT. HE WAS PANICKING AND ON THE VERGE OF JUMPING AGAIN.
HE PROBABLY HAD NO IDEA HIS MULTIVERSAL TRAVEL LEFT A RADIATION FOOTPRINT.
JUMPED AROUND TO SEE WHAT THERE WAS TO SEE, CAME BACK HOME, DISCOVERED HE'D IRRADIATED HIS HOME SITE, THE FURIES WERE SET ON HIM...
YES.

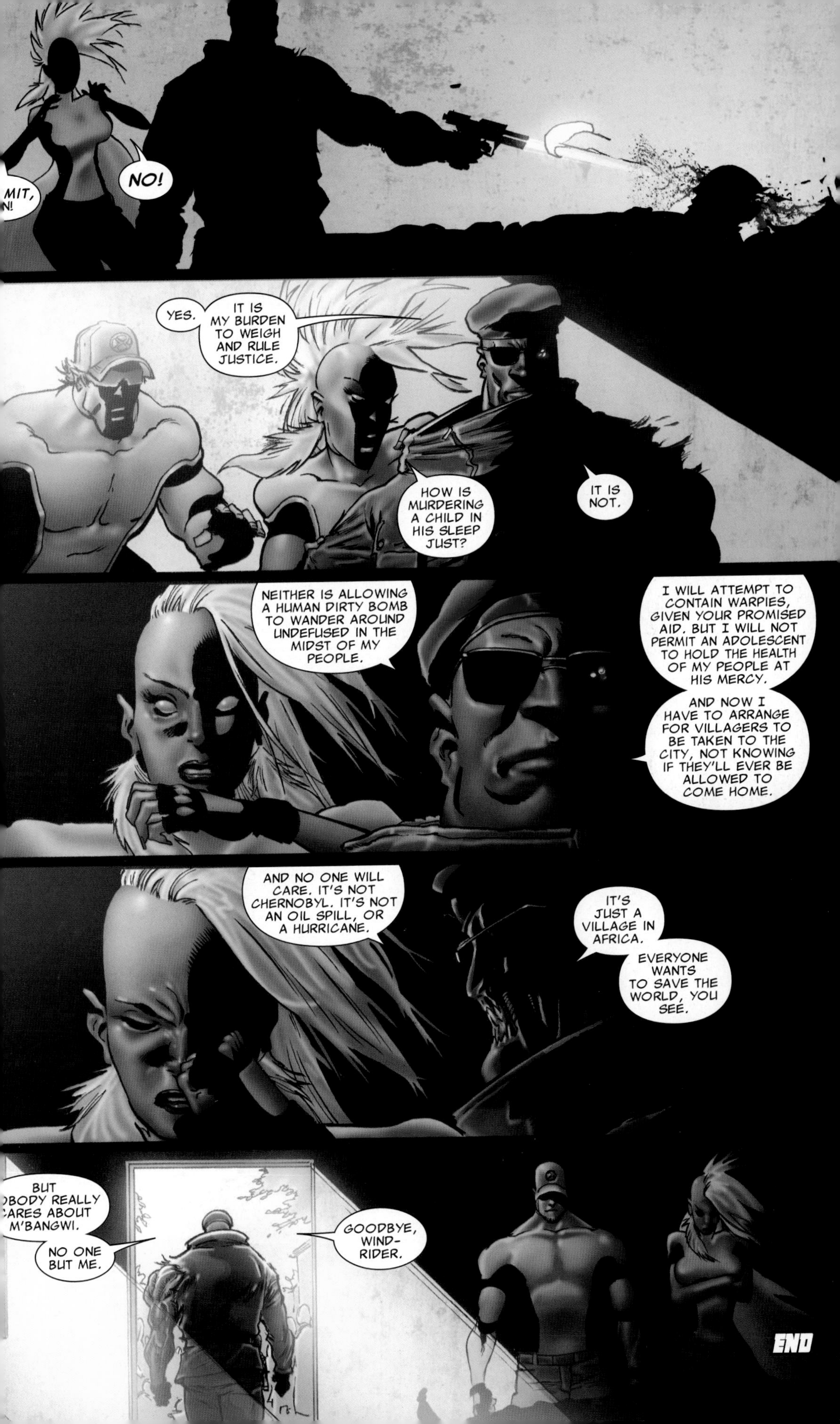
MIT, N!
NO!
YES.
IT IS MY BURDEN TO WEIGH AND RULE JUSTICE.
HOW IS MURDERING A CHILD IN HIS SLEEP JUST?
IT IS NOT.
NEITHER IS ALLOWING A HUMAN DIRTY BOMB TO WANDER AROUND UNDEFUSED IN THE MIDST OF MY PEOPLE.
I WILL ATTEMPT TO CONTAIN WARPIES, GIVEN YOUR PROMISED AID. BUT I WILL NOT PERMIT AN ADOLESCENT TO HOLD THE HEALTH OF MY PEOPLE AT HIS MERCY.
AND NOW I HAVE TO ARRANGE FOR VILLAGERS TO BE TAKEN TO THE CITY, NOT KNOWING IF THEY'LL EVER BE ALLOWED TO COME HOME.
AND NO ONE WILL CARE. IT'S NOT CHERNOBYL. IT'S NOT AN OIL SPILL, OR A HURRICANE.
IT'S JUST A VILLAGE IN AFRICA.
EVERYONE WANTS TO SAVE THE WORLD, YOU SEE.
BUT OBODY REALLY CARES ABOUT M'BANGWI.
NO ONE BUT ME.
GOODBYE, WIND-RIDER.
END

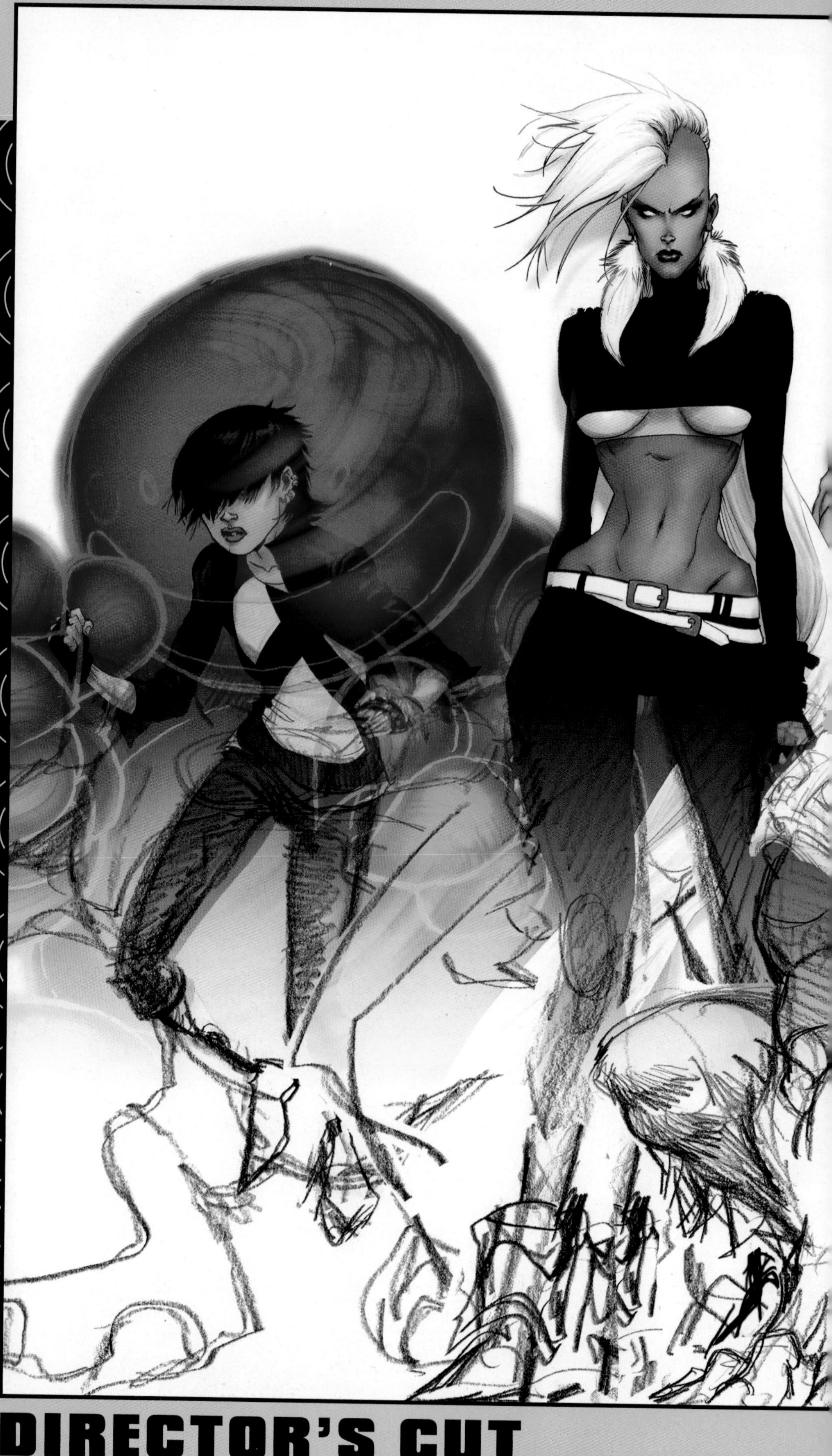

DIRECTOR'S CUT

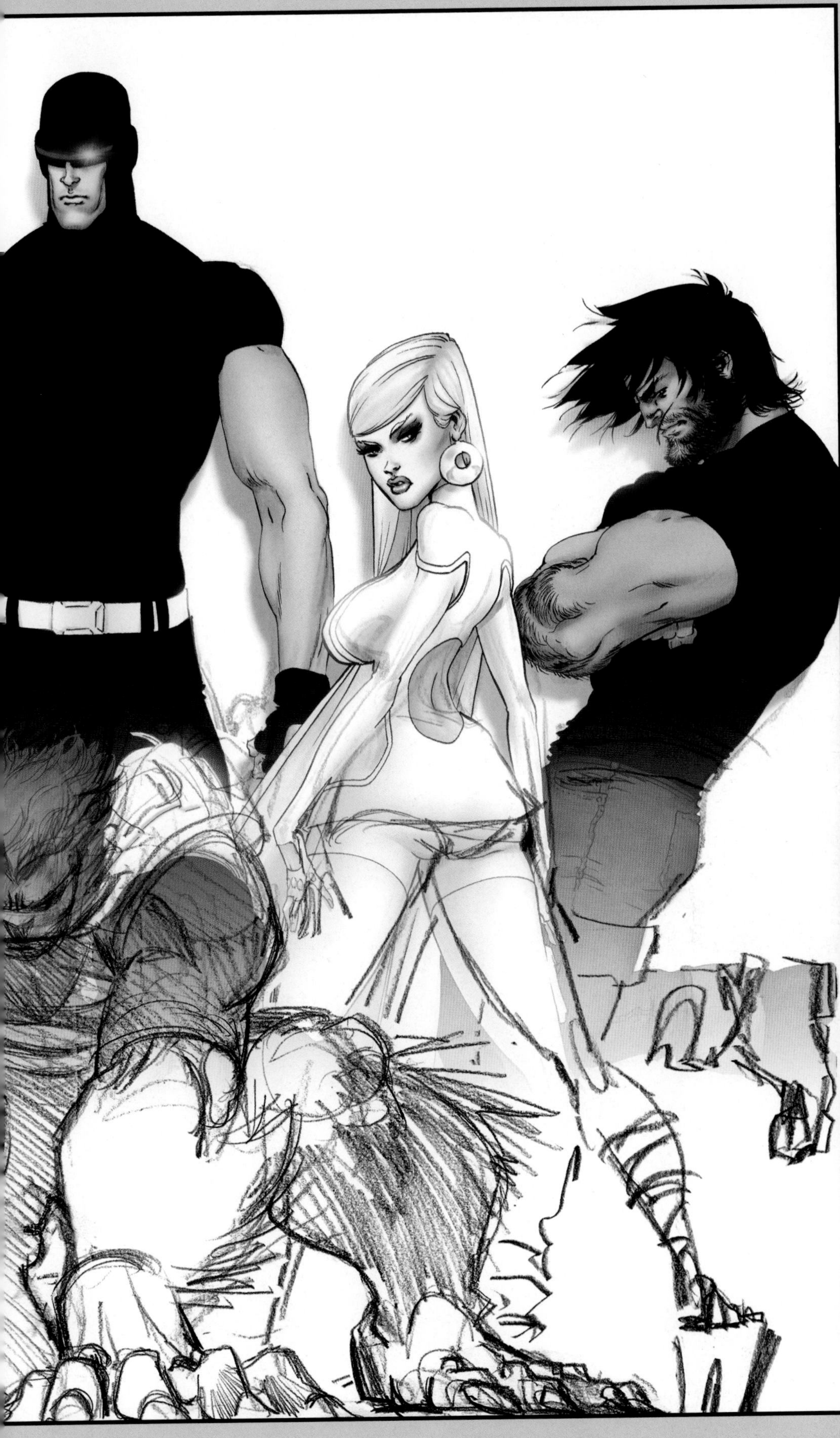

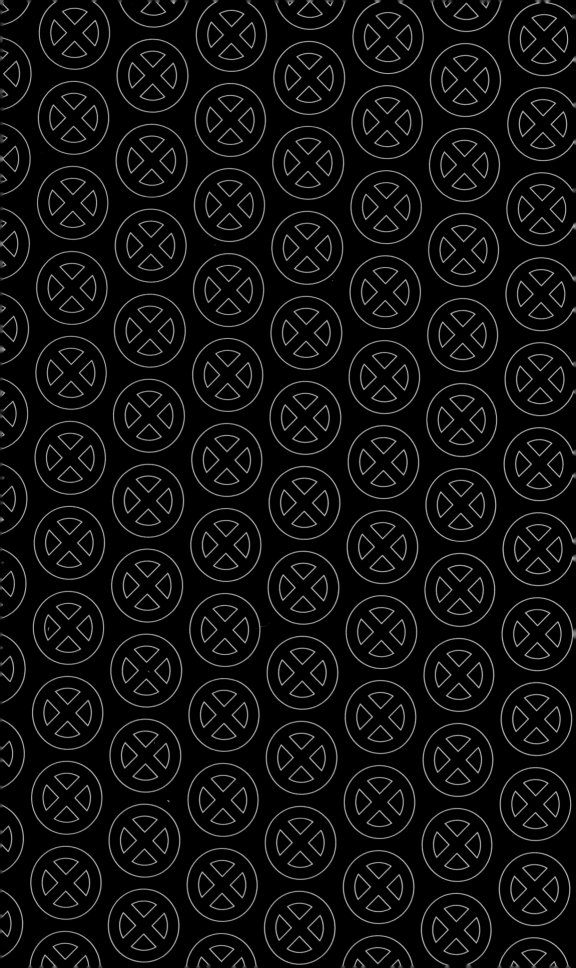

Book ASTONISHING X-MEN Issue 31 Story Page # 01 Line Up Page # kaare andrews

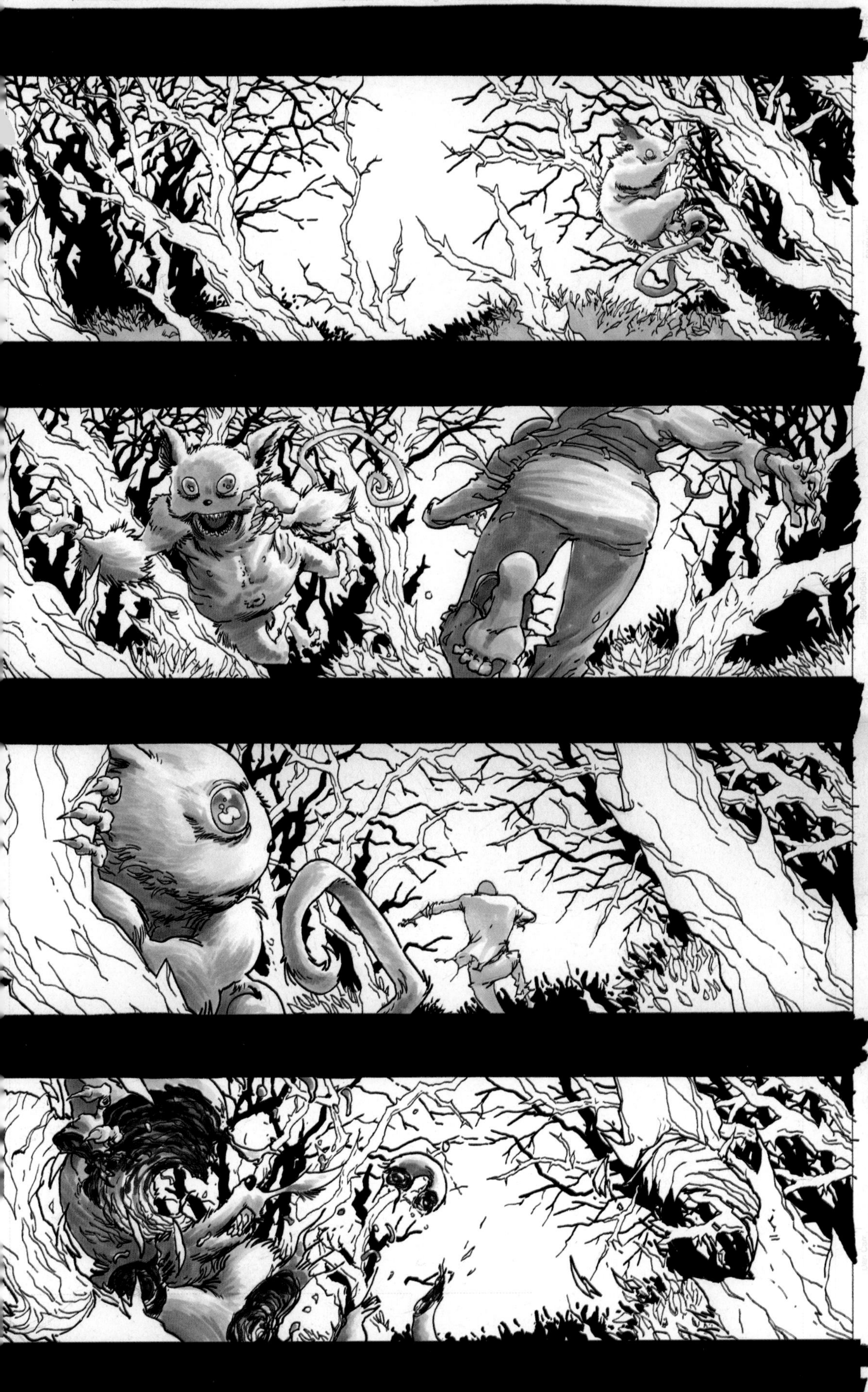

INSTRUCTIONS FOR DOUBLE PAGE SPREAD: CUT AS SHOWN, ABUT PAGE EDGES, TAPE ON BACK. DO NOT OVERLAP.

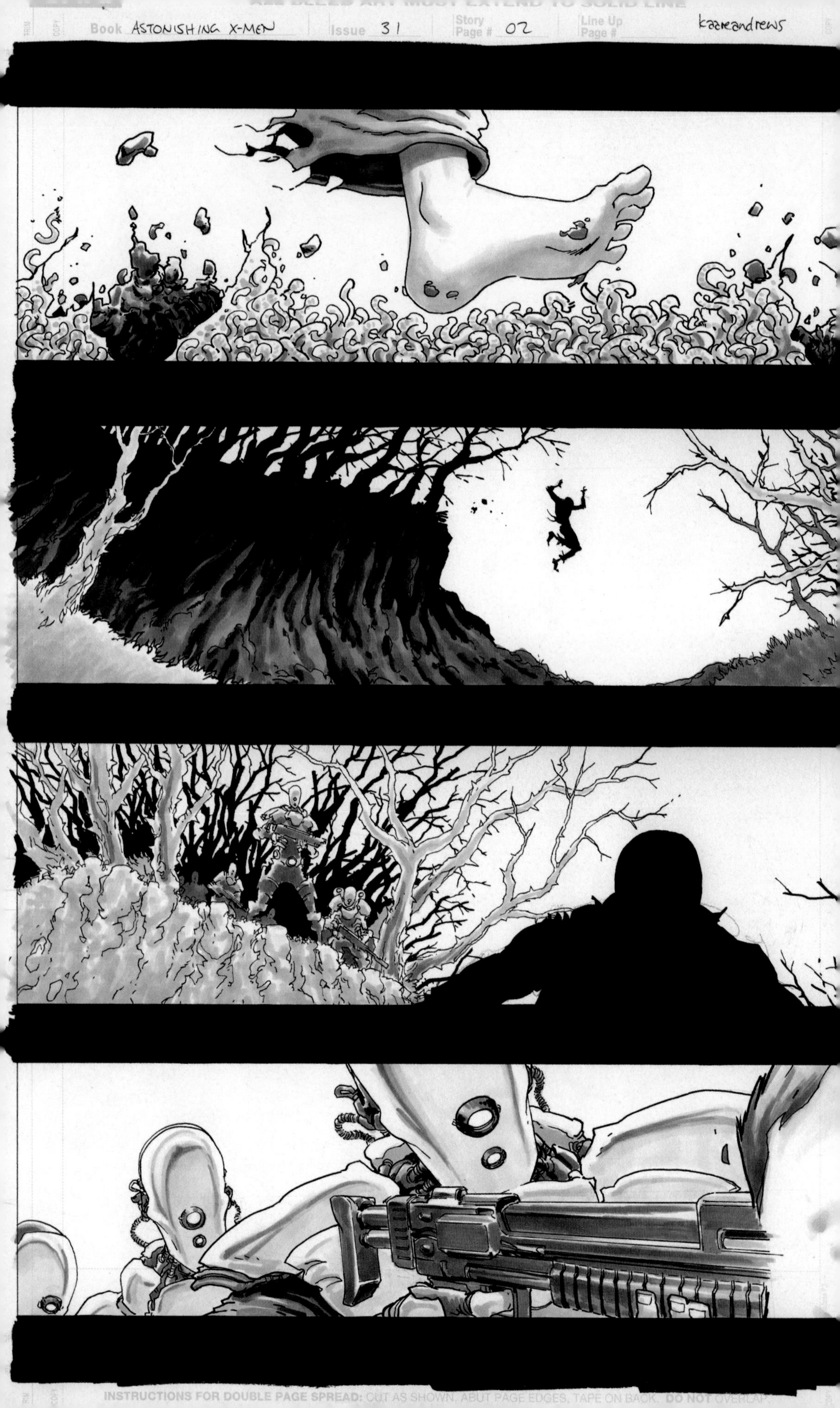
Book ASTONISHING X-MEN
Issue 31
Story Page # 02
Line Up Page #
kaareandrews
INSTRUCTIONS FOR DOUBLE PAGE SPREAD: CUT AS SHOWN, ABUT PAGE EDGES, TAPE ON BACK. DO NOT OVERLAP

Book ASTONISHG X-MEN Issue 31 Story Page # 03 Line Up Page # kaareandrews

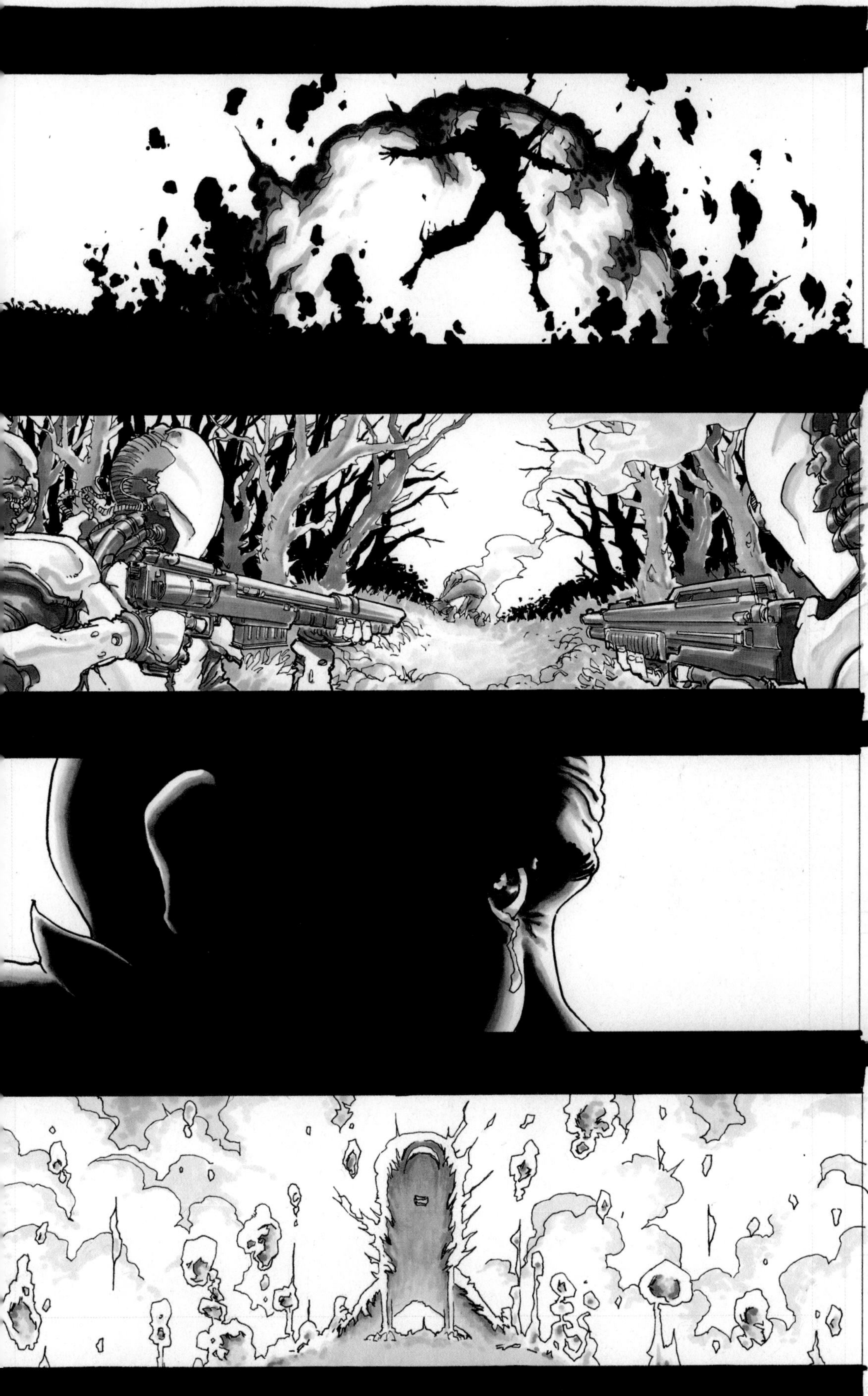

INSTRUCTIONS FOR DOUBLE PAGE SPREAD: CUT AS SHOWN. ABUT PAGE EDGES, TAPE ON BACK. DO NOT OVERLAP.

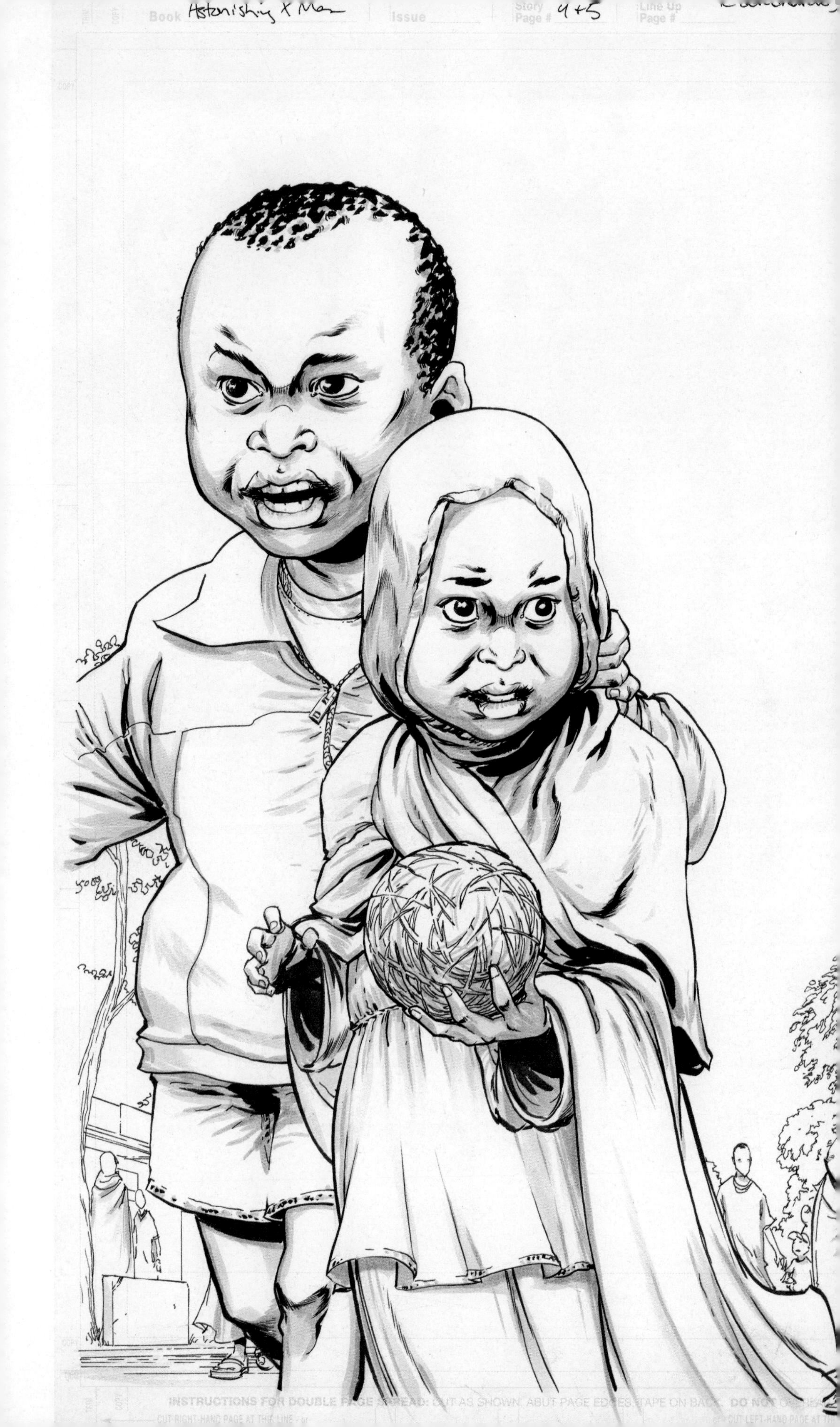
Book Astonishing X Men
Issue
Story Page # 4+5
Line Up Page #
INSTRUCTIONS FOR DOUBLE PAGE SPREAD: CUT AS SHOWN, ABUT PAGE EDGES, TAPE ON BACK.
CUT RIGHT-HAND PAGE AT THIS LINE

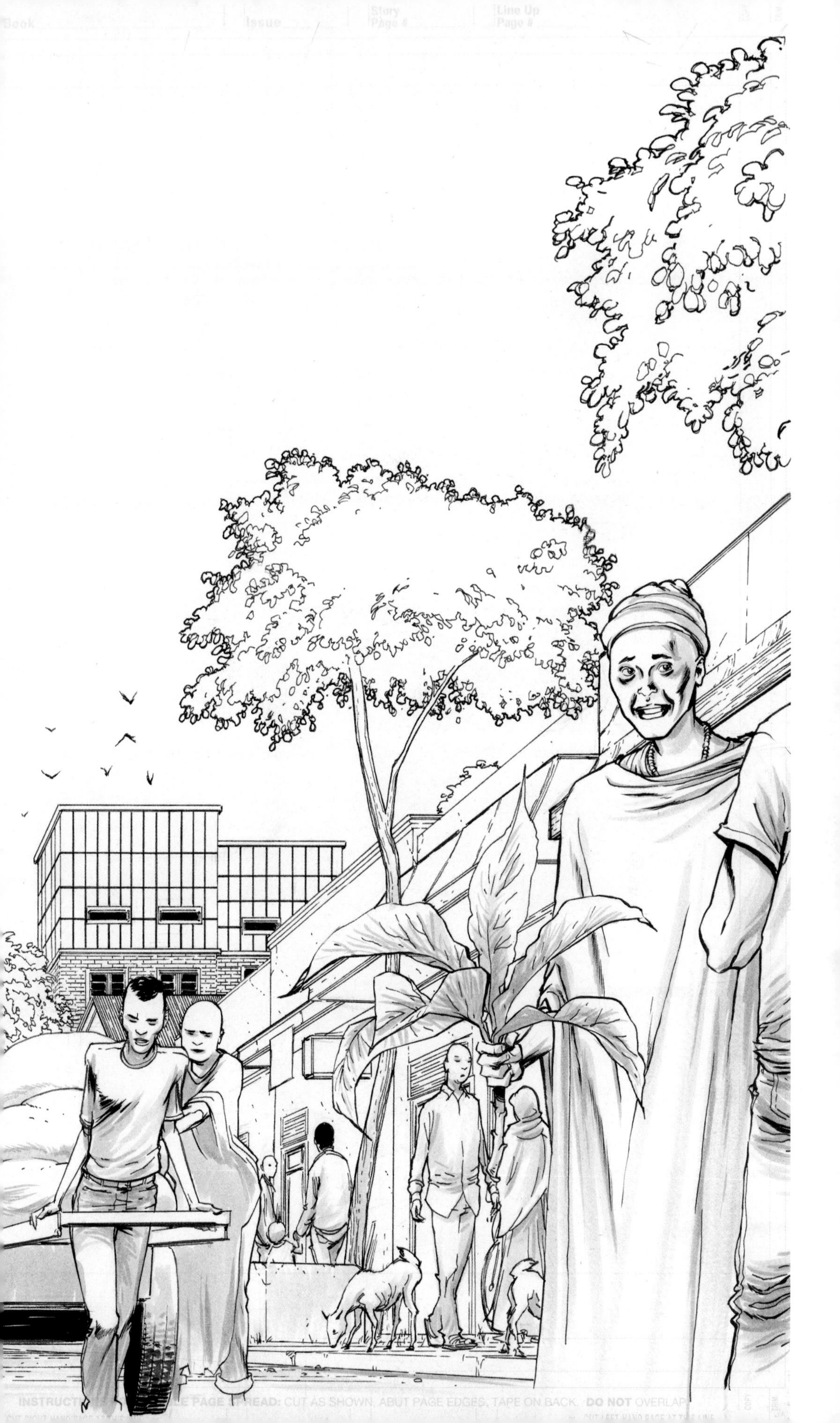
Book
Issue
Story Page #
Line Up Page #

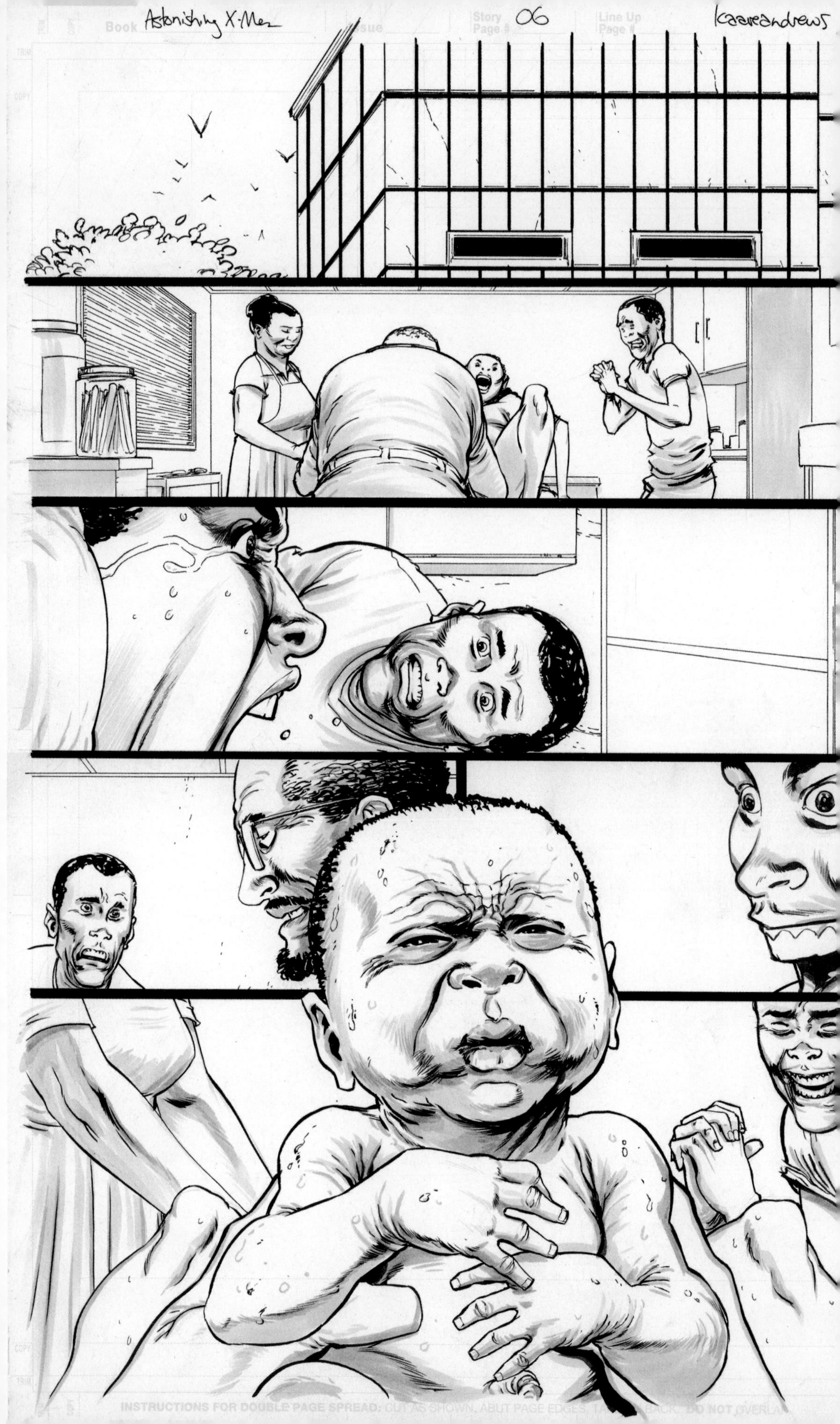
Book Astonishing X-Men
Issue
Story Page # 06
Line Up Page #
kaareandrews
INSTRUCTIONS FOR DOUBLE PAGE SPREAD: CUT AS SHOWN, ABUT PAGE EDGES,
DO NOT OVERLAP

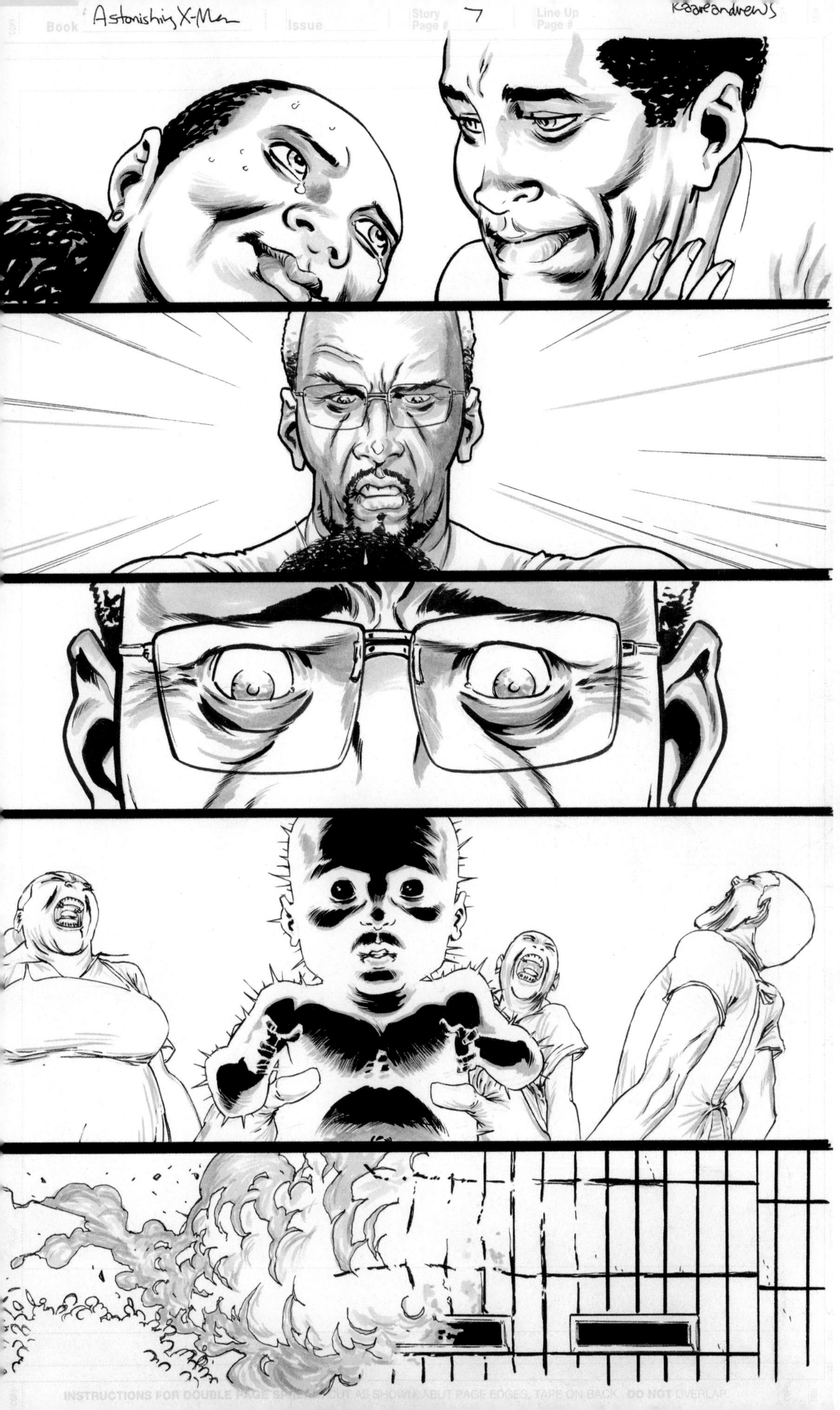
Book Astonishing X-Men
Issue
Story Page # 7
Line Up Page #
kaareandrews
INSTRUCTIONS FOR DOUBLE PAGE SPREAD: CUT AS SHOWN, ABUT PAGE EDGES, TAPE ON BACK. DO NOT OVERLAP

Book Astonishing X-Men Issue Story Page # 8/9 Line Up Page #

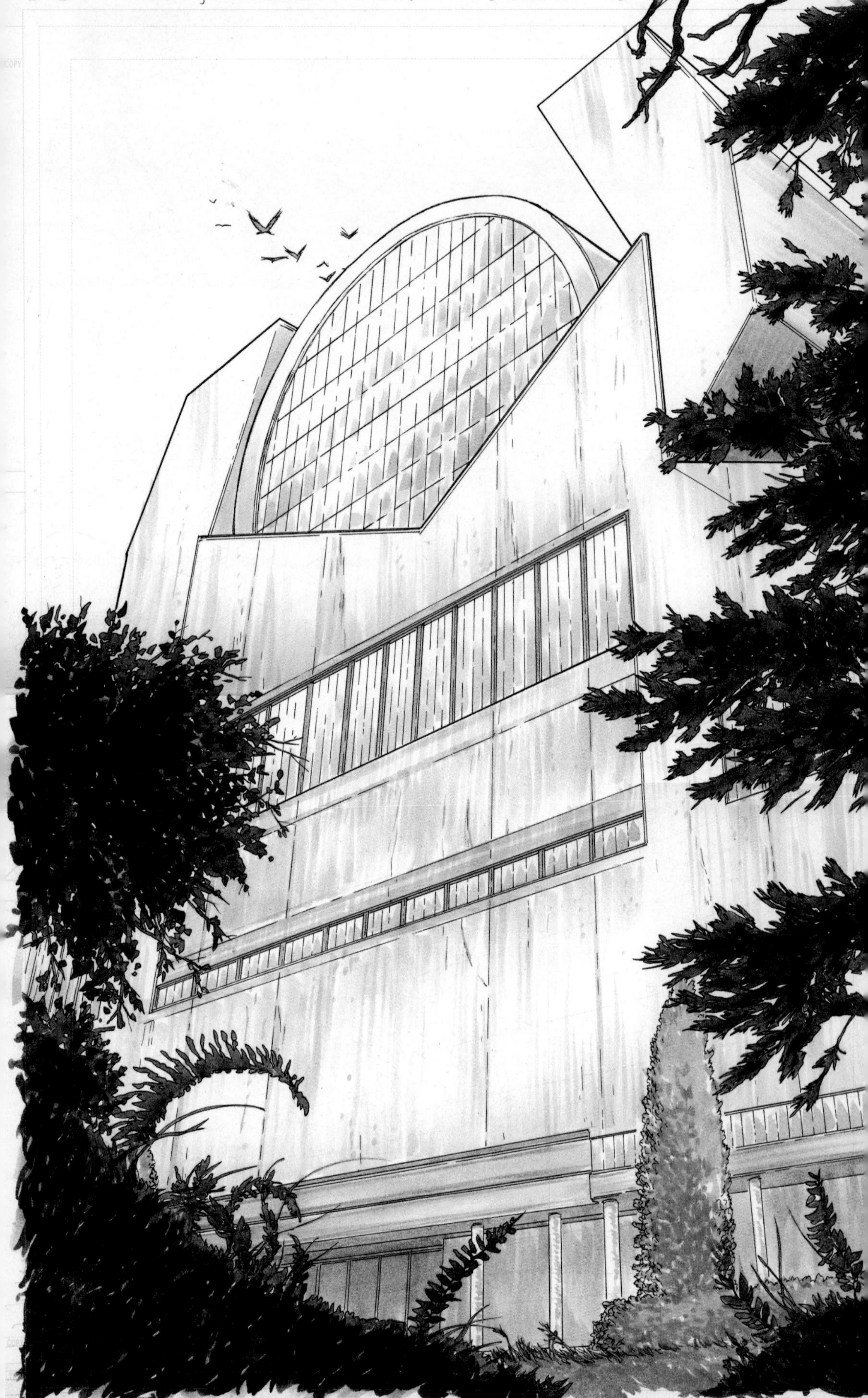

INSTRUCTIONS FOR DOUBLE PAGE SPREAD: CUT AS SHOWN ... TAPE ON BACK. DO NOT OVERLAP

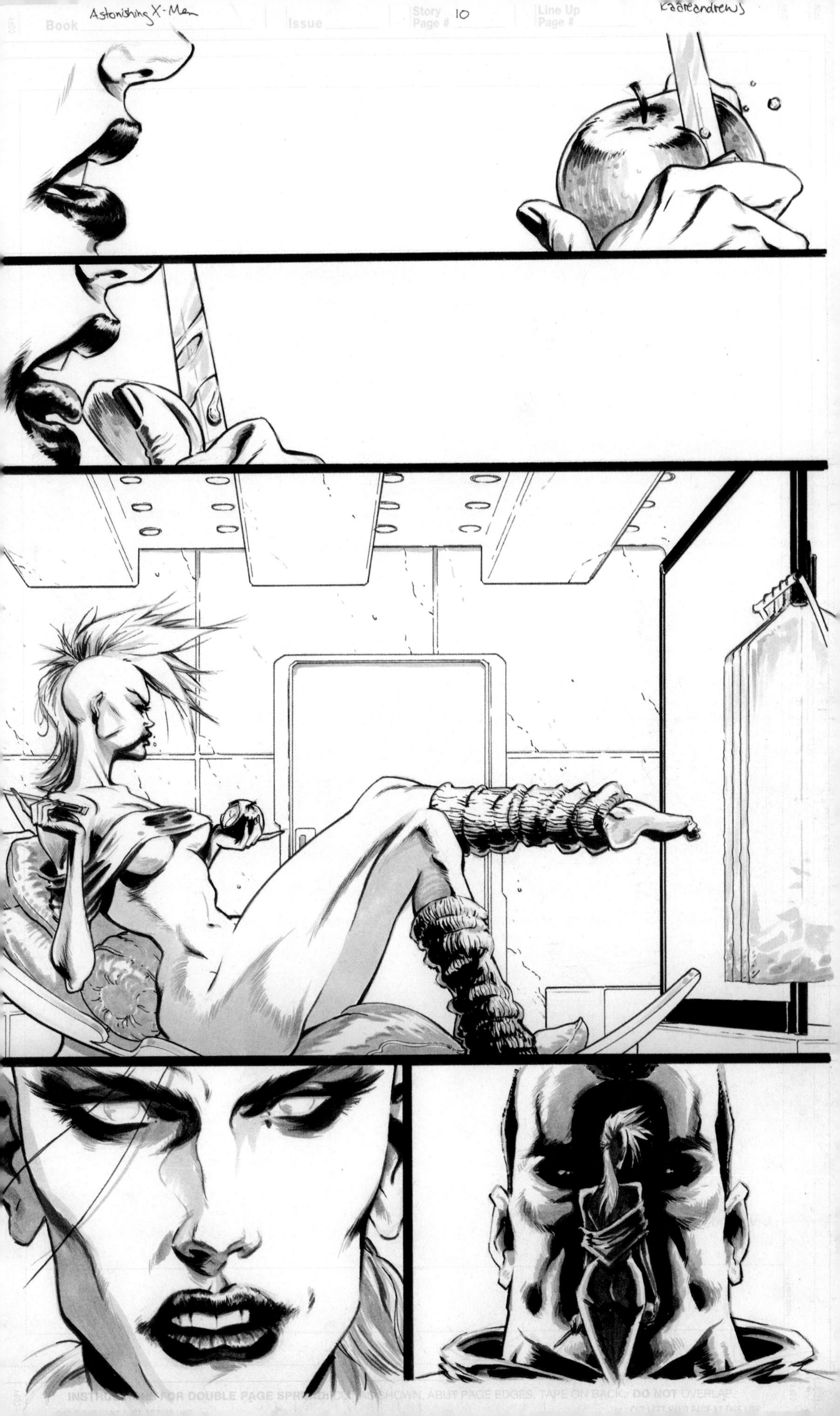
Book Astonishing X-Men
Issue
Story Page # 10
Line Up Page #
kaareandrews

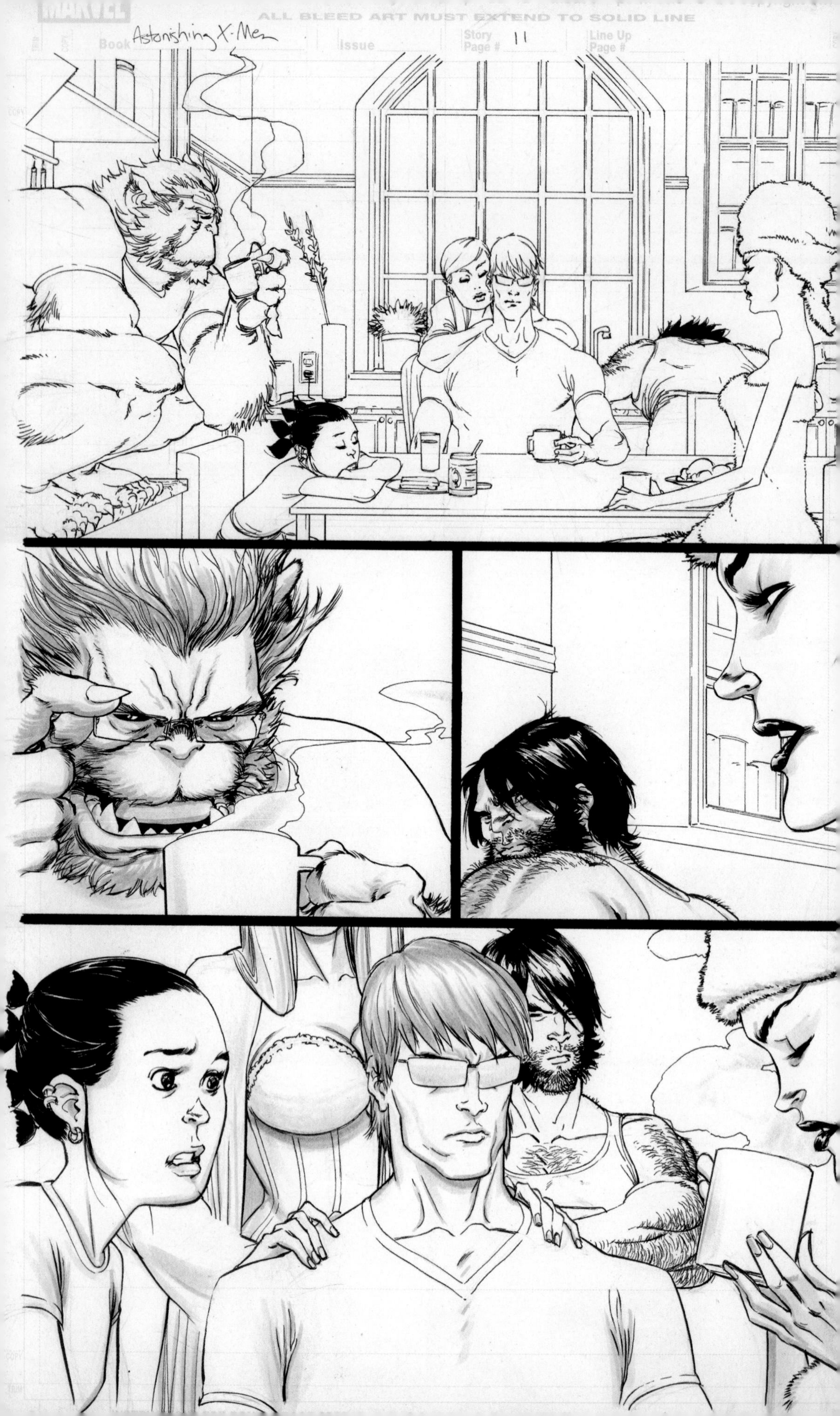
MARVEL
ALL BLEED ART MUST EXTEND TO SOLID LINE
Book Astonishing X-Men
Issue
Story Page # 11
Line Up Page #

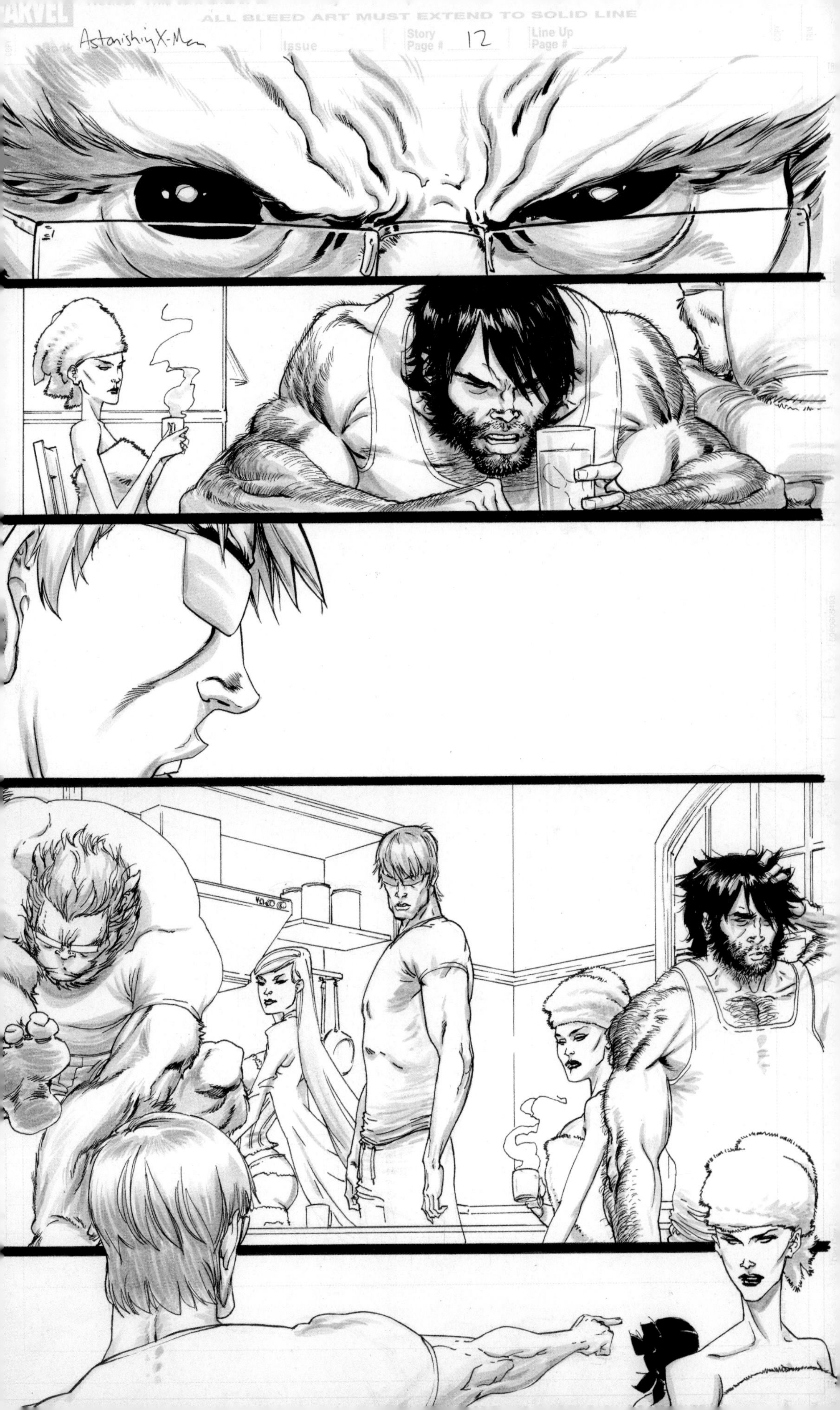
ALL BLEED ART MUST EXTEND TO SOLID LINE
Astonishing X-Men
Issue
Story Page # 12
Line Up Page #

Book Astonishing X-Men Issue Story Page # 13 Line Up Page #

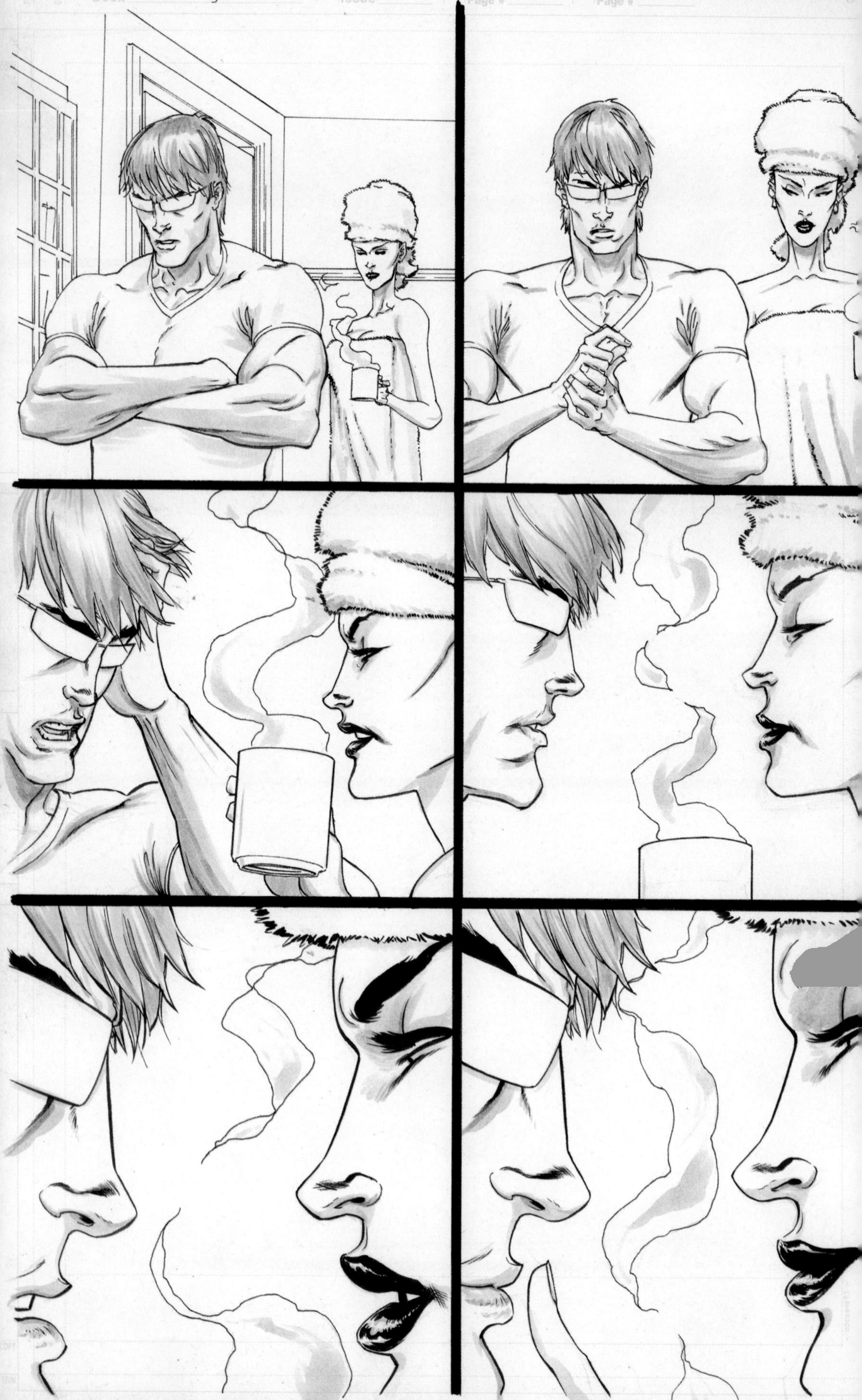

INSTRUCTIONS FOR DOUBLE PAGE SPREAD: CUT AS SHOWN, ABUT PAGE EDGES, TAPE ON BACK. DO NOT OVERLAP.

Astonishing X Men #1 136 Kaare andrews

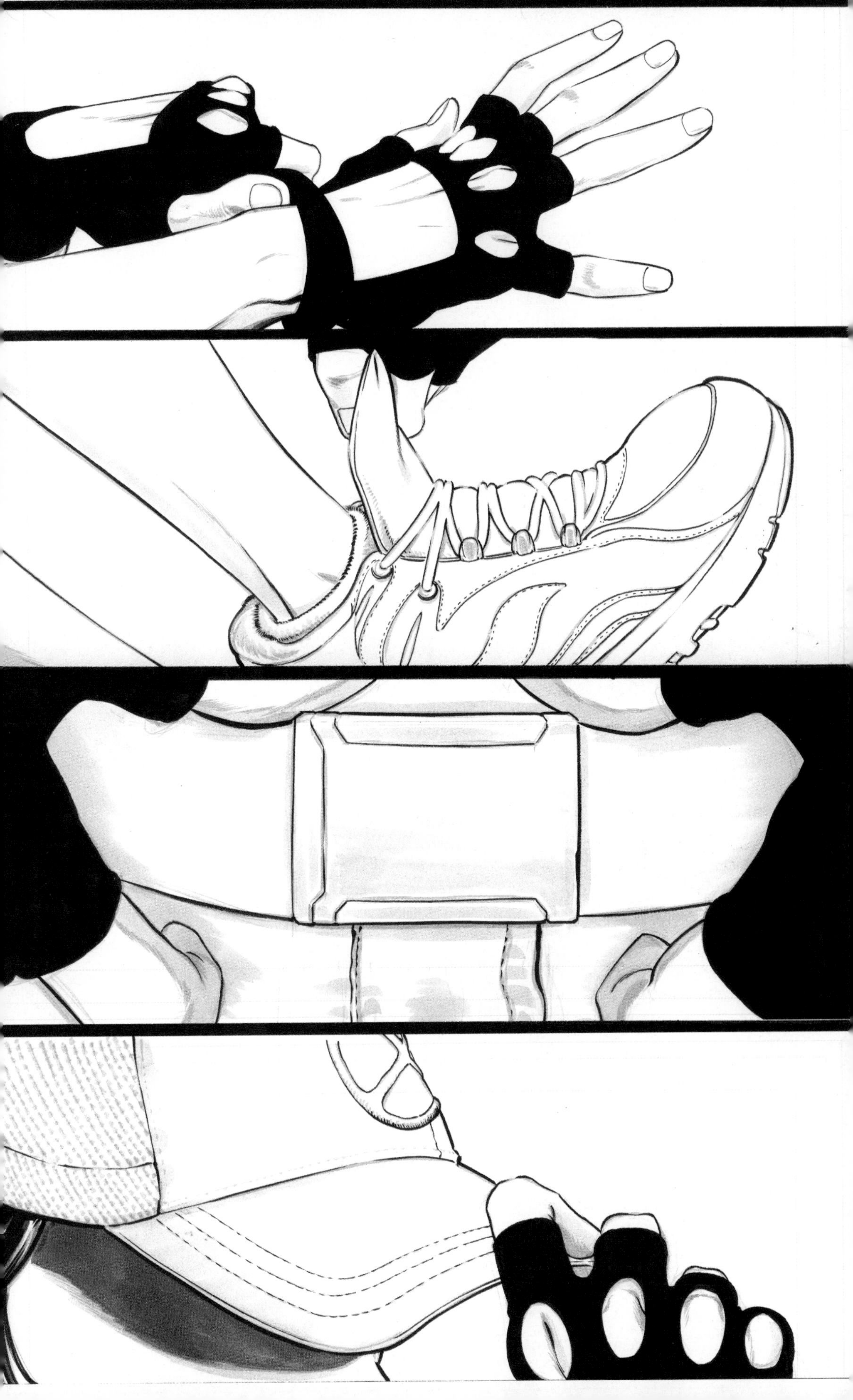

Book Astonishing X-Men Issue Story Page # 14 Line Up Page #

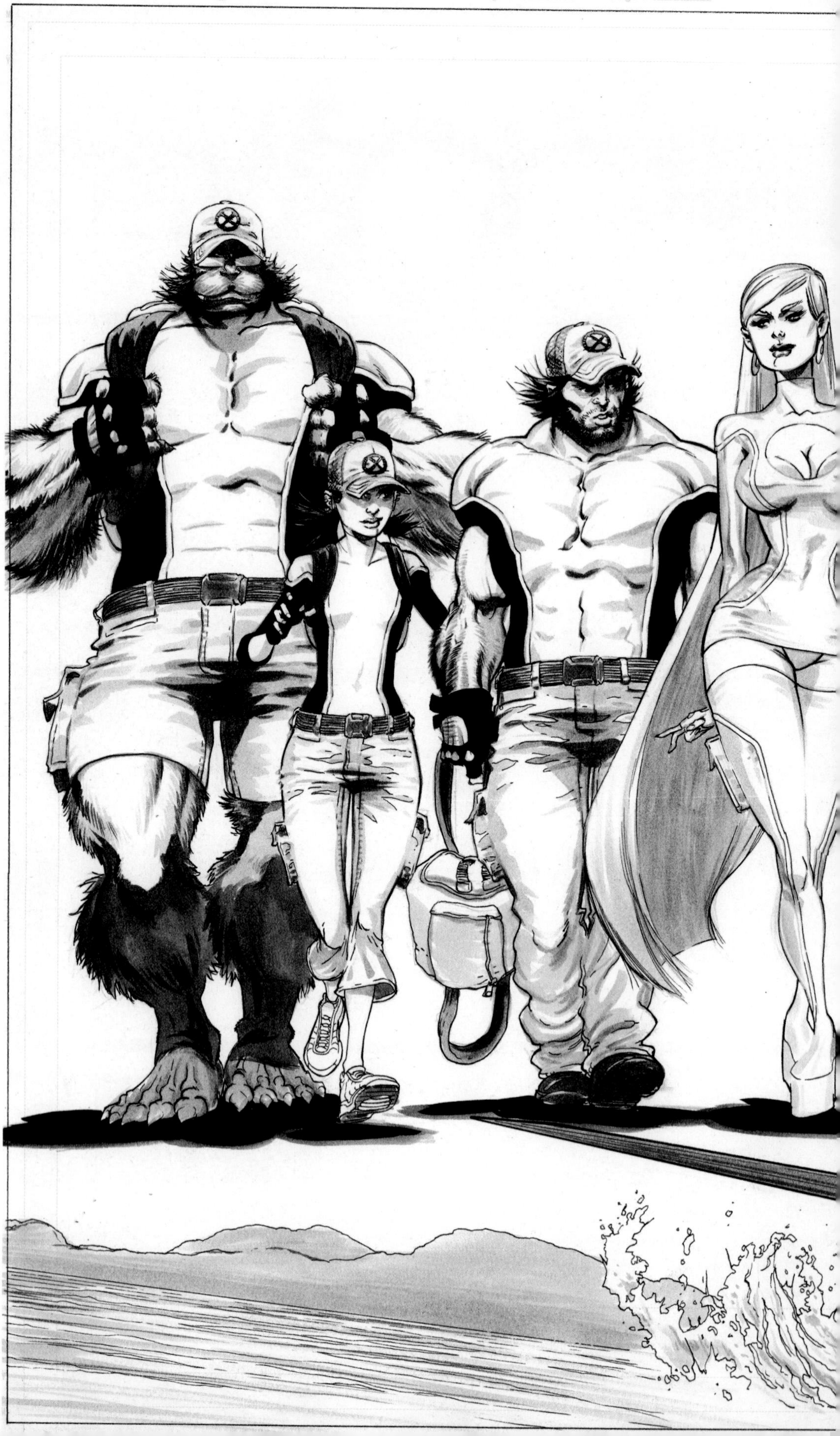

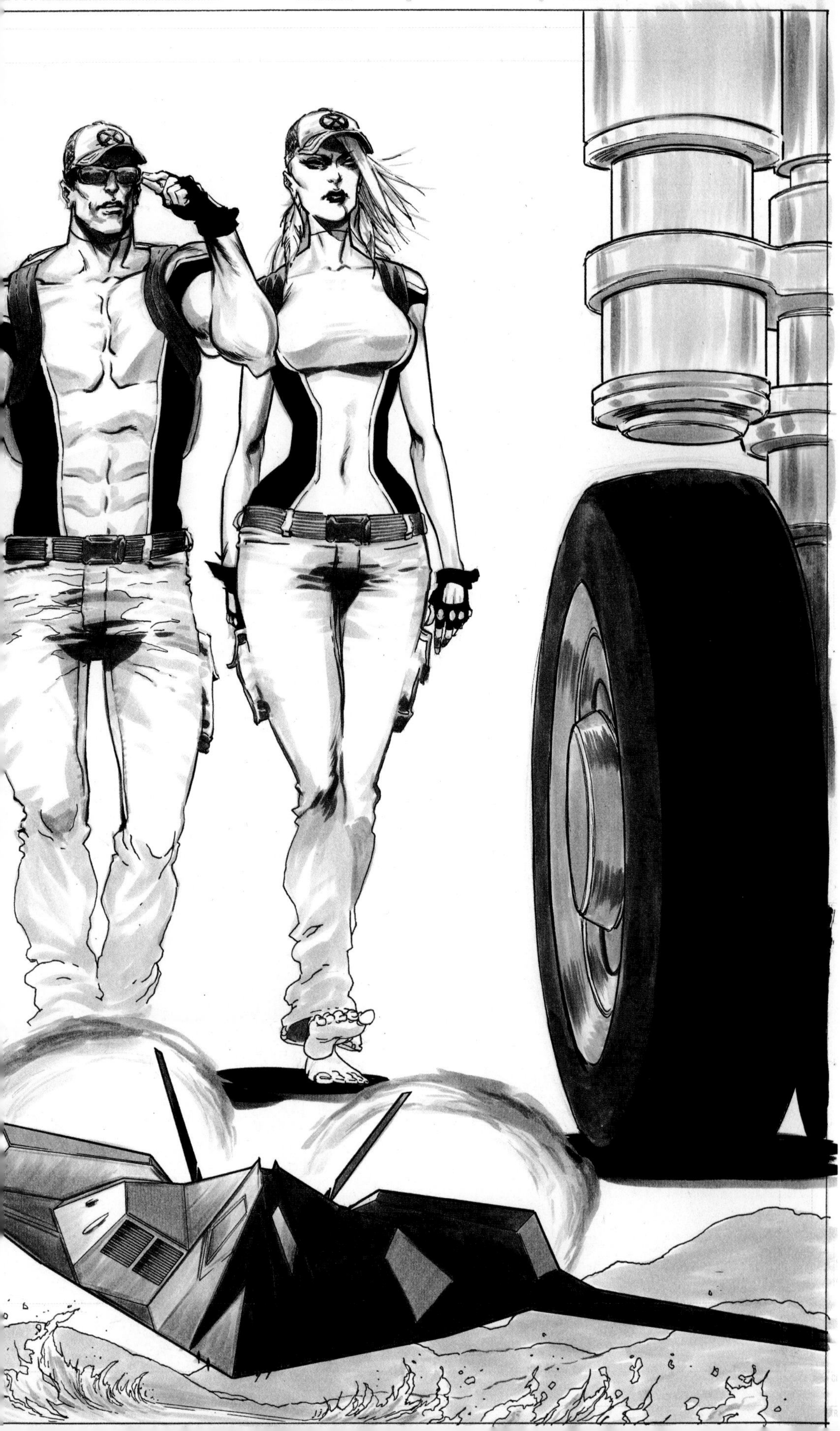

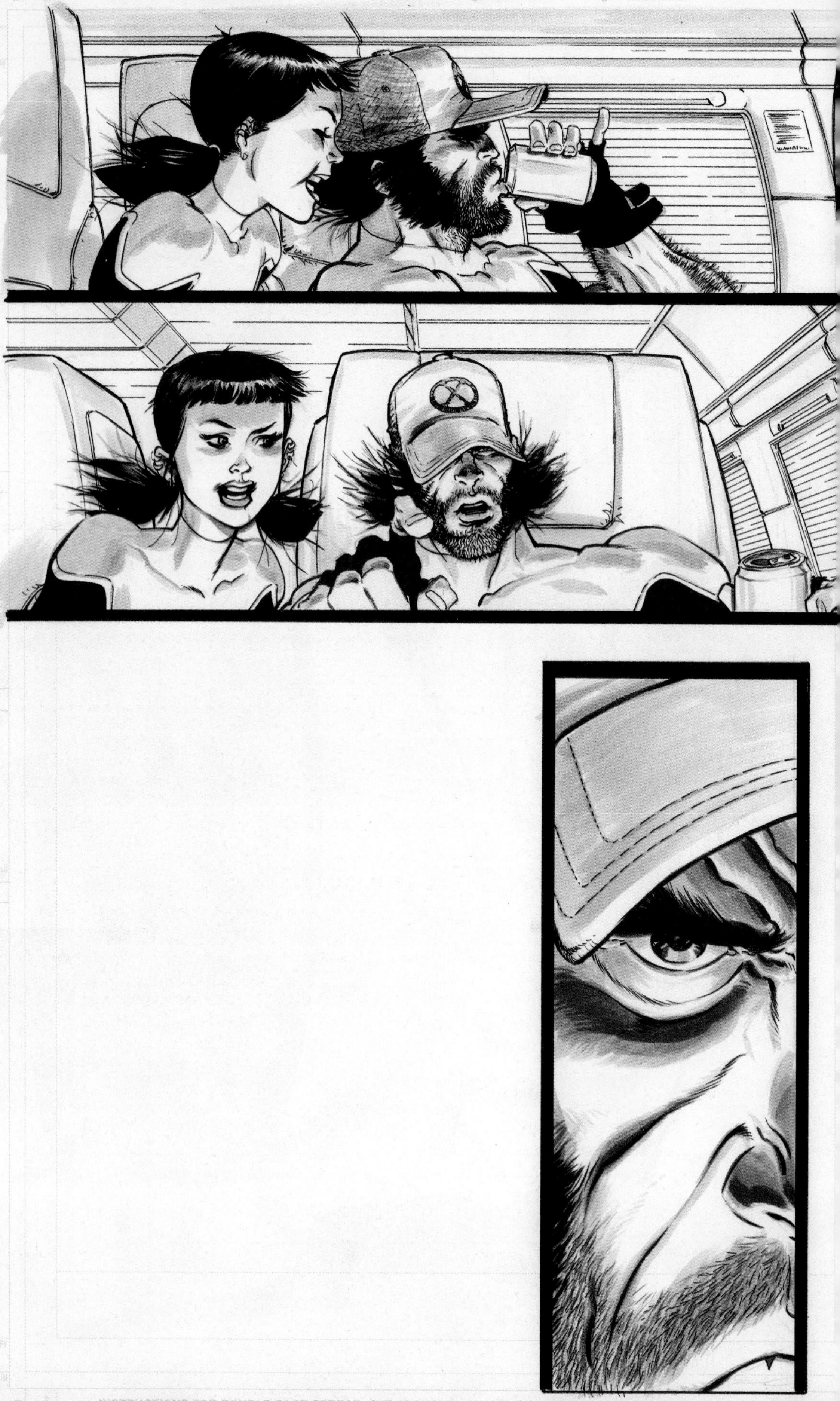

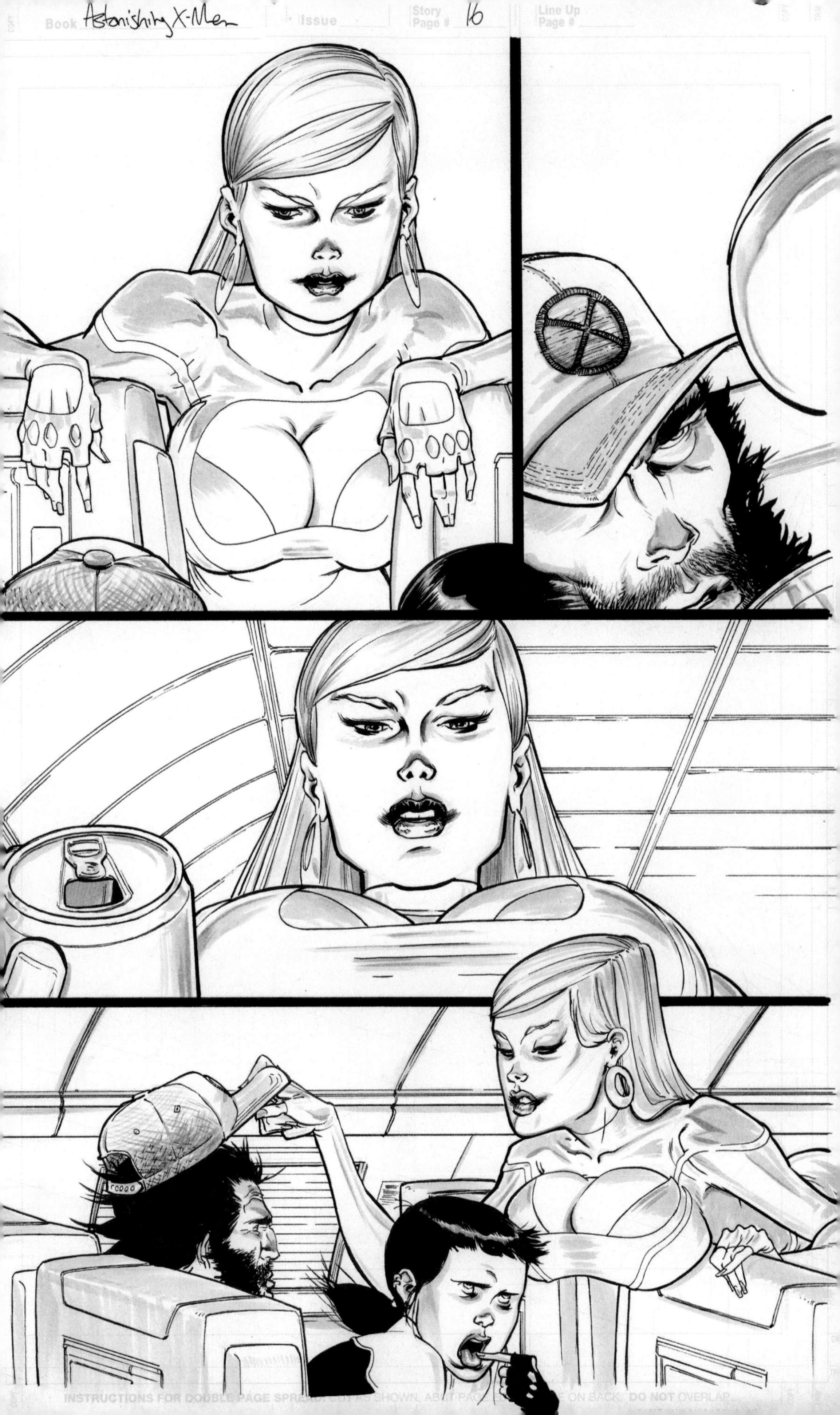
Book Astonishing X-Men
Issue
Story Page # 16
Line Up Page #
INSTRUCTIONS FOR DOUBLE PAGE SPREAD
AS SHOWN
ON BACK. DO NOT OVERLAP

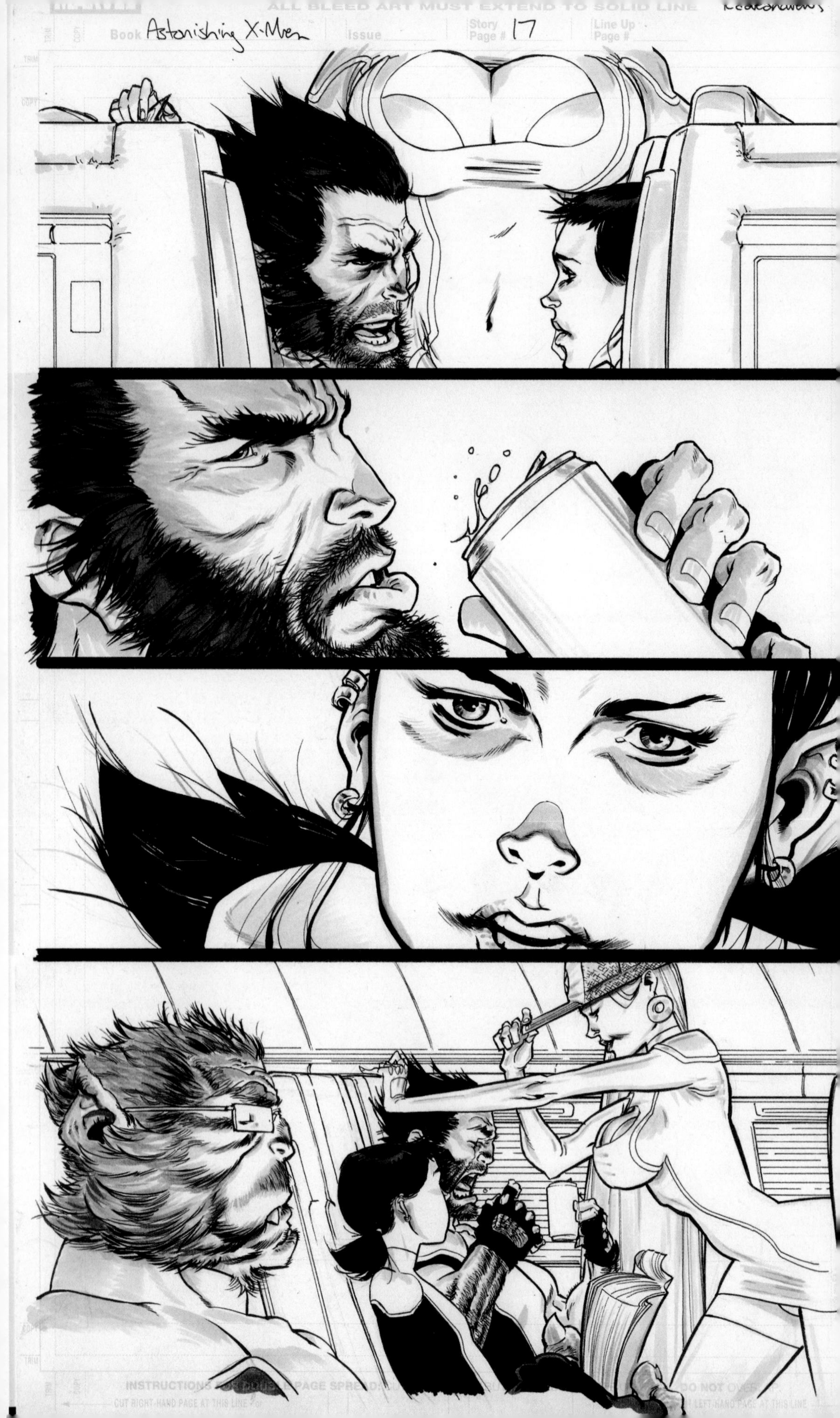
ALL BLEED ART MUST EXTEND TO SOLID LINE
Book Astonishing X-Men
Issue
Story Page # 17
Line Up Page #
INSTRUCTIONS FOR DOUBLE PAGE SPREAD
DO NOT OVER
CUT RIGHT-HAND PAGE AT THIS LINE
LEFT-HAND PAGE AT THIS LINE

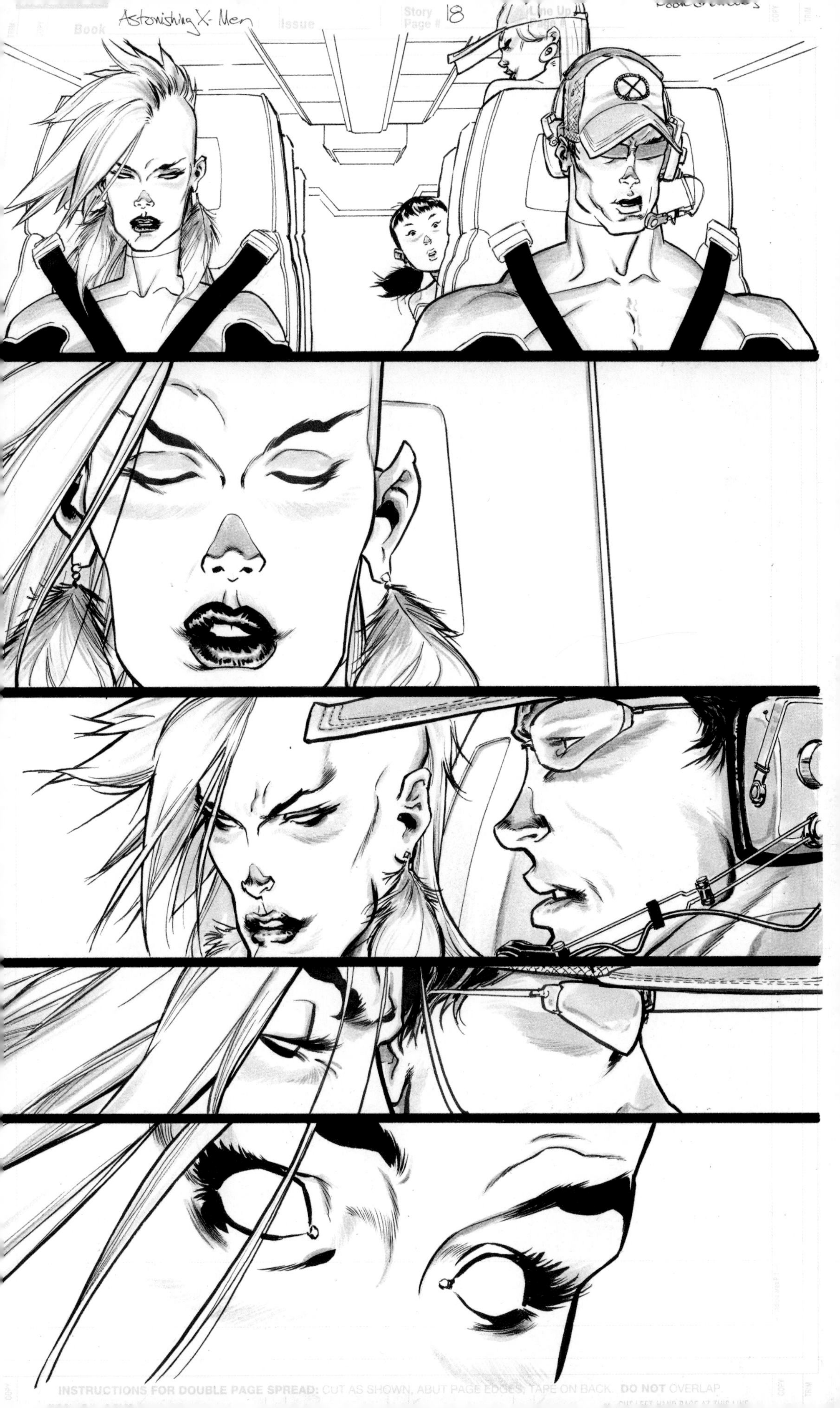
Book Astonishing X-Men
Issue
Story Page # 18
Line Up Page #
INSTRUCTIONS FOR DOUBLE PAGE SPREAD: CUT AS SHOWN, ABUT PAGE EDGES, TAPE ON BACK. DO NOT OVERLAP

ALL BLEED ART MUST EXTEND TO SOLID LINE

Book Astonishing X-Men | Issue | Story Page # p19 | Line Up Page # | kaareandrews

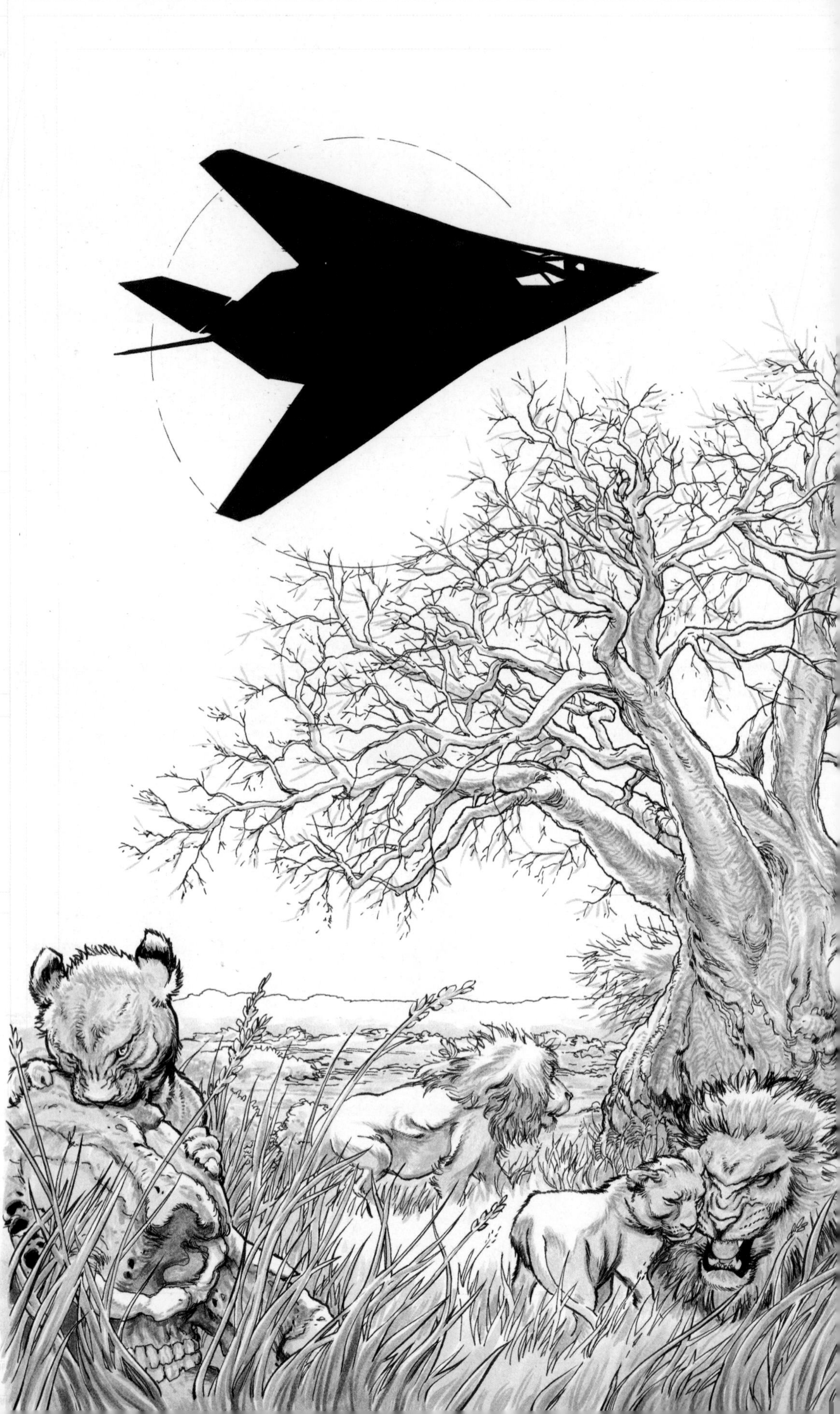

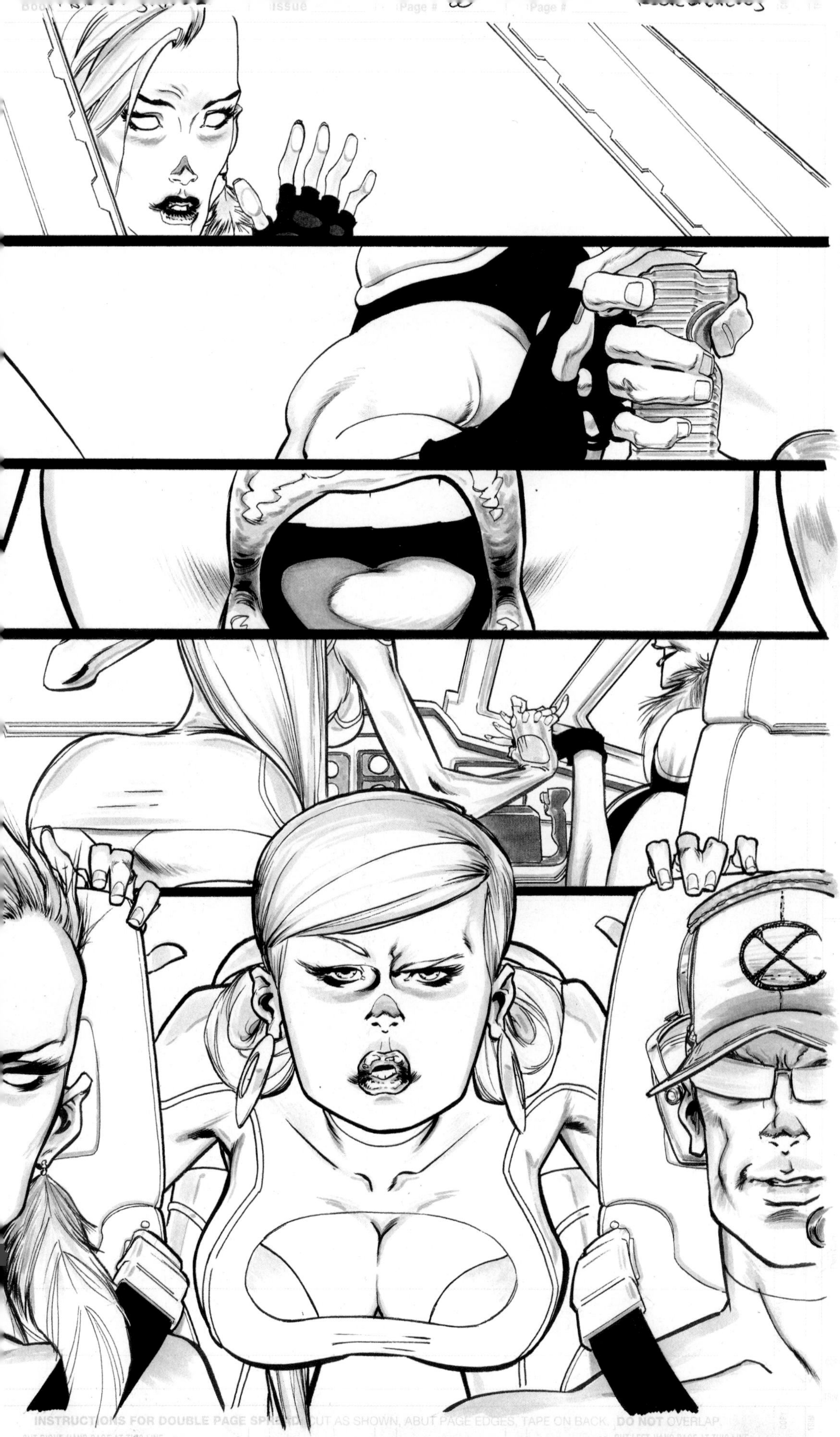
INSTRUCTIONS FOR DOUBLE PAGE SPREAD: CUT AS SHOWN, ABUT PAGE EDGES, TAPE ON BACK. DO NOT OVERLAP.
CUT RIGHT-HAND PAGE AT THIS LINE
CUT LEFT-HAND PAGE AT THIS LINE

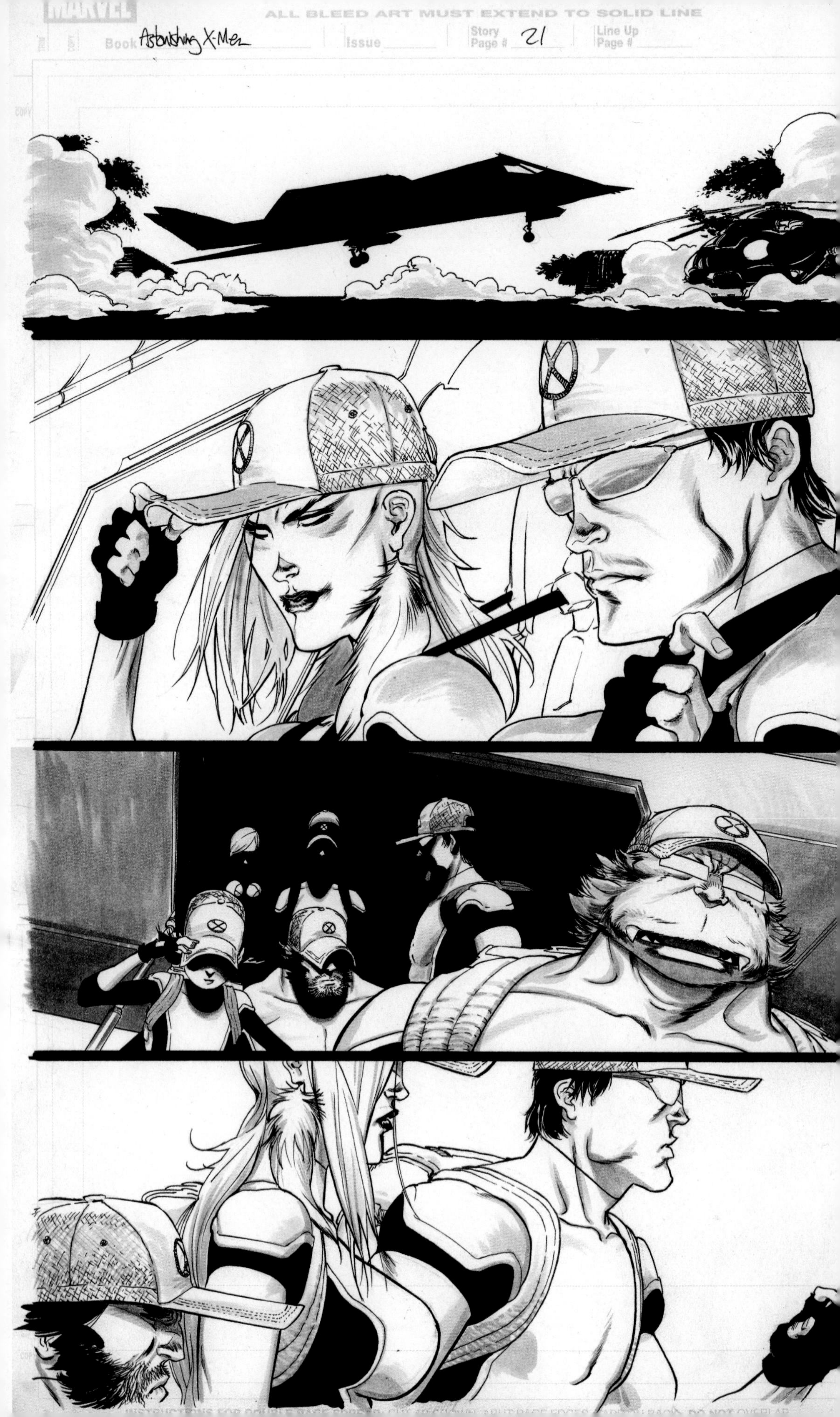
MARVEL
ALL BLEED ART MUST EXTEND TO SOLID LINE
Book Astonishing X-Men
Issue
Story Page # 21
Line Up Page #

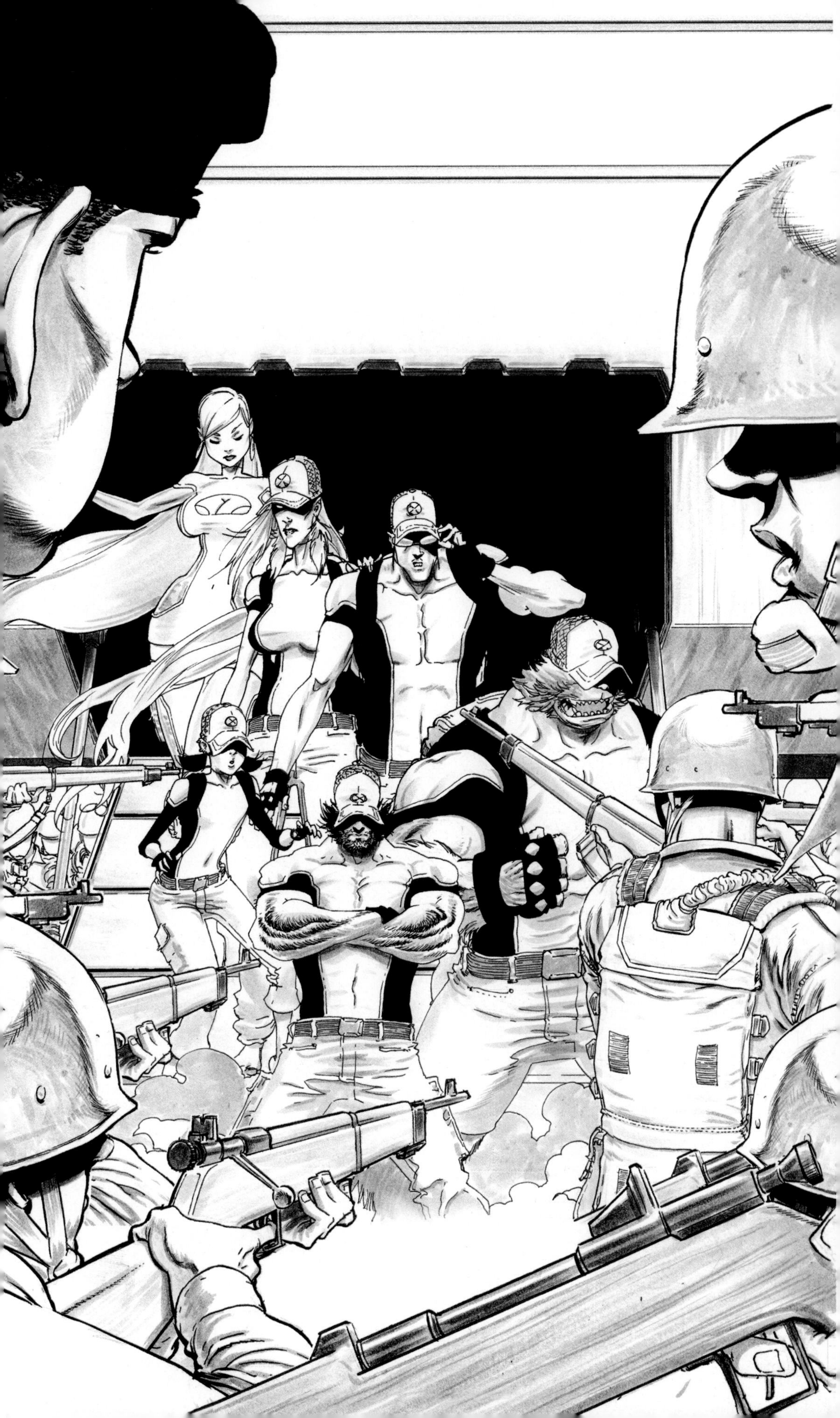

PAGE ONE

Pic 1

OPEN ON: red trees. Metallic. A forest of strange, thin, lumpy, alien red trees. At night. Almost abstract.

(no dialogue)

Pic 2

A thin man, wearing simple and slightly ragged black clothes, a little hard to make out in the dark -- is he black, too? -- dashes between the red trees.

(no dialogue)

Pic 3

He keeps running, away from us, in wild panic. A little creature, like a blue lemur with fluorescent eyes, curls around a tree, looking ahead at us with its huge eyes.

(no dialogue)

Pic 4

GUNFIRE strikes the trees around him, and they shatter like glass, the lemur-thing leaping.

(no dialogue)

PAGE TWO

Pic 1

The running man's tattered shoes hammer down on the undergrowth -- weird fleshy plants that tear and squirt under his feet as he runs.

(no dialogue)

Pic 2

And he ducks into a thicker part of the forest, dodging more gunfire, as we glimpse his pursuers, heavily armored figures with heavy rifles, a metallic horde rumbling through the forest after him. The armor appears to be electrically charged, there are often sparks at the joints, little spiders of lightning running across the surfaces.

(no dialogue)

Pic 3

And pan around, to look at the figures in the front of that horde. The one in the FRONT cycles a big grenade-launching tube slung under the rifle barrel.

FRONT: STOP.

FRONT: JUST STOP NOW.

Pic 4

And he fires into that thicker part of the forest, and on contact there's a great explosion, trees shattering like glass, and we can see the figure of th running man go flying, kicked to one side by the shockwave.

(no dialogue)

PAGE THREE

Pic 1

Smoke blows away, and we see the running man, knocked to the ground, laying at the edge of the crater dug o by the grenade shot. His back to us.

RUNNING MAN: DON'T...

XENOGENESIS
SCRIPT BY WARREN ELLIS